# Murder, Magic, Madness

# Murder, Magic, Madness

## The Victorian Trials of Dove and the Wizard

Owen Davies

PEARSON

Longman

Harlow, England • London • New York • Boston • San Francisco • Toronto
Sydney • Tokyo • Singapore • Hong Kong • Seoul • Taipei • New Delhi
Cape Town • Madrid • Mexico City • Amsterdam • Munich • Paris • Milan

PEARSON EDUCATION LIMITED

Edinburgh Gate
Harlow CM20 2JE
United Kingdom
Tel: +44 (0)1279 623623
Fax: +44 (0)1279 431059
Website: www.pearsoned.co.uk

**First edition published in Great Britain in 2005**

© Pearson Education Limited 2005

The right of Owen Davies to be identified as author
of this work has been asserted by him in accordance
with the Copyright, Designs and Patents Act 1988.

ISBN–13: 978–0–582–89413–6
ISBN–10: 0–582–89413–1

*British Library Cataloguing in Publication Data*
A CIP catalogue record for this book can be obtained from the British Library

*Library of Congress Cataloging in Publication Data*
A CIP catalog record for this book can be obtained from the Library of Congress

10 9 8 7 6 5 4 3 2 1
09 08 07 06 05

Set by 3
Printed in Great Britain by Henry Ling Ltd, Dorchester

*The Publishers' policy is to use paper manufactured from sustainable forests.*

# Contents

# Introduction

This book is not a whodunnit. William Dove killed his wife. Nevertheless at the heart of this book is a mystery. What led the scion of a prosperous and widely respected Methodist family to commit murder? Yet it was not this question that first attracted me to the case. It was Dove's curious involvement with a wizard named Henry Harrison that caught my attention. Much of my work has been dedicated to demonstrating the continued relevance and social importance of magic in nineteenth-century England, and this seemed, at first, to be 'just another' example to prove my point. Once I began to research the backgrounds of Dove and the wizard, however, it became clear that their respective life histories, and the consequences of their relationship, provided an extraordinary insight into many more facets of mid-Victorian society. Indeed, when deciding on the title for this book I kept juggling with alliterative nouns. I decided on 'murder, magic, madness' but it could just as appropriately have been 'Methodism, medicine and marriage'.

There is nothing new in the use of a murder case as a window on to the social and cultural milieu in which it was committed. Few subjects are better at luring people into studying the past than 'true crime'. The murderer, as Angus McLaren has put it, can act as a grim 'guide' through the society of the time. McLaren examined the case of the late nineteenth-century serial killer Thomas Neill Cream to provide insights into the cultural role of the medical man, the development of police procedure and perceptions of female sexuality. Others have successfully used the trial in 1857 of the poisoner Madeleine Smith as a means of exploring Victorian newspaper reportage, middle-class society and Scottish jurisprudence. The trial of another poisoner, William Palmer, who plays no small part in this book, has proved a fascinating means of exploring the contentious role of expert medical witnesses in Victorian courts.[1] For an example of how a murder case can illuminate the world of popular beliefs, particularly with regard to magic and witchcraft, we can turn to two books on the sensational Irish trial of Michael Cleary who, in 1895, with the help of other family members, burned his wife to death believing she was a fairy changeling.[2] Jack the Ripper, of course, dominates the popular discourse on Victorian crime. The legion of populist books and films on the subject concentrate on unmasking the identity of the misogynistic serial killer, but the academic focus has been on what the press reports of the murders tell us about middle-class conceptions of morality and sexuality.[3]

This book is not, though, just about the act of murder and its cultural significance. It is also a work of biography, an attempt to show how two individuals' lives were shaped, categorised and condemned by a complex web of social, cultural, religious, intellectual and legal forces. Biography is a strong aspect of history publishing. Indeed, look at the history section of any high street bookshop or the book review pages of any broadsheet and you will find its disproportionate presence. This is quite understandable, but if there is a problem with biography as history, it is that the lives recounted and examined are usually those of the rich, famous or influential. It is rare, indeed, to read the life stories of the humble labourer, artisan or farmer. Of course, we have fine biographies of those of 'lowly birth', such as the poet John Clare and Charles Dickens, who rose to fame through their literary or artistic talent.[4] Historians are also fortunate to have the autobiographies of the autodidactic, politically conscious working classes, and also the religiously inspired, particularly the Methodists, who often desired to have their spiritual journeys recorded in memoirs. The latter have proved particularly valuable for reconstructing William Dove's early life.[5] What historians rarely do, though, is focus on the biographies of the ordinary, or even the ordinary whose lives may have been briefly illuminated by fleeting notoriety. The reason is primarily, but not solely, to do with the paucity of sources. Without diaries or artistic works to interpret, you cannot get very far with the basic facts provided by parish records and censuses. When the sources are sufficient to build up the life histories of the illiterate, the poor, or people like Harrison, who left no personal record of their lives, it is often only because they have committed a serious crime. From the mid-nineteenth century, in particular, with the growing importance of defence counsels in major trials, the biography of the accused became an integral aspect of both prosecution and defence cases.

In the case of Dove and Harrison, however, nearly all the relevant court records are lost. The assize depositions are missing from the boxes where they should be in the Public Record Office, and there are no surviving Leeds coroners' papers for the period. This may seem to be a serious setback in reconstructing events but it is not – thanks to newspapers. The court records would certainly have been helpful in confirming specific details but they rarely provide information not reported by the sensation-hungry press. In fact, newspaper reports of prosecutions often provide far greater detail because they covered the actual trials. Evidence given by witnesses under cross-examination can provide many more details about events leading up to a crime, and about the behaviour and relationships of the individuals concerned, than those gleaned from depositions. Court reports also provide us with information about the physical characteristics of defendants, witnesses, judges, jurors and lawyers. But newspapers were not only essential to this book as a source material. As an increasingly powerful cultural force at the time, they also profoundly shaped the development of the relationship between Dove and the wizard, and ultimately their fate.

Finally, I should also note that considerable use has also been made of censuses, birth, marriage and death certificates, trade directories and maps. To avoid cluttering the text, however, I have not cited them every time they have been used to double-check or correct facts printed in the newspapers, or used to find out such information as the age, occupation, place of residence and marital history of the actors in this extraordinary story.

## Notes and references

1 Angus McLaren, *A Prescription for Murder: The Victorian Serial Killings of Dr Thomas Neill Cream* (Chicago, 1993); Douglas Macgowan, *Murder in Victorian Scotland: The Trial of Madeleine Smith* (Westport, 1999); Sheila Sullivan, '"What is the Matter with Mary Jane?" Madeleine Smith, Legal Ambiguity, and the Gendered Aesthetic of Victorian Criminality', *Genders* 35 (2002); Ian Burney, 'A Poisoning of No Substance: The Trials of Medico-Legal Proof in Mid-Victorian England', *Journal of British Studies* 38 (1999), pp. 59–92. See also Michael Alpert, *London 1849: A Victorian Murder Story* (London, 2004).

2 Joan Hoff and Marian Yeates, *The Cooper's Wife is Missing: The Trials of Bridget Cleary* (New York, 2000); Angela Bourke, *The Burning of Bridget Cleary: A True Story* (London, 1999).

3 L. Perry Curtis, *Jack the Ripper and the London Press* (New Haven and London, 2001); Judith Walkowitz, *City of Dreadful Delight: Narratives of Sexual Danger in Late-Victorian London* (London, 1992); Walkowitz, 'Jack the Ripper and the myth of Male Violence', *Feminist Studies*, 8 (1982) pp. 543–75. For broader discussion on the relationship between press reporting of murders, sensationalism and the Victorian novel see, for example, Judith Knelman, *Twisting in the Wind: The Murderess and the English Press* (Toronto, 1997); Grace Moore and Andrew Maunder (eds), *Victorian Crime, Madness and Sensation* (Aldershot, 2004); Richard D. Altick, *Victorian Studies in Scarlet* (New York, 1970); Altick, *Evil Encounters: Two Victorian Sensations* (London, 1987); Thomas Boyle, *Black Swine in the Sewers of Hampstead: Beneath the Surface of Victorian Sensationalism* (New York, 1989).

4 See, for example, Jonathan Bate, *John Clare* (London, 2004). The biographies on Dickens are too numerous to mention.

5 On working-class autobiographies see David Vincent, *Bread, Knowledge and Freedom* (London, 1981).

# Acknowledgements

First and foremost I give my thanks to those closest to me for their love and support. They know who they are. I would also like to thank my colleagues at the University of Hertfordshire for help and advice, and also Peter Nockles of the John Rylands Library and Peter Forsaith for answering questions on Methodist matters. My research was made all the easier by the service provided by the staff at the Wellcome Library, British Library and the Newspaper Library at Colindale. I would also like to thank Michelle Petyt of York Castle Museum for her solicitous responses to my queries. Moreover, this book has been written at a time when the internet is becoming an increasingly important academic research resource, and I have benefited considerably from a range of websites that deserve mention. Some are only accessible through libraries or educational institutions, in particular the Thomson Gale online digital archive of *The Times* newspaper and the *New Oxford Dictionary of National Biography*. Others are freely available, such as: Leicester University's impressive searchable collection of trade directories (www.historicaldirectories.org); GENUKI, the genealogical information service (www.genuki.org.uk); Leodis, the history of Leeds website (www.leodis.info); A2A, the archives database (www.a2a.org.uk); Yorkshire birth, marriage and death indexes (www.yorkshirebmd.org.uk); and for nineteenth-century Ordnance Survey maps (www.old-maps.co.uk). Other more specific websites have been acknowledged in the endnotes.

# Publishers' Acknowledgements

We are grateful to the following for permission to reproduce copyright material:

Plates 5 and 6: Leeds Library and Information Service; Plate 7: National Portrait Gallery, London; Plate 8: Wellcome Trust, London; Plate 9: by permission of the British Library, Image 7411.aa.4; Plates 10 and 11: York Museums Trust (York Castle Museum); Plate 12: reproduced with permission from www.imagineyork.co.uk © City of York Council.

In some instances we have been unable to trace the owners of copyright material, and we would appreciate any information that would enable us to do so.

# List of Illustrations

# CHAPTER 1

# An inauspicious start in life

*'... pious parentage and religious training are not the infallible guarantees of virtuous maturity'*[1]

Even if William Dove had lived a quiet and unremarkable life he would still have secured a small place in the historical record by virtue of his family's business and religious activities.[2] His grandfather Christopher Dove was a yeoman's son brought up in the North Yorkshire village of Newby Wiske. Like many young men from his social group, at the age of fifteen Christopher was apprenticed and sent to York to learn currying, a skilled job involving the treatment and dressing of tanned leather. Christopher stayed and worked in York after the end of his apprenticeship, but in the early 1780s he set up his own currying and leather-cutting firm in Prebend Row, Darlington, a town that had long been a centre of leather manufacturing in the northeast.[3] Christopher's business prospered and when he died in 1816, aged seventy-one, he bequeathed a substantial sum of money. In the words of Henry Spencer, who wrote a large tome on the worthies of Darlington, he 'passed a sober quiet life, unmarked by extraordinary incidents'.[4] The family firm was taken over by three of his ten children, Christopher junior, and his younger brothers William and Thomas. Only a year later, though, tragedy struck when Thomas died aged only thirty. The two remaining business partners set about building up the firm with considerable success. Spencer remarked that they 'pushed their trade with tact and energy', and were a good demonstration that the accumulation of wealth was achievable 'without the possession of eminent intellectuality'.[5]

Christopher junior converted to Wesleyan Methodism in his twenties and met his first wife through his business and religious connections. She was Mary Steele, a grave and sedate young woman from Barnard Castle whose family were also curriers and Methodists.[6] The couple were married in the spring of 1814, and a friend of the Steeles wrote that when she left the town 'sorrow was portrayed on many countenances, and some wept aloud, on account of their losing so kind and generous a friend.'[7] Less then a year later she was also lost to the world, entering 'the haven of eternal blessedness' on 13 February at the age of twenty-four. Christopher's austere response to her death was shaped by his puritanical Methodism. On her deathbed, when she asked Christopher if 'he had not remarked in her a backwardness, and an apparent aversion to our entering into close conversation on the subject of Christian experience,' he replied he 'certainly had, and lamented it.' Her last wish was to become Christopher's guardian angel if God permitted. Hours after her death he wrote a memoir of her character and last days in which expressions of love mingled with evangelical criticism. 'She was, perhaps, naturally too diffident and reserved,' he observed, 'which disposition the enemy sometimes availed himself of; and which, no doubt, prevented her from enjoying at all times that clearness of experience which is so highly desirable.'[8]

Christopher married Mary Dunn the following year. She was the daughter of William Dunn, a Durham ironmonger and fellow Wesleyan Methodist. It was said that she 'possessed considerable literary ability', though her only published writing was a pamphlet on the quality of sober dressing entitled *Thoughts upon Dress*, which was presumably a reflection upon John Wesley's essay of the same title.[9] Henry Spencer had the opportunity to read a copy and remarked that her 'antiquated' views would have been 'read with astonishment' by the 'fair wearers of gaily-trimmed bonnets, and extensive crinolines' of his day.[10] We gain some insight into her early years of marriage from the correspondence of her only sister Margaret Burton, who died of a long lingering illness in 1830. Her letters and diaries are full of references to the kind attentions of her sister and Christopher. When, one time, he was very seriously ill with an 'attack of inflammation', she wrote to her sister expressing the hope that 'thy invaluable husband shall yet for many years continue to grow in grace, and to be a general blessing. Amen, Lord Jesus.'[11]

It was a sign of their increasing prosperity and upward mobility that around 1820 the Dove's moved to a newly built rented house in Wellington Place. Darlington was about to undergo something of a housing boom, due initially to population pressure as the economy attracted new migrants, and then in response to the opening of the Stockton to Darlington railway in 1825, which led to considerable urban development. New commercial streets were built on the outskirts of the town, and the small residential development of Wellington Place, named in honour of the general, was one of the first of a series of new middle-class residential areas in the town.[12] Not long afterwards Christopher moved to the newly built Grange House. It was here that William was born on 1 July 1827. He was the eighth of Mary and Christopher's nine children, six girls and three boys. Their first was Mary, born in 1818. She later married Benjamin Marsden, son of John Marsden, a Leeds hosier and glover. Jane was born in 1819 but died eight years later. Their first son, Christopher, was delivered on 6 April 1820. The following year Elizabeth was born. Sarah came next in 1824 and was to be the longest lived of the Dove children. Anna was born in 1825 and Margaret the following year. William was three when the last of the Dove children, Samuel, died aged only eleven months.

Samuel's death happened not long after the family had moved to Leeds. The difficult decision to uproot from Darlington was in response to Leeds' growing prominence in the leather trade. The booming population generated demand for large quantities of meat, which in turn generated large quantities of hides, while the textile mills that fuelled the expansion of Leeds required a constant supply of heavy leathers for their machinery.[13] The industry expanded rapidly, with all grades of leather being produced, from industrial drive belts to fine morocco leather.[14] From 1827 quarterly leather fairs were held at the newly built South Market, and soon became the largest outside London. It made good business sense, therefore, for the Doves to remove to Leeds; besides, they already had premises in the town at 37 Boar Lane. But the decision was not taken 'without much prayer and deliberation'. The Doves were well integrated into the religious and commercial world of Darlington, but ultimately Christopher felt that the 'finger of Providence' pointed in the direction of Leeds.[15]

The Doves settled at 3 Park Square, one of several red brick developments built for the gentry and prosperous merchants on the western edge of Leeds during the late eighteenth and early nineteenth century. It was initially a highly desirable area but as the woollen mills and dye houses spread westwards along the banks of the River Aire a thick pall of smoke replaced the country air and workers' cottages encroached on the genteel suburb.[16] In 1824, Park Square householders had taken legal action against the biggest of the offending factory owners, Benjamin Gott, but to no avail.[17] So around the time the Doves moved in, the wealthiest of the middle classes were beginning to move out of the neighbourhood and relocate to villas further westwards and northwards where the air was cleaner and the working classes not so evident. Nevertheless, Park Square and other such residential areas near the town centre remained home to many professionals and businessmen. The Dove's neighbours included the likes of the barrister Thomas Horncastle Marshall, the borough engineer Thomas Walker, the banker Thomas Blayds, and the Rev. Edward Cookson.[18] Christopher soon established himself as an influential member of the Wesleyan Methodist community. He became the secretary of the Auxiliary Wesleyan Missionary Society for the Leeds circuit[19] and was instrumental in the construction of Oxford Place Chapel, one of the largest Wesleyan chapels in the country, which opened in the autumn of 1835 and provided places for 2,600 worshippers, with 1000 seats being offered free to the poor.[20] Its plans were determined at a meeting held in the Doves' drawing room, Christopher contributed significant sums to its construction, and he was its treasurer for many years. Yet he was not a staunch sectarian and was also widely respected by the local Anglican clergy and other Nonconformists through his involvement with and donations to such bodies as the Evangelical Alliance, Bible Society, Leeds Town Mission and the Strangers' Friend Society.[21]

Leeds was described in the 1830s as a town 'favoured with many signal revivals of religion; and in which many truly religious people are to be found.'[22] Indeed, as a recent comprehensive survey of Victorian religion has shown, Wesleyan Methodism flourished more than any other denomination in the rapidly expanding northern towns of Victorian England.[23] A census of Leeds taken by the town council in 1839 revealed that Methodism was running a close second to Anglican churches regarding the provision of places, with Wesleyan chapels providing 11,160 seats to the Church of England's 13,255.[24] By 1851 there were significantly more people attending the various Methodist chapels in Leeds than the Anglican churches. The situation was similar in other large towns in Yorkshire such as Hull and Bradford.[25] At the time of the Doves' move to Leeds, however, the town's Wesleyan community had only recently settled down after the acrimonious schism generated by the installation of an organ in Brunswick Chapel in 1827. Such an apparently innocuous move was taken as a grave mark of religious vanity by some and led a small group to break away from the Wesleyan Connexion.[26] 'Embarrassed finance, diminished congregations, disruption of friendships, depressed hopes, and many melancholy instances of backsliding, were the sad fruits,' wrote one observer.[27] Christopher, who remained loyal to the Connexion, proved himself a key figure in restoring confidence, raising money and healing personal and public rifts.

## Working hard and giving generously

The Methodist environment in which Christopher brought up his children did not mirror his own upbringing. Christopher senior had been opposed to the Wesleyans but considered there were some good men among them and sent his sons to a local preacher's school. Christopher junior did not, however, immediately follow in the devout footsteps of one of his brothers, John, who trained as an Independent minister and wrote a biography of the Wesley family.[28] It was said that once out of school Christopher forgot God, and his life until the age of twenty-five was 'spent in the follies and vanities of the world' – a not uncommon story in male Methodist biographies and autobiographies of the time.[29] His father's resistance to his son's conversion was not solely on religious grounds, he was also concerned that Christopher's attendance at Methodist meetings would interfere with the running of the family business. Christopher was determined to allay his concerns. He made a point of being the first to arrive at the workshop in the morning and the last to leave at night. He may have mixed religion with business but he ensured that the one did not interfere to the detriment of the other. Anthony Steele, his brother-in-law and business companion in these early years, recalled with great respect and affection their first trip to London in 1815: 'For between two and three weeks, we acted together in business affairs during the day, and at night cast up our spiritual accounts. I well remember how, during our journey by coach, he watched for opportunities to do good, distributing religious tracts, and holding serious conversation with coachmen and passengers.'[30] When leather markets were occasionally held on Mondays, instead of travelling the day before like most merchants, he would avoid profaning the Sabbath by rising at one o'clock in the morning on the Monday and hiring a post-chaise. At the end of the day he would avoid staying in large hotels where he 'might be exposed to worldly customs and company.'[31]

During the early nineteenth century artisans, trades people and independent businessmen like the Doves were the most active group in the Methodist movement.[32] It is no surprise, then, that Methodism seems to have been particularly strong in the currying trade in Yorkshire. As well as the Doves in Darlington and Leeds, the Steeles in Barnard Castle, one of the leading lights of the Wesleyans in York was Joseph Agar, a prosperous currier and generous benefactor to worthy causes, who, like Christopher, was converted to Methodism in his mid-twenties.[33] The appeal of Methodism to successful men like Dove and Agar, whose families had come from humble backgrounds, was that it presented itself as embracing the life and outlook of the 'common man and woman'. It was an independent religion for the self-employed who worked in small close-knit groups. It recognised the nobility of hard, honest toil and espoused a vision of social equality before God that contrasted with Anglicanism, where social hierarchy and deference was enforced through seating plans and patronage.[34] This Methodist conception of social levelling was not only an aspect of the church's philosophy, it was also a guiding principal for personal social relations. When he took over the business from his father, Christopher had the apprentices lodge in his own house, and even though he had to give up this arrangement as his family grew, he continued to join his workers in daily prayer. On Sunday evenings he would also invite the servants into the parlour to join the family in reading aloud from the Scriptures and to discuss the incidents of the day.[35]

Methodism also provided its members with a close-knit network of friends and acquaintances among whom business and religion were inextricably intertwined. This was apparent in Christopher's first marriage and the marriages of his offspring, whose spouses came from Methodist families engaged in leather-related trades, such as gloving and shoe making. Indeed, it was unusual for Methodists to marry outside the faith. In 1823 the Wesleyan Conference had deemed 'the marriage of a preacher with a female not belonging to our society to be an instance of culpable imprudence, perilous to the comfort and usefulness of the preacher himself, and likely if not discountenanced to be greatly injurious to the spiritual interests of our people.'[36]

Charity was central to the Methodist way of life. Working hard and giving generously was a guiding principal, and once again Christopher and his wife strove to exemplify this Christian duty. A typical example of his charitable impulse occurred one Sunday morning when he suddenly turned to his wife and said:

> *I am not satisfied with my givings to the Missionary cause; and as I have £50 in the house, for which I have no immediate call, I wish you to hand it to the Superintendent, that he may send it to the Mission-house tomorrow. I always find it best immediately to follow the intimations of the Good Spirit. Perhaps, if I keep it till tomorrow, the enemy may suggest, and my own evil heart may concur in the suggestion, that a smaller amount will be quite sufficient.*[37]

His sister-in-law, Margaret Burton, also bequeathed to him a large sum of money 'to increase his ability to relieve the destitute and afflicted, and to help yet more extensively to support the best of causes upon earth'.[38] He not only gave money but also much of his spare time. Both he and Mary conducted religious classes for the poor and visited the sick. He taught his children to do likewise. On reaching a certain age the Dove children were encouraged to teach in Sunday school and distribute religious tracts. While Anna lay ill in bed her favourite occupation was making garments for the poor, the material for which she purchased from her own savings.[39] Each child was given a sum of money to be used for 'charitable and useful purposes', and they were required to keep a regular account of receipts and disbursements – a classic example of the Methodist harmony between good business practice and charitable principles.[40]

## Family life

William's parents were described by one who knew them well as being 'strict without being severe, and kind without being over-indulgent'.[41] The children were brought up in an atmosphere of religious austerity and daily devout contemplation: in the Dove household 'the domestic altar was magnified'.[42] From an early age the children received constant religious instruction and were taught to develop a serious and, to the modern eye, rather depressing view of life. By the early years of the Victorian period the asceticism of early Methodism was being diluted, and card playing and dancing were being conducted in increasing numbers of Methodist homes. In the 1830s the Wesleyan authorities in Manchester disciplined a number of such 'dancing Methodists' and lost members as a result, but in the opinion of some, 'members who patronised dancing were better lost than found.' A couple of decades later the Wesleyan authorities decided to reinforce the ban on such sinful activities. The Rev. J. Scott commented 'that as the evil was chiefly among the younger members of Methodist families, he hoped they would with great affection as well as firmness enforce the rule, so as not to lose their hold upon the younger people.' [43]

There was certainly no dancing or card playing in the Dove household; 3 Park Square was free of all worldly amusements. Leisure time in such homes was built around religious contemplation and charitable works. As to reading, the Wesleyan Methodist T. Jackson, writing in 1839, said that Methodists 'had no time for light literature, and chiefly read the Methodist Hymn-Book and the Bible'.[44] In the first thirty years or so of Woodhouse Grove School, a highly respected Wesleyan establishment founded in 1812 to educate the sons of ministers, the only other reading matter available to the boys were old copies of Methodist magazines. It was only with the arrival of a new geography teacher, Peter M'Owan, that some edifying historical novels were introduced to the library, 'to the horror' of some of the masters. The Rev. William Lord, a friend of the Doves, who was the school's governor between 1842 and 1858, even initially banned the reading of Harriet Beecher Stowe's *Uncle Tom's Cabin* when it was published in England in 1853, although he later realised it was an edifying book and bought copies for the library.[45] Back in the Dove household William's sister, Margaret, was ever ready to reprove her sisters if she found them with a book 'which was not manifestly of an improving character.' 'Would our parents like us to read this book?' she would chide them. An instance is recorded when one of the Dove children brought home some books from a circulating library, the content of which their father disapproved. He confiscated them and had them placed in Margaret's bedroom, 'but perceiving that these volumes were a temptation to her sisters, who occasionally came to peep into their contents, she crept out of bed unperceived, and concealed them.'[46]

We gain an intimate insight into this loving but austere childhood environment from two rare memoirs published to commemorate three of William's siblings. When his elder brother Christopher died on 6 February 1836, aged sixteen, his parents requested the Wesleyan minister Peter M'Owan to set down his brief life in print.[47] Before becoming a teacher of geography at Woodhouse Grove in the 1850s, M'Owan had spent much of his life preaching around England and abroad, and it was presumably during his stint on the Leeds circuit that he became friends with the Doves. He was certainly not the most gifted of writers but as a former pupil of his remembered, 'he had a rare quality of making us learn and think for ourselves'.[48] Following the death of Margaret on 14 April 1838 the Doves once again turned to M'Owan. Although a man of tremendous energy, he had difficulty finishing the memoir sufficiently swiftly for his own conscience, and sent an apologetic letter to Christopher that June in which he wrote: 'I esteem you too highly, and love you too tenderly, ever to forget you long together.' By this time Anna had also apparently fallen ill, for M'Owan went on to ask: 'I have scarcely adverted to the affliction of dear Anna, lest it would be inappropriate, but I wish to know how she is, and how you all are.'[49] She died in early January the following year and the commemorative book that eventually came out concerned both daughters and was given the rather sweet symbolic title of *The Two Doves*. M'Owan wrote both memoirs not only as private remembrances but also as public exemplars for Methodist children, and it was for this purpose that the *Memoir of Christopher Dove* went through three editions, the last in 1850, and *The Two Doves* was republished in New York in 1843 at the request of the Sunday School Union of the Methodist Episcopal Church.

The memoirs were as quick to point out the children's faults as to praise their good points. From an early age the children of staunch

Methodists like the Doves were taught the necessity of self-criticism to achieve piety. The danger was that self-criticism could turn to destructive self-loathing. 'Many were the errors' that Christopher committed, wrote M'Owan, 'through the volatility of his mind; but in none of them did he obstinately persevere, after their true character had been exposed.'[50] What these errors were is not divulged, but they presumably referred to the usual childhood pranks, such as the time he overturned a toy carriage in which his sisters were riding. This episode led to his being chastised by his tutor, Jacob Smith, whose admonishment triggered an outpouring not only of childish guilt in Christopher but also a more disturbing premature sense of his own worthlessness. He confessed to Smith that he was 'afraid he was growing worse instead of better'. When asked how long it was since he committed his first sin, Christopher replied that he could not tell exactly, but thought it must be three years. 'How often do you sin, on an average, each day?' inquired Smith. 'At least fifty times,' admitted Christopher.[51] The boy's views on the 'exceeding sinfulness of sin', according to M'Owan, 'were vivid; his self-loathing was deep', and though 'there was little to condemn in his life, he knew that he had a depraved nature.'[52] This was apparently a good thing. Margaret too, when about nine years of age, was convinced that she was mired in sin: 'her soul was filled with distress; she saw herself to be a lost sinner, and refused to rest till she found redemption in the blood of Jesus.'[53]

William makes a brief appearance in both these memoirs, and there are indications that even by the age of ten he was displaying certain tendencies of cause for concern not only to his parents but also his brothers and sisters. A year or two before Christopher's death a religious awakening was held at the Doves. Christopher had already given himself up to Christ but he 'yearned with concentrated pity over his brother William, who still remained in distress of soul, shut up in unbelief', and so while the company took tea he led his younger brother into another room and prayed for him. According to the memoir, Christopher's prayers were answered and 'William found that his load of guilt was gone, and that his soul was strangely filled with peace and joy.' Christopher ran to his parents and exclaimed in rapture, 'O mother, all your children are converted to God!'[54] Several years later we get a tantalising inkling that Christopher's joy was, perhaps, premature. On her deathbed, Anna wished to speak to each member of the family in turn. When she came to

William, who stood near, she exclaimed, 'O William! – William!' but was unable to say any more.[55] She had once tried to instruct her brother on the advantages of dedication to God, and William, who was not yet in his teens, asked, 'And have you always felt that your sins were pardoned since you did so, Anna?' 'Sometimes,' she replied. The answer may not have been entirely reassuring.[56]

Other sources also indicate that William was a wild and wayward child, who could not be readily taught his religious lessons. One of the family servants, Mary Wood, spent much of her time looking after him when he was five or six years old, and found him a real handful. When she undressed and put him to bed he would often sit in front of the bedroom door to prevent her from leaving and would grin and scream if she tried to pick him up. On several occasions he put a lit candle in a basket and then locked it in a closet. He was also punished for putting candles and salt in the coffee mill. His taste for malicious pranks continued over the next few years. He once chased his sisters with a red-hot poker, and on another occasion locked them in their room and threatened to burn them. Another time his twisted sense of fun led him to hang a cat out of his bedroom window by its tail.[57] Nevertheless, as their only surviving son, William was apparently treated much more leniently than his older brother and sisters, and was once described as 'the spoiled child of a fond father and an indulgent mother'.[58]

## Growing up in Leeds

By the time William was thirteen he had experienced the death of his two brothers and two of his sisters. Of the nine Dove children only Mary and Sarah were alive to suffer the tragedy William was to inflict on the family. The Doves' experience of infant mortality and illness was, in fact, nothing unusual at the time, even for middle-class families. Nevertheless, as a prosperous family living in a comfortable part of town they were more sheltered than most from the ravages of the influenza that struck Leeds and elsewhere in 1830–31 and the national cholera epidemic that plagued the town in 1832 killing seven hundred people, and which struck again two years later.[59]

Leeds was expanding rapidly at the time. Between the first national census of 1801 and that of 1831 the population had grown from around

53,000 to 123,393. By this time the poor health of its population was a cause for vociferous concern. In 1831 the respected Leeds doctor Turner Thackrah wrote a book on the subject that painted a very bleak picture:

> *I should think that not 10 per cent of the inhabitants of towns like Leeds enjoy full health. Were we to ask, indeed, those we see around us, the major part would say that they are quite well. But a close examination would prove that there are few individuals who have not either disease of some organ, or an evident disposition to disease.*[60]

In Thackrah's extensive survey of occupational health, curriers actually came out as one of the healthiest groups of workers. 'The smell of the leather produces no disagreeable effect,' he noted, and the 'men are generally very healthy; and a considerable proportion live to old age,'[61] which was better than the gloomy prospects for the employers of curriers. According to Thackrah it would seem that Christopher was in an unhealthier occupation than his workers. Thackrah shared our present day recognition of the value of cardio-vascular exercise and varied diet, and observed that it was an unfortunate arrangement that such mercantile and manufacturing men had their houses and warehouse within 'a stone's cast of each other', for it severely restricted the opportunity for exercise. The only exercise such men got was 'a day's shooting, or drive on business to a neighbouring town'. Furthermore, 'the way in which men of business take their meals is also highly injurious to health. It is far too hasty.'[62]

The family may have avoided the influenza and the cholera epidemics, but they could not avoid that most prevalent, persistent and indiscriminate of nineteenth-century killers: tuberculosis. While cholera grabbed the headlines and the public imagination, consumption or phthisis, as tuberculosis was known at the time, was the biggest killer of all.[63] The Doves were no exception. William's elder brother Christopher died of the disease in 1836. Doctors applied leeches – a common but patently ineffectual cure. His sister Margaret was the next victim in April 1838. She was twelve years old. The poor girl's throat was so ulcerated as a result of tuberculosis that for the last few months of her life she was unable to talk. The following year Anna also succumbed.

## William's education

Between the age of ten and twelve William was sent to Richard Hiley's school in Leeds. Hiley found him difficult, nigh impossible to teach. William was nearly always bottom of his class. He was fond of mischief, badly tempered and while intellectually limited he nevertheless possessed 'a low cunning'. On one occasion he was found to have stolen some drawings from one of his sisters and sold them. When confronted with this, he said they were his own productions. Hiley replied, 'that can soon be ascertained,' and made him sit down and make a copy of them. William began to do so but as it was soon apparent that he had little artistic ability, he stopped and feebly claimed, 'Oh, sir, I forget.' Another of his teachers at this time, Charles Hanmer, stated that 'he had a great want of moral power to resist evil and vicious propensities.' Corporal punishment had no effect; he 'would hold out his hand for fifty strokes as easily as for one.' [64] His one redeeming feature at this stage, as far as his teachers were concerned, was a certain generosity, and he would give away all he had to fellow pupils. This was one aspect of his religious upbringing that shone through.

Not long after the exposure of William's painting racket he got into more serious trouble due to an early fascination with guns. As an act of revenge he brought a gun to school and boasted to his fellow students that he was going to shoot Hiley, and then his own father. Some of the boys quickly informed Hanmer, who confiscated the pistol and sent word to William's father, who duly arrived and administered a severe flogging. This did nothing to deter William's love of firearms though. Later in life he possessed a double-barrelled shot gun, a brace of pistols and a six-barrel revolver. He was in the habit of carrying them around with him, much to the consternation of others, particularly as he used to fire them off for no apparent reason.[65]

William was expelled from Hiley's school because of the gun incident, and he was then packed off to the newly established Wesleyan Proprietary Grammar School (later changed to Wesley College in 1844) in Sheffield, which his father had helped set up. The school had opened its doors in 1838, and its prospectus advertised its 'many advantages to families of wealth and influence among the Wesleyans', providing a 'generally superior and classical education, combined with religious training in the principles of Methodism.'[66] Its headmaster was the Rev. John Manners, and at the time William was there, there were around 150 boarders, some from overseas. William avoided mathematics and studied Latin, history, chemistry and drawing, but apparently achieved little. In class he would adopt a vacant stare and cared little about threats of punishment or its application. Manners thought he 'partook more of the animal than of the rational creature.'[67] After about a year the college requested William's parents to remove him, and so he was then sent to Mr Kay's school in Oxford Street, Leeds, to complete his ill-starred education.[68]

It was by now 1842 and William was fifteen years of age. It was clear to Christopher and Mary that their son was not fit to take over the family business and was also ill-prepared to enter any other profession due to his lack of social graces. He could not, it was said, be 'introduced into company without great mortification to the family'.[69] Distressed by their son's behaviour Christopher consulted officers at the York County Asylum regarding his son's mental state and whether he should be admitted as a patient.[70] He also sent him to Woodhouse Grove School to see his friend the Rev. William Lord. 'I made myself acquainted with the state of his mind,' Lord recalled, but 'could make no impression upon his heart or head. He listened quietly, but I could get no rational answer.'[71] In the circumstances it was decided that he should take up farming, and so he was articled to Aaron Frankish, an acquaintance of his father who managed two farms at Ganton, a village on the edge of the North York Moors, a few miles south of Scarborough.

For the next five and a half years Frankish had nothing but trouble with William, who showed little interest in and no aptitude for farming. But life on the farm certainly gave William a free rein to indulge his sadistic delight in inflicting pain on animals. Oil of vitriol, otherwise known as sulphuric acid, was his favourite tool of torture. Not long into his apprenticeship Frankish discovered that Dove had burned several of his cows and their calves by pouring vitriol over them. He had initially denied responsibility but then confessed and apologised for his behaviour. Frankish, curious as to why William neglected to injure one of the calves, received the reply that it was his favourite. On another occasion, William poured vitriol into the eyes of two kittens and sent the frantic, blinded creatures into the farm kitchen to scare the maids. He also once poured vitriol into the horses' trough, though fortunately the horses refused to drink from it. He once poured phosphorus on some cats to 'make them bright and on fire'. Another great pleasure was pyromania. He set two of Frankish's wagon covers alight and also burned an area of grass. When he returned to his parents on holiday one time, he poured alcohol on his bedroom curtains and set light to them. William also found other ingenious means of tormenting livestock. One day he tied some cows' tails together, and another time put a rope around a cow's back legs, threw the rope over a beam and commenced to hoist the rope as far as he could, which was not far, but nevertheless left the cow standing on its forelegs in much distress.[72]

Frankish disapproved of the way William sought the company of the farm labourers. On one occasion William treated the farmhands to some beer and when Frankish's wife chided him about it, Dove brandished a knife and said, 'Mrs Frankish, you may think yourself well off you have a husband this morning.'[73] He threatened to 'destroy' Frankish but it was just his familiar teenage bravado and bluster rather than real intent. Frankish lectured him and sent for his father. Christopher punished his son and persuaded Frankish to keep him on. The farm servants were also the targets of William's unstable and violent temperament. One of them, James Rowell, recalled how one day Dove ran at him with a pitchfork after he refused to give him some straw, and on another occasion threatened, 'Damn you, if I had a gun in my hand I would have shot you!'[74]

To Frankish's considerable relief, Dove left his farm on turning twenty-one. Yet at the end of his apprenticeship he was no better equipped to start farming than he was when he first arrived. Frankish farmed using a system of crop rotation, but even after five years Dove could not understand the workings of a four-course and six-course rotation farm. 'He knew sowing from reaping, and mowing from harrowing, but that was all,' said Frankish.[75] As a result, William's father asked another farming acquaintance, Jonathan Gibson of Hedley Hall, near Tadcaster, to further his son's agricultural education. He looked after the young man for nearly a year, paying him nine pence pocket-money a week. Gibson may have been understating the situation when he said that he did not consider William 'one of the brightest farmers'. He managed to teach him something of the practical side of the business, but was less successful in teaching him farming theory. So with six years of agricultural training, albeit largely wasted, William was set to become a farmer in his own right, but he had other plans. Wanderlust led him to America, and one can imagine that his father readily paid for the passage.

He travelled mainly through the northern states and Canada, paying a visit to Niagara at one point, but also spent some time in the south where he observed the slavery system.[76] Otherwise all we know of his two years in America is from the amazing stories he told to his acquaintances on his return. There was the time, for example, when he got to be a chief of the 'Red Indians' and travelled around with his tribe. During this time he had a brave fight with a bear. The bear clasped him with its paws and tried to suffocate him, but he managed to free his knife and disembowel it. His tribe celebrated this heroic feat. In another adventure he described how he was caught in a prairie fire. The fire raged behind him but quick wittedly he set fire to a stretch of prairie before him and when the two fires met they burnt out. The Rev. Lord found his 'accounts were not in accordance with my own personal knowledge of the country.'[77] Others were more willing to believe. A local schoolmaster, John Thompson, 'thought there was probability in his story about the Red Indians – it was told coherently, but romantically. He told the story in such a way as to induce me to believe it. He talked to me about things that had transpired abroad, great feats and miracles he had done. The Red Indian story was the best; I cannot remember the next best.'[78]

## Farmer Dove [79]

Not long after William's return to England his parents asked Jonathan Gibson to find a suitable farm for William to rent. White Well Farm, which belonged to the Becca Hall estate, near Aberford, was chosen. It lay in a rather isolated position south of Bramham Park, next to the turnpike road from Tadcaster to Leeds. William moved there in February 1852, and was joined by James Shann and Robert Tomlinson, hired by Christopher to help run the farm, along with a housekeeper named Mary Peck. It was not long before the servants were acquainted with their young master's peculiar and capricious ways. There was good reason for Shann to describe him as 'odd' and for Tomlinson to observe 'something strange about him'. He would get angry with them for no apparent reason and made them the target of his malicious pranks. He set fire to Mary

Peck's cap while she was wearing it, and on another occasion threw a can of water over her. He also fired off a pistol next to the ear of the charwoman for fun. He continued to tell tall tales to impress, telling Peck, for example, how four men on the road had waylaid him. He knocked two down, the third he left sprawled in the road and the fourth ran away. Yet he was unduly concerned about robbers, and regularly claimed men were prowling around the farm at night. On these occasions he would wake Shann to accompany him to look around the farm, but no nocturnal intruders were ever encountered. He inevitably took a gun with him on these night watches. On one occasion during daytime Shann stopped Dove from threatening to shoot a man who was in his garden for purely innocent purposes. Shann was so shocked by the careless way his master brandished his guns while fully cocked that he eventually refused to accompany him. Nevertheless, despite this volatile behaviour he continued to display that streak of generosity and lack of social condescension that had marked him out in his youth. One night, for example, while the household were at prayer, a female tramp came to the door. Dove invited her in to join them and let her sleep the night in the barn, much to the disapproval of his employees.

As to farming, William not unsurprisingly made a poor start. Headley Hall was only four miles from White Well Farm, enabling Gibson to pay frequent visits over the next three months to help William get himself started. But things did not go well. He ignored Gibson's advice and 'did not farm it as he ought'. This would seem to have been something of an understatement. He planted an apple orchard, for example, and then within a couple of weeks he decided to uproot and move some of them, and then decided to have some of them cut to pieces for no apparent reason. He mowed an acre of barley when it was still green and unripe because he did not want to be behind the other farmers in bringing the crop to market. One night he sent the boy to get two linseed cakes from Mr King, a neighbouring farmer, which he gave to two cattle he was taking to Leeds market the next day. He believed they would fatten them up overnight. He tried to innovate with the ploughs by putting some pegs into their shafts for the ploughmen to put their thumbs in, believing it would help them get a better grip. According to Shann, though, 'it made the ploughs worse, and they could not be worked with.'

# Marriage

On his return from America William had continued to mix in Methodist social circles in and around Leeds. He was a periodic visitor at the social events organised at Woodhouse Grove School. At times William could behave with decorum, but his lack of education and social graces were painfully apparent to the refined sensibilities of middle-class society. Lord, who was a kindly man, affectionately called 'Daddy Lord' by the schoolboys, recalled that William's 'conduct was such that he could not visit us without mortifying us by his conversation and his poverty of intellect.'[80] William thought himself very clever, said Lord, but he could not 'follow out a subject to its results.' Nevertheless, it was at the social gatherings at Woodhouse Grove that he caught the eye of a young woman named Harriet Jenkins. She was the same age as William and the daughter of Elisabeth and Richard Jenkins, a Plymouth shoemaker and leather merchant. Harriet periodically travelled up to Woodhouse Grove to see her brother the Rev. John Sloggett Jenkins, who taught mathematics at the school, and who a couple of years later married William's sister Sarah.[81] William proposed to Harriet not long after their first meeting but she made no decision for several months, during which time William continued to pay his addresses to her. The scenario echoes a far more auspicious wooing that took place on exactly the same spot forty years earlier. It was at Woodhouse Grove School that the parents of the Brontë sisters first met. Patrick Brontë, who was curate at Hartshead, some twelve miles away, was invited by his good friend John Fennell, headmaster of the newly opened school, to inspect the teaching of classics. While there he was introduced to Fennell's niece Maria Branwell, who like Harriet had travelled up from the West Country, although Maria's trip would have been rather more arduous in the age before the railway.

Of Harriet's life and physical appearance we know very little. Although once a healthy young woman, she had developed an occasionally debilitating nervous disposition resulting from the shock over the untimely death of one of her brothers when she was seventeen or eighteen. Since then she had suffered from what her friends and family called 'hysterics'. During these fits, which lasted around a quarter of an hour, there was a sound like wind rattling in her stomach, her hands grew stiff and her arms twitched. She became insensible but was physically none the worse once the fits had passed, though 'her mind would be pained by any circumstance.'[82] Unfortunately her husband was an engine of circumstance, and eyebrows were raised in some quarters regarding the suitability of the match. Lord told Harriet's brother that he ought to enquire as to William's character before the marriage took place, but Harriet was of age to decide her own future. Besides, the Doves were a highly esteemed family, and John deemed it an honour to be allied to it. The couple were married in Plymouth in August 1852, and so began a brief, tempestuous and ultimately tragic marriage.

The couple returned from Plymouth to White Well Farm and a succession of housemaids was taken on to help the new mistress. None of them stayed for long. Emma Wilkinson was there for six months after the married couple arrived, but found her master's conduct 'not that of a reasonable man'. The next, Emma Spence, said she was 'frightened of the man'. Three weeks after their marriage William and Harriet were already quarrelling, reducing each other to tears at times. Their relationship was one of emotional extremes, stemming, in part, from William's violent mood swings. When John Sloggett Jenkins visited the couple at White Well he never quite knew how he would find his brother-in-law. He was sometimes 'miserably depressed', sometimes 'highly elated'. 'I have known him most devout and religious one day, and a reprobate the next,' he observed.[83] William would conduct family prayer in an orderly, solemn fashion and then fly into an inexplicable rage. Out of the blue he would suddenly pick up his gun and go and shoot rabbits.

A typical incident occurred on a visit to Aaron Frankish a few weeks into their marriage. In the evening William asked Harriet to play a tune on the piano for them. She refused, and William grew angry, ordered a candle and stormed off to bed. When his wife went up a little later she found the bedroom door locked. He only opened it when Mrs Frankish threatened to break it down. The next morning he apologised and the young couple cuddled and fondled each other, with William affectionately calling her 'my love' and 'my dear'. Back at White Well Farm the couple would frolic in the fields 'like children', with William carrying his wife under his arms and over his shoulders. In the mornings he would carry Harriet downstairs on his back and feed her with a spoon. Such intimate and open displays of love were too much for the straight-laced John Jenkins, who described his disgust at William's 'intense and foolish affection' for his sister.

A more serious and ominous example of William's erratic behaviour occurred on 16 January 1853 while Harriet's mother was staying with them. The young couple had gone into Leeds where William got rather drunk, and on the way back he was in a demonic mood, riding the carriage furiously and telling her he would 'drive her soul to eternity.' On their return a frightened and tearful Harriet told her mother what had happened and she turned to William and upbraided him for making her daughter cry. In response William went off to get two pistols. He found Emma Spence in the cellar and announced, 'Now, Emma, we are going all into eternity tonight. I have three balls, one for each, but I will not hurt you.' When he went upstairs to the parlour brandishing the pistols all three women fled the house and ran to the brewhouse. Shortly after, Harriet went back to the house to reason with him. William cornered her in a room and threatened to blow her brains out if she moved. He fired the pistols out of a window instead and then went off for some matches saying he would burn the place down.

Yet, from accounts provided by the Doves' servants at White Well it is clear that sudden mood swings and an unstable temperament were also as much a part of Harriet's character as her husband's, and the servants at White Well were patently sick and tired of both of them. Shann thought her 'full as bad as he was.' Emma Spence described her as a 'bad 'un', tormenting William with her jealousy. On one occasion she accused him of having an affair with someone called 'Emma'. Spence at first thought that this referred to her, but was later relieved to find she had some other Emma in mind. Another housemaid, Annie Wilson, who worked for the Doves in 1853 thought Mrs Dove was the cause of some of William's queer behaviour: 'She used to treat him like a beast sometimes. Called him a fool.' Wilson often 'heard her scolding him, and he used to go into the fields and cry like a man not right in his mind.'[84] These verbal put-downs seem to have followed her frequent hysterical fits.

William's drinking hardly helped matters. Harriet frequently chided him about it, and she had good reason to, for his binges not infrequently led to wild gun-wielding rampages. On one occasion in 1852 while he and Harriet and Robert Tomlinson and his wife were together in a room, he took a loaded pistol, put the barrel in Tomlinson's mouth and threatened to blow his brains out. Tomlinson took the pistol off him, leading William to make one of his periodic vows to blow the place up. From time to time, though, he would try to turn a new leaf. In January 1854, for example, he told his farm servant William Tomlinson that he had signed the teetotal pledge and asked him to help carry two barrels of ale out of the cellar, the contents of which he then poured down the sink. Afterwards he wondered aloud whether coffee would serve as well as ale for drinking. It evidently did not, and his teetotal days were short in number.[85] He was heavily under the influence that summer when, on 11 August, he was arrested for threatening behaviour. He had been to see his parents in Park Square and brought his pistols with him. He announced to the family he was going to shoot his parents and then kill himself. He then ran off and a guest of the family, the Rev. Theophilus Woolmer, bravely went after him. He found William nearby in the cottage of a poor and frightened family. William was armed and still babbling about destroying himself and his parents. Woolmer sent for the police. William was arrested and charged with attempted suicide and lodged in prison. When brought before the magistrates he was heavily reprimanded and then discharged.

## Notes and references

1 Henry Spencer, *Men that are gone from the households of Darlington* (Darlington and London, 1862), p. 151. The quote refers to William Dove.

2 Graham Prattens' genealogical notes on the Dove family have been a very helpful resource in piecing together the history of William's family. See http://www.prattens.co.uk/FAMILIES/DOVE/NOTES.HTML.

3 See Gillian Cookson, *The Townscape of Darlington* (Woodbridge, 2003).

4 Spencer, *Men that are gone*, p. 149.

5 Spencer, *Men that are gone*, p. 149.

6 Her brother, Anthony Steele, was the author of a *History of Methodism in Barnard Castle* (London, 1857).

7 'Memoir of Mrs. Christopher Dove, Jun.', *Arminian Magazine*, 39 (1816), p. 532.

8 'Memoir of Mrs. Christopher Dove', p. 534.

9 I have been unable to trace a copy of Mary's pamphlet.

10 Spencer, *Men that are gone*, p. 150.

11 John Dungett (ed.), *Life and Correspondence of the late Mrs. Margaret Burton, of Darlington* (Darlington, 1832). p. 171.

12  See Cookson, *Townscape of Darlington*, ch. 3.

13  R.J. Morris, *Class, sect and party: The making of the British middle class, Leeds 1820–50* (Manchester, 1990), p. 33.

14  W.G. Rimmer, 'Leeds Leather Industry in the Nineteenth Century', *Thoresby Society* 46 (1960), p. 133; *A Historical Guide to Leeds and its Environs* (Leeds, 1858), pp. 44–5.

15  Peter M'Owan, 'Memoir of Mr. Christopher Dove', *Wesleyan-Methodist Magazine*, 5th S., 11 (1856), p. 969.

16  See M.W. Beresford, 'Prosperity Street and others', in M.W. Beresford and G.R.J. Jones (eds), *Leeds and its Region* (Leeds, 1967).

17  Morris, *Class, sect and party*, p. 49.

18  On social segregation and communities in Leeds at this period see D. Ward, 'Environs and neighbours in the "Two Nations", residential differentiation in mid-nineteenth century Leeds', *Journal of Historical Geography*, 6 (1980), pp. 132–62; Robin Pearson, 'Knowing one's place: Perceptions of community in the industrial suburbs of Leeds, 1790–1890', *Journal of Social History*, 26 (1993), pp. 221–44; M. Beresford, *East End, West End: The Face of Leeds During Urbanisation 1684–1842* (Leeds, 1986).

19  A circuit consisted of around twenty or so preaching places served by several itinerant ministers in conjunction with local preachers. Ministers were periodically moved to different circuits around the country, of which there were over 400 by the 1850s.

20  Colin D. Dews, *Oxford Place Methodist Centre, Leeds, 1835–1985: a history of one hundred and fifty years of worship and witness* (Leeds, n.d.).

21  *Wesleyan-Methodist Magazine*, 3rd S., 13 (1834), p. 940; *Leeds Mercury*, 30 December 1854.

22  Peter M'Owan, *The two Doves: or, Memoirs of Margaret and Anna Dove, late of Leeds* (London, 1839), p. 5.

23  Keith Snell and Paul S. Ell, *Rival Jerusalems: The Geography of Victorian Religion* (Cambridge, 2000), p. 398.

24  William Beckworth, *A Book of Remembrance: Records of Leeds Primitive Methodism* (London, 1910), pp. 102–3.

25  See E. Royle, 'The Church of England and Methodism in Yorkshire, *c.* 1750–1850: From Monopoly to Free Market', *Northern History*, 33 (1997), pp. 137–61.

26  See John Barr, *A statement of facts, being a brief history of the measures adopted by the Leeds Wesleyan Methodist Society, in their opposition to the introduction of an organ into Brunswick Chapel* (Leeds, 1827). On the

consequences see R. Currie, *Methodism Divided: A Study in the Sociology of Ecumenicalism* (London, 1968).

27 M'Owan, 'Memoir of Mr. Christopher Dove', p. 969.

28 Spencer, *Men that are gone*, pp. 152–3. John Dove, *A Biographical History of the Wesley Family; More particularly its earlier branches* (London, 1833).

29 M'Owan, 'Memoir of Mr. Christopher Dove', p. 966.

30 M'Owan, 'Memoir of Mr. Christopher Dove', p. 968.

31 M'Owan, 'Memoir of Mr. Christopher Dove', p. 969.

32 See C.D. Fields, 'The social structure of English Methodism: Eighteenth–twentieth centuries', *British Journal of Sociology*, 28 (1977), pp. 199–225; Michael Watts, *The Dissenters: The Expansion of Evangelical Nonconformity*, vol. 2 (London, 1995), pp. 319–27.

33 John Lyth, *Glimpses of Early Methodism in York* (York, 1885), pp. 167–8; Royle, 'Church of England and Methodism in Yorkshire', p. 155.

34 See David Bebbington, 'Gospel and culture in Victorian Nonconformity', in Jane Shaw and Alan Kreider (eds), *Culture and the Nonconformist Tradition* (Cardiff, 1999), pp. 43–62; David Hempton, *The Religion of the People: Methodism and Popular Religion c.1750–1900* (London, 1996), ch. 1; G.M. Ditchfield, *The Evangelical Revival* (London, 1998), p. 76.

35 M'Owan, 'Memoir of Mr. Christopher Dove', p. 971.

36 Cited in J.M. Turner, 'Methodist Religion 1791–1849', in Rupert Davies, A. Raymond George and Gordon Rupp (eds), *A History of the Methodist Church in Great Britain* (London, 1978), p. 111.

37 M'Owan, 'Memoir of Mr. Christopher Dove', p. 972.

38 Dungett, *Life and Correspondence*, p. 176.

39 M'Owan, *The two Doves*, p. 68.

40 Peter M'Owan, *Memoir of Christopher Dove* (London, 1837), p. 69.

41 M'Owan, 'Memoir of Mr. Christopher Dove', p. 970.

42 M'Owan, 'Memoir of Mr. Christopher Dove', p. 970

43 Wesleyan Methodist Conference 1856, reported in the *Leeds Mercury*, 19 August 1856.

44 T. Jackson, *Centenary of Wesleyan Methodism* (London, 1839); cited in J.M. Turner, 'Methodist Religion 1791–1849', in Rupert Davies, A. Raymond George and Gordon Rupp (eds), *A History of the Methodist Church in Great Britain* (London, 1978), p. 104.

45 J.T. Slugg, *Woodhouse Grove School: Memorials and Reminiscences* (London, 1885), pp. 143–4. For discussion on initial responses to Stowe's

book see Robert S. Levine, 'Uncle Tom's Cabin in Frederick Douglass' Paper: An Analysis of Reception', *American Literature* 64 (1992), pp. 71–93.

**46** M'Owan, *The two Doves*, p. 22.

**47** M'Owan, *Memoir of Christopher Dove*.

**48** Slugg, *Woodhouse Grove School*, p. 143.

**49** George Osborn, *A Man of God: or, Providence and Grace exemplified in a Memoir of the Rev. P. M'Owan, compiled chiefly from his letters and papers* (London, 1873), p. 159.

**50** M'Owan, *Memoir of Christopher Dove*, p. 6.

**51** M'Owan, *Memoir of Christopher Dove*, p. 9.

**52** M'Owan, *Memoir of Christopher Dove*, p. 36, p. 12.

**53** M'Owan, *The two Doves*, p. 9.

**54** M'Owan, *Memoir of Christopher Dove*, p. 68.

**55** M'Owan, *The two Doves*, p. 61.

**56** M'Owan, *The two Doves*, p. 50.

**57** *Leeds Mercury*, 19 July 1856; *The Times*, 19 July 1856.

**58** *Leeds Times*, 15 March 1856.

**59** David Sellers, *Hidden Beneath our Feet: The Story of Sewerage in Leeds* (Leeds, 1997), p. 2.

**60** C. Turner Thackrah, *The effects of the principal arts, trades and professions and of civic states and habits of living, on health and longevity. With a particular reference to the trades and manufactures of Leeds* (London, 1831), p. 15.

**61** Thackrah, *The effects of the principal arts*, p. 23.

**62** Thackrah, *The effects of the principal arts*, p. 84.

**63** See Robert Woods and John Woodward (eds), *Urban Disease and Morality in Nineteenth-Century England* (London, 1984); Asa Briggs, 'Cholera and Society in the Nineteenth Century', *Past and Present*, 19 (1961), pp. 76–96.

**64** *Leeds Mercury*, 19 July 1856.

**65** *Leeds Mercury*, 19 July 1856.

**66** Philip E. Robinson, 'The Origins of Wesley College', www.homepage.ntlworld.com/pc1dmn/KES/WesleyCollege.html.

**67** *Leeds Mercury*, 19 July 1856.

**68** *Manchester Guardian*, 17 March 1856.

**69** *Leeds Mercury*, 19 July 1856.

70 Caleb Williams, *Observations on the Criminal Responsibility of the Insane; Founded on the Trials of James Hill and William Dove* (London and New York, 1856), p. 15.

71 *Leeds Mercury*, 19 July 1856.

72 *Leeds Mercury*, 19 July 1856; *The Times*, 19 July 1856.

73 *The Times*, 19 July 1856.

74 *The Times*, 19 July 1856.

75 *Leeds Mercury*, 19 July 1856.

76 *Leeds Times*, 15 March 1856.

77 *Leeds Mercury*, 19 July 1856.

78 *Leeds Mercury*, 22 July 1856.

79 The following section is based on the *Leeds Mercury*, 19 July 1856.

80 *The Times*, 19 July 1856.

81 His teaching skills are briefly mentioned in Slugg, *Woodhouse Grove School*, p. 142. They were married at Oxford Place Chapel in June 1854.

82 *Leeds Mercury*, 19 July 1856.

83 *Leeds Mercury*, 19 July 1856.

84 *The Times*, 19 July 1856.

85 *The Times*, 19 July 1856.

# CHAPTER 2

# A wizard's business

*'The black art can wear a white surplice'*

One day in September 1854, while out in the fields mowing barley, William fell into conversation with one of his farm labourers, a man named John Hardcastle. Talk turned to the subject of 'wise-men' and their ability to identify thieves. William asked whether such people might help him find a dog that had recently gone missing. Hardcastle believed they could and named Henry Harrison, also known as the 'Wizard of the South Market', as a wise-man worth consulting. He recalled how at a previous place of work two guns had been stolen, and so he had consulted Harrison to find out the identity of the culprits. The wise-man said that one of the thieves would pass by him the next evening and shoot a rabbit. This prediction turned out to be true and the man was arrested. The missing dog was not the most pressing matter on William's mind that day, however, and displaying his usual openness with his social inferiors he explained to Hardcastle that he had recently given notice to quit White Well Farm, but was now reconsidering. The problem was whether the steward Mr King would let him renew the tenancy. After all, William had given ample reason for him not to do so. Hardcastle hit upon a solution. Why not employ Harrison to use his magical powers to influence King? The wise-man had also helped him out in a similar tricky position. At one time Hardcastle had owed money and he heard that the bailiffs planned to enter his house and seize his possessions. So he went off to see Harrison who said he would use his magic to prevent the bailiffs' visit. True enough, while on their way to Hardcastle's place the bailiffs' horse took sudden fright, causing them to be thrown out of their cart. They were badly injured and confined to bed for so long that Hardcastle had time to remove his possessions to a safe place. These anecdotes of Harrison's abilities clearly impressed William, and so he asked Hardcastle to arrange a meeting with the wizard the next time they went to Leeds market.[1]

## Wise-men and wise-women

Who were these 'wise-men' that William and Hardcastle talked about? They were certainly familiar figures in mid-Victorian England. In 1856 the *Leeds Intelligencer* exasperatedly reckoned that 'there are few under whose notice this paper will come, who cannot recall to their minds the name of some friend or acquaintance, who does not devoutly believe in the power which these "wise men" are assumed to possess.'[2] The power of such people, who were sometimes called wizards, and were also known as cunning-folk and conjurors in the southern half of England, lay in the depth of their magical and divinatory knowledge and the breadth of their services. They offered to detect thieves, recover stolen property, divine the future course of one's life, promote good fortune in business, induce the love of men and women, cure the sick and bewitched with herbs, and ward off the powers of evil spirits and witches with charms. These were just their main services; as Hardcastle's story of the bailiffs indicates, they could do much more besides.[3]

Cunning-folk remained popular in mid-Victorian England because of the precariousness of life. For the majority of people absolute poverty was either a reality or an ever-present possibility. Local authorities and charities were able to provide a basic level of help and support. The total expenditure on poor relief in mid-nineteenth-century Leeds was considerable, averaging around £28,000 a year. For the sick there were also several charitable institutions such as the Leeds General Infirmary, which dealt with 2000 inpatients and 3000 outpatients annually.[4] There was also the House of Recovery for dealing with those struck down with infectious diseases, the Hospital for Women and Children, and The Eye and Ear Infirmary. But such institutions provided relief for those who had already fallen into destitution and sickness. What most people at the time lacked, though, was the independent security to get through the bad times and overcome the misfortunes incurred through ill health, marital breakdowns and theft. There was no sick pay and unemployment benefit. Personal banking and insurance were available to few. Sanitary conditions were awful in both rural and urban areas, and medical science had yet to find effective cures for the vast majority of diseases and ailments. In such a world cunning-folk not only offered resolutions to misfortune in all its guises, but also the security of averting misfortune and divining and ensuring a better future.

At a time, for example, when the vast majority of people kept their savings in the home a burglary could prove a disaster. With no insurance and with police detection rudimentary, particularly in rapidly expanding towns like Leeds, magic proved a popular alternative for restoring stolen goods. When, in the early 1850s, a Leeds lodge of the Oddfellows Friendly Society found money missing from their funds they decided to employ a 'wise-man' to detect who had stolen it. Their next annual financial report recorded 'fees' paid, but whether he was successful was not mentioned.[5] At a time when women's social status and financial security was dependent on marriage, it is no wonder that many young women turned to cunning-folk and fortune-tellers to hear of their marital prospects, while those already married resorted to magic to ensure the obedience and love of their spouses. In Leeds in 1864 an elderly female fortune-teller told an undercover policeman that for ten shillings she could bring back his wife who he said had deserted him. Another of her clients, a young woman, was informed that she would be married 'on the first of next holiday' and would have four children, two of which would die. This was at least a realistic assessment of mortality rates, if not an accurate prediction.[6] The depth of their boasted divinatory knowledge was sometimes quite remarkable. A couple of years later, Mary Ann Walker of St Luke Street paid £2 to a 'deaf and dumb' Leeds 'planet ruler' or astrologer named Henry Hardy to hear the following forecast:

> *Mrs Walker must be on her guard against a certain deceptive female;*
> *that she would be twice a wife; that she would be the mother of one*
> *child, a daughter; that her affections were placed on a young man*
> *whose name was William; that she must be careful in whose company*
> *she was on the 17 March 1868; that she was a person who would several*

*times in her life be in contact with the police authorities, and that she*
*would not always live outside the walls of a prison; that she would have*
*to live a great deal in Scotland, would change her name in 1868, would*
*live to a ripe old age, and that she had yet many years of great*
*happiness before her.*

A mixed bag of news indeed and evidently not one that pleased Walker as she subsequently reported him to the police.[7]

While theft detection and marital issues generated the bulk of urban cunning-folk's trade, it was the identification, cure and prevention of witchcraft that set them apart from astrologers and fortune-tellers. The relevance of witchcraft as an explanation for misfortune was no doubt diminishing fairly quickly in such rapidly growing urban areas as mid-Victorian Leeds. The ill health of livestock and the failure of the domestic processing of food and drink, such as butter, cheese, beer and bread, had been a common source of witchcraft accusations, and so as the population of Leeds became increasingly divorced from such agricultural activities so explanations in terms of witchcraft became increasingly irrelevant. Yet the cure and prevention of witchcraft was still an essential element of urban cunning-folk's business, with much of the trade being generated by rural folk from surrounding villages, who would come knocking at their doors on market days – which is no doubt why Harrison settled near the South Market.[8] Furthermore, the belief in witches was certainly by no means extinct in the rapidly expanding towns of the period, as the following case shows. At around eleven o'clock one May morning in 1856 a police constable arrested two women in Myton Street, Kingston-upon-Hull. The women were causing a disturbance outside the house of an old wise-woman named Betty Gofton. They accused her of having bewitched them and their families for six or seven years past. She kept dead toads and frogs, they said, on which their names were written. A child of one of the women was at that moment ill in bed, as cold as clay with the appearance of death, all thanks to Gofton's spells. One of the women, known as 'Blind Frank's wife', a nut seller, had been to Leeds and other more remote places, but Gofton's witchcraft still bothered her. The police later discharged the two women while Gofton was arrested and sentenced to one month in prison for fortune-telling.[9] We should not suppose that the clients of cunning-folk were predominantly uneducated, working class and female. Farmers made up a significant portion of the clients of both urban and rural cunning-folk, and we can turn to the experience of one of William's contemporaries to show that his intended visit to the Leeds wizard was not an exceptional occurrence for someone of his social position.

In the year 1856 Thomas Charlesworth, a young farmer the same age as William, and also recently married, began to experience a series of misfortunes on his small farm at Bromley Hurst near Rugeley in Staffordshire. He and his wife felt unwell, the cheese they made fell to pieces and the butter failed. A neighbour, a tollgate-keeper, advised Thomas to see a local cunning-man named James Tunnicliff who 'could do anything'. Thomas and his wife Elizabeth paid a visit to Tunnicliff, who ran a pub near Newborough called the Royal Oak. Using his occult powers the cunning-man confirmed what the young couple already suspected, that they and their farm had been bewitched by Thomas's widowed mother who had left the farm, angry at his marriage. Tunnicliff offered to visit the farm to see what he could do, and ended up staying for several months, making witch-hazel crosses to place on all the doors and conducting other rituals to ward off the witchcraft. All the time he was extracting more and more money from the Charlesworths for his services, and also travel expenses for trips to confront wizards residing in other towns in the region who, he said, had been employed by Thomas's mother. Despite having a cunning-man as a permanent member of the farm staff the Charlesworths' health did not improve and Elizabeth had two miscarriages. After nearly a year, and having paid nearly £30 to Tunnicliff, Thomas was so ill that a lawyer was called in to make his will and a surgeon was consulted. Tunnicliff was subsequently dismissed and two weeks later was arrested for the suspected drugging of Thomas, the root of the toxic white bryony, used by herbalists as an abortifacient in cows, having been found in his house. He was eventually found guilty only of the crime of false pretences and sentenced to a year in prison.[10] Would William's dealings with Harrison end in a similar calamitous way?

What do we know of the motivation and character of people like Tunnicliff? There is no doubt that Tunnicliff was an outright rogue playing on the fears and anxieties of the Charlesworths, and archival research suggests that numerous other cunning-folk were little better, though sincere and conscientious practitioners certainly existed. The mid-Victorian phrenologist Frederick Bridges made an extensive study of cunning-folk, and his appraisal of their character tallies well with many of those one finds in the historical record, though his analysis was based on rather different means to that of the historian. From his phrenological investigations, in other words studying the shape of their heads, Bridges concluded that the main characteristic of the 'wizard type' was a grave deficiency 'in the moral region'.[11] In phrenological terms they had a particularly small organ of 'conscientiousness', which was located above the left ear. People with such a small organ were 'courteous and affable, or repulsive and harsh'. They were 'never to be relied on. They misrepresent and extort in dealing – as buyers they depreciate, as judges they are unsound, as friends unreasonable.'[12] James Tunnicliff, whose trial Bridges attended, was a good specimen of the 'type'. Regarding wizards in general, 'Self-assurance, low cunning, and a practical knowledge of the credulity and weakness of a certain class of people, and how to play upon them' were, he thought, 'the prominent features of their character.' He had interviewed numerous cunning-folk and fortune-tellers and had 'been both amused and astonished at their unblushing effrontery, as they revealed the tricks they adopted to work on the feelings of the credulous and superstitious.' They expressed considerable glee in recounting the way in which they manipulated their clients, and openly told Bridges that what they told their clients and professed to do for them was all 'gammon'. When he asked how they could justify such a means of making a living a typical reply was, 'Well, you see, sir, people are fond of being humbugged, and there is more or less of it in every trade and profession, and I do not see any harm in one trying to make an honest living, if people are willing to pay me for my knowledge.'[13] We shall see throughout the rest of this book how far Harrison matched Bridges' archetype.

## Harrison

Henry Harrison was born in Boar Lane, Leeds, in 1816, to a wool-sorter named Edward Harrison and his wife Elizabeth. He had two elder sisters, Hannah and Ann. A few years later the family removed to Printer's Row in the Isle of Cinder. Like many cunning-folk, he was not brought up in the magic trade. He began his working life as a dyer in one of the town's factories. Around the age of sixteen or seventeen his father had either left or died, for we find him living with his mother in School Close, Leylands, an area of dense housing and poor sanitation in the centre of town. The house was also shared by Hannah and her husband, who was a stuff and woollen printer named William Mitchell. Henry's other sister had by this time married Joseph Giles and was living nearby in Gower Street.

In August 1833, Henry married Jane, the daughter of a fellow dyer named Richard Brayshay. The witnesses to the marriage were Hannah and Joseph Giles. The young couple moved in with her father in Dawson's Yard, Holbeck, where they stayed for three or four months before moving into a house in Denison Row. Here they stayed for at least two years during which time Jane gave birth to a boy and a girl. In the autumn of 1837 Harrison evidently lost his job and the family became destitute. Henry applied for poor relief from the Holbeck overseer of the poor and wrote the following statement: 'I, Henry Harrison, with my wife Jane, and two children, born in lawful wedlock, are now chargeable to the township of Holbeck.' The overseer, William Ellis, decided it was economical to pay the cost of having the family removed to Harrogate workhouse. Richard Brayshay later recalled seeing them driven off in a cart. They returned to Leeds the following Christmas and once more lodged with Jane's father. After a few weeks, however, Harrison abandoned his young family.

Over the next few years Harrison drifted into crime. In July 1840 he was sentenced at the Leeds Borough Sessions to three months in Wakefield House of Correction for stealing fifty yards of black lustre (a dress fabric consisting of silk and worsted) from Joseph Rowling.[14] Then in April 1841 he was back in the House of Correction for a month as a rogue and a vagabond for neglecting to support his wife and children. Around 1844 he took up lodgings in Moor End, Holbeck, with Elizabeth Brown, the widow of Benjamin Brown, a butcher who had kept a shop in Hunslet Lane, and her children George and Sarah Ann. Harrison and Brown evidently formed a relationship and Elizabeth began to give out her name as Harrison even though they were not married. Sometime in the next couple of years the Brown family and their lodger removed to a house in the Dewsbury Road. Then, around 1850, Elizabeth, her son and Harrison settled at 5 North Row, just opposite the South Market, in Bridge End. Elizabeth and George set up a grocer's shop at the end of the street and also took in a couple of other lodgers to supplement their income.

How Harrison came to be a wizard is not clear but he seems to have begun on his new career path in the mid-1840s. At this time he was still calling himself a dyer, but according to Elizabeth Brown he was also selling herbs and drugs. It was not long before he branched out to detecting stolen goods, for it was around 1846 that he was apparently reported to the police by a disgruntled working man who had consulted him about the theft of some celery from his vegetable plot, which was adjacent to one worked by Harrison on Hunslet Moor. When he went to see Harrison in his lodgings the man espied his missing celery in the corner of the room. Harrison's light fingers had been at work, but evidently not his wits.[15] As an advertising card shows, by the end of the decade he was well established in the Dewsbury Road as an 'astrological doctor' and 'dentist', and in the 1851 census the former pauper and 'rogue' grandly described himself as a 'Doctor & Water Caster'. In a Leeds trade directory of 1854 he was entered as an 'astrologer'.[16] Harrison's heavy and inexpressive features clearly masked a lively and intelligent mind, and he was well educated for someone of his background. His signature shows a confident hand, and his use of language was sophisticated. He also considered himself a bit of a philosopher. On one occasion, when William was still at White Well Farm, he was accompanied on a visit to Harrison by a schoolmaster named John Thompson. As Thompson recalled, Harrison expounded his own distinctive theory of the formation of man, and believed he could have done a better job than God. He used the example of a mason to prove his point. If he had made him, he would have placed the calves of his legs in front, and then he would not knock his shins in going up ladders.[17]

Harrison was by no means the first notorious practitioner of the magic arts in town. 'Unfortunately,' the *Leeds Intelligencer* commented in 1856, 'Leeds has for many years been notorious as the residence of "wise men".'[18] Much of that notoriety actually stemmed from a wise-woman, namely Mary Bateman, a farmer's daughter from the Yorkshire village of Asenby. As a young woman she worked as a dress-maker in York but her constant petty thievery got her into trouble and around 1788 she fled to Leeds. It was here that she began to practise as a fortune-teller and soon moved on to detecting and curing witchcraft. A manipulative and devious woman, she seems to have prospered, but her career was cut short in 1809 when she was hanged for poisoning one of her clients. The public dissection or 'anatomization' of Bateman's corpse proved immensely popular with £80 14s being raised from entrance charges.[19] Her trial and execution was a sensation in Leeds, the national press reported the case and pamphlet accounts were also sold around the country.[20] Such was the exposure that several decades later the name of Mary Bateman was still remembered far beyond Yorkshire. Prior to the infamy generated by Bateman's trial, however, the most well known magical practitioner in Leeds was a wise-man named 'Rough Robin'. For much of his career he could be found in an isolated spot on Rombalds Moor some twelve or so miles from Leeds. People travelled from across the Pennines to consult him regarding stolen goods and the secrets of futurity.[21] In the summer of 1806 Rough Robin decided to take advantage of the commercial prospects of expanding Leeds and set up a consulting room in Meadow Lane, where he reportedly made around eighteen shillings in one morning alone. The *Leeds Mercury* was not impressed, and gave public warning that 'if he did not beat a quick march out of the town he would before Monday night be tipped with a magic wand called a constable's staff, and lodged in an enchanted castle, where he may confer with his familiars without danger of interruption except from the turnkey.'[22]

Moving forward to Harrison's time, there were a number of competitors in the magic and divination market in Leeds. We know of their existence only because of their appearances in court. Prosecution was one of the risks of the trade, as the commercial practice of magic and divination was illegal under the Witchcraft Act of 1736 and under the more frequently implemented section four of the Vagrancy Act of 1824, which concerned 'persons pretending or professing to tell fortunes, or using any subtle craft'. Sometimes they were prosecuted by unsatisfied clients, but the Leeds police, like most other urban forces, periodically took a proactive stance and entrapped unsuspecting fortune-tellers. From this prosecution evidence only one other fully fledged wise-man can be identified as practising in Leeds at the same time as Harrison. He was Isaac Rushworth, a man the same age as Harrison, who seems to have settled in the Dewsbury Road after Harrison had moved out. Although he described himself as a 'planet ruler' he offered the full array of services, selling magic charms, curing witchcraft and providing herbal remedies and drugs. He had built up a considerable reputation during the early 1850s, which had spread as far as Sheffield. We shall see him in action later on.

Other 'planet rulers', who may or may not have extended their services beyond astrology and herbalism were James Trenham and Alfred Broughton. Trenham had been in practice for many years and was well known in the town. He was one of those practitioners who managed to evade prosecution despite his local reputation. We get a brief glimpse of him from his appearance at the Leeds Court House in December 1854 to press charges against George Scott and Maria Davis, who assaulted and robbed him of £2 10d. and other articles in Ebenezer Street one rainy night. No doubt there were some in court who wondered why he had not foreseen the attack.[23] Alfred Broughton was a less established planet ruler. He was the son of William Broughton, who ran a druggists and chemists shop at 46 Meadow Lane. Alfred initially worked for his father but around 1856, when he was in his early twenties, he set himself up in business as a herbalist and druggist with a shop at 33 Call Lane. He initially gained a reputation for simple fortune-telling but quickly moved on to astrology. It was from an upstairs room above the shop, fitted out with globes and astrological paraphernalia, that he ruled the planets.

Broughton did not have the most auspicious of starts as he was charged under the Vagrancy Act in August 1857. His upstairs business came to the attention of Superintendent Graham, who employed two young women to visit his shop to entrap him. They entered and asked if he would tell their fortunes. He replied that he no longer told fortunes but could rule their planets for five shillings. The police had only given the two women two shillings each, so they told Broughton they would think about it and left. They met up with Graham in Meadow Lane and he gave them four marked half-crowns. The two women returned to Broughton's shop and he asked them for their names and date of birth and told them to return on the following Wednesday night to hear the results of his planet ruling. Shortly after they left, Graham, and detectives Musgrave and Bramley, searched Broughton's premises, recovered the marked half-crowns from the till and arrested him. He was brought before the Leeds magistrates where he was defended by the well-established solicitor Francis Ferns, who explained at length to the Bench that astrology was merely an adjunct of the study of astronomy and was a science 'in which many great men had and still believed'. It was, he stated, 'perfectly legitimate, whatever the prejudices against it.' The magistrates disagreed.[24]

# Water caster, doctor, dentist

Like most cunning-folk, Harrison did not advertise himself as a 'wizard' or 'wise-man' in trade directories, newspapers, handbills or business cards. Reputations for magic were best developed discreetly by word of mouth. He generally adopted instead the more respectable title of doctor, but as we have seen he was certainly not a formally trained and licensed general practitioner. Yet he was in good company in this respect. Until the Medical Act of 1858, which established the General Medical Council and a Medical Register of all qualified practitioners, there was essentially a free market in medical practice. The Apothecaries Act of 1815 had instituted regulations that those calling themselves apothecaries had to hold a certificate confirming they had served a five-year apprenticeship in the trade, but druggists and chemists, who had originally been included in the Bill, successfully petitioned for their exemption. The title of doctor remained free for anyone to use. There was nothing to stop druggists, herbalists, cunning-folk, vendors of patent medicines seventh sons and daughters and a variety of other healers giving themselves the title. In the fishing villages and towns of the Yorkshire coast there were the 'Greenland Doctors', for example, who were disdainfully dismissed as a 'set of failed mechanics who learn to bleed, and are then qualified for the place on board a Greenland ship.'[25] Bone-setters, who specialised in the healing of broken and fractured limbs, also sometimes adopted the title. Leeds was served by the Bird family throughout the first half of the century. From the 1820s through to his death in the mid 1840s John Bird plied his skills from 7 Harper Street. His widow Hannah continued in his footsteps, and built on the family reputation by setting up a druggist's shop a few doors down at no. 3, which was run by her son-in-law George Frobisher.[26] People from Leeds would also have gone to the well-known Crowther family of Wakefield.[27]

One consequence of the lack of restrictions on medical practice was that it allowed women like Hannah Bird to achieve popular if not official medical respectability. Women may have been barred from obtaining a medical licence but they could still adopt the title of 'Doctress'. Popular culture was far more accepting of female medical skills than the male-controlled medical profession of the Victorian middle classes, enabling entrepreneurial women like Mrs Drummond to compete successfully with general practitioners. In her adverts Mrs Drummond gave herself the title 'MD' and bogusly claimed to be a Member of the Royal College of Surgeons. From her base in Park Square she and her assistant 'doctors' would visit surrounding West Riding towns on market days to sell her 'Famed Herbal Tonic' and 'Aperient Canada Pills', which could cure any disease.[28] Rapid urbanisation offered considerable opportunities for such alternative healers, both male and female. Considering that around mid century there was roughly one doctor for every two and a half thousand people in Leeds, and bearing in mind the terrible sanitary conditions, it is no surprise the medical market was diverse and thriving. Those who took best advantage were druggists and herbalists, like Harrison, who provided medical services but often had no formal medical training.[29] In towns such as Wakefield and Huddersfield, for example, the number of druggists tripled between 1822 and 1853, far outstripping the increase in qualified medical men.[30] In Leeds they more than quadrupled over the same period. In 1822 there were nineteen druggists and chemists listed in trade directories, but by 1854 there were eighty-four, compared to only sixty-five surgeons.[31] This figure does not even take into account unlisted back-street herbalists like Harrison, Rushworth and Frobisher.[32]

It is no wonder the medical profession felt under siege and often undervalued. 'I wish it emphatically to be observed that herb-shops abound in poor neighbourhoods, and that herbs are chiefly the medicines of the poor, taken and administered empirically and ignorantly' asserted one letter-writer to the press. He went on to single out 'the densely populated manufacturing districts, where medical quackery and medical superstition take disastrous effect upon the working classes, chiefly through the medium of herbs and herbalists.'[33] The well-established Leeds surgeon George Wilson, of 8 North Street, gave vent to his frustrations in a letter to *The Lancet* in April 1854. He observed that although 'the time is happily past when quacks could do me much harm' he was concerned about a number of his talented younger colleagues in Leeds, 'who are trailing along a dull round of poverty and disappointment, under the double pressure of a treacherous Government and a rampant quackery.' The treachery referred to the government's lack of regulation of untrained medical practitioners. In Wilson's opinion there should be 'summary and severe ordeal and punishment for those who, being totally ignorant of the body and its ailments, as they are of everything else, have the impudence and rascality to sacrifice the public health for their private emolument.'[34]

Wilson may have had Harrison in mind, but of more direct concern were the likes of James Lawrence Ward. He had been practising as a cancer curer for many years. He was listed as a surgeon in the trade directories but he had no formal qualification and his practice was far removed from the likes of Wilson. Back in 1838 Ward had written to *The Lancet* defending his methods of curing cancer by using herbs and criticised the profession for needlessly resorting to surgery.[35] In August 1854, though, Wilson would have been deeply satisfied to read in the local newspapers that Ward had been arrested for manslaughter. The circumstances were as follows. Mary Lambert, who lived in Croft Street, Bradford, was diagnosed as having breast cancer. A local surgeon suggested an operation to remove the tumour but she was too afraid. She got to hear about Ward and so paid a visit to Leeds and consulted him at his premises at 24 Wellington Street. The sign-plate on his door read 'curer of cancer without cutting'. His mode of treatment consisted of first spreading an unguent around the nipple of the affected breast with a feather, then sprinkling white powder over it from a bottle. Cloth was then laid on the breast. The mixture was caustic and burned into the flesh – a process Ward described as 'eating out' the cancer. She made six visits for this treatment, paying five shillings a time. When she was too ill to go, Ward sent her some herbs to put on the breast. She died in great pain in early August. It was difficult to prove that Ward's methods were directly responsible for her death and at the winter assizes he was found not guilty.[36]

While it was commonplace for unqualified medical providers like Harrison to call themselves 'doctors', in the Victorian period it was certainly rare for such people to describe themselves as 'water casters' in formal publications like trade directories. Up until the early seventeenth century water casting, 'urine scrying' or 'uroscopy' as the practice was also known, had been a widely accepted method of diagnosis in the medical fraternity. The basic principle behind the practice was that through the observation of the colour and consistency of a patient's urine the cause of most illnesses could be detected. There was and is some sound medical basis for the practice, albeit very limited, but it became discredited during the late seventeenth century, partly because of greater medical understanding and partly because there were a host of practitioners who went beyond straightforward medical diagnosis and prescription and claimed they could determine the sex of unborn children, whether a patient would die and whether he or she was bewitched.[37] Despite the best vituperative efforts of the medical establishment, such 'piss prophets', as they were branded, seem to have remained widespread up until the end of the eighteenth century.[38] Around 1800, for instance, James Roberts of Black Bank, Leeds, displayed a sign outside his cottage that read with rather original orthography:

> *Black Bank Doctor and Urin Castor and Botonist NB By the elp of God and erbs of british Growth cures all manner of disorders inhuman and cattle And as performed vara greet cures all our this country.*[39]

London was equally as enamoured of water casters. In the 1770s Dr Theodore Myersbach drove a thriving trade among all social classes at his uroscopic surgery in Soho. Among his clients were the renowned actor and theatre manager David Garrick, the Duke and Duchess of Richmond and several lords and ladies. His success attracted severe criticism in the press and among the medical establishment. One critic sought to expose him by sending along a stooge with a flask of cow's urine, which he pretended belonged to his wife.[40] During the Victorian period water casting certainly continued as a significant aspect of magical practice, usually as a means of detecting witchcraft, but to what extent it was still practised by medical dispensers such as druggists and herbalists is unclear.[41] Most would not want to advertise as much, though in 1856 we find Joseph Turton, a Sheffield 'apothecary', listed in a trade directory as a 'water caster', and in 1858 William Broughton, the father of Alfred, listed himself as a 'druggist and water caster' in a Leeds directory.[42]

One wonders what water casters like Broughton and Harrison used to train themselves in urine scrying. No new English texts on the art had been published since the late eighteenth century, and these were very rare. More likely they discovered the art through reading old seventeenth-century astrological-medical texts such as William Salmon's *Synopsis Medicinæ: or, A compendium of astrological, Galenical, & chymical physick* (1671). We know, for example, that the early nineteenth-century Lincolnshire cunning-man John Parkins made notes on urine scrying from Salmon's works.[43] The most influential of these medical books was undoubtedly Nicholas Culpeper's *Astrologicall Judgement of Diseases* (1655), which contained a 'compendious treatise of urines'. It was repackaged and published several times during the late eighteenth and early nineteenth centuries along with Culpeper's enduringly popular *Herbal*.[44] Copies would not have been difficult or expensive to get hold of in the Victorian second-hand book market.

When William Dove became acquainted with Harrison he was also describing himself as a dentist. Indeed in 1854 he is listed in a trade directory as one of seventeen dentists practising in Leeds.[45] In the early 1850s he also distributed advertising cards which ran as follows:

> *REMOVAL. – DENTIST SURGERY*
>
> *H. Harrison, astrological doctor and water caster, announces that he has removed from Dewsbury-road, where he has practised dental surgery and astrology for the last fifteen years, to 5, North-row, South-market, Meadow-lane, Leeds.*
>
> *Nativities calculated and horary questions definitively solved on any subject connected with life, death, sickness, marriage, travelling by land or sea, the welfare of absent friends, &c., &c.*
>
> *H. H. may be consulted on all diseases incident to the human frame by letter or in person; questions by letter containing a fee punctually attended to.*[46]

Dentistry was the perfect professional front for a cunning-man like Harrison. It was an even more uncontrolled medical practice than the druggist trade. Until the 1878 Dentists Act, which instituted a register of qualified practitioners, and the advent of the British Dental Association in 1880, anyone could set up a dentist's surgery and advertise their services.[47]. Harrison may have been listed alongside Thomas Dixon of 27 East Parade, for example, but there was a huge gulf between their respective practices. We have no record of Harrison's dentistry skills but one suspects that they extended to no more than pulling the teeth of the local poor. In contrast, Dixon, who had been operating in Leeds since the 1830s, publicised his services 'to the Nobility, Gentry, and Clergy visiting Leeds'. His laboratory was 'complete with first-class dental materials, which will be found to embrace everything requisite in the scientific practice of the profession.' He was able to provide pure gold foil for filling decayed teeth, and sold a variety of American dental products, including 'improved curvature gum teeth' for restoring the 'contour of the lips and face'.[48] Harrison's laboratory probably contained little more than tooth powder, a set of pliers, alcohol and some herbal remedies. Then again, Harrison made most of his money in other ways.

## Working magic

About a month after William's conversation with Hardcastle the two men took some potatoes to market in Leeds. After having sold them, they made their way to Harrison's lodgings in North Row, and arranged to meet a few minutes later in a room at the Old Red Lion Inn at the top of Meadow Lane, near the Leeds Bridge. It was not long after midday when Harrison turned up and the three men sat drinking for the next six hours, much of the beer being paid for by William. He told Harrison of his desire to retake the farm and arrangements were made for the wizard to visit White Well to see what he could do. Meantime, Harrison asked for William's date of birth so that he could draw up his horoscope.

Ten days later Harrison, along with Mr Orrell, landlord of the Old Red Lion, who was obviously complicit in the wizard's business, turned up at the Fox and Grapes Inn, in Kiddal Lane End, about a mile west of White Well Farm along the turnpike road towards Leeds. About nine o'clock in the morning Harrison went on to Dove's farm, leaving Orrell at the inn. He was met by William and Hardcastle at the farm gate leading on to the turnpike road. William told the wizard that he wanted to keep the reason for his visit from his wife, and then the three men went on to the farm buildings. In the granary Harrison began his magic. He produced a mahogany box containing a mariner's compass and proceeded, he explained, to determine the farm's 'cardinal points'. He then took out of his pocket five copper pieces the size of halfpennies, and, as William described it, marked each one with some sort of 'hieroglyphical form'. William asked what they were for and Harrison replied, 'Your house and farm are bewitched; I'll show you what they are for.' As they went down the stairs of the granary he placed the first of the five copper pieces in between the steps. Once down in the yard Harrison asked whether there was any other way into the yard other than through the large fold gates. William said there was a way through the cowhouse, and so the party set off in that direction.

Once in the cowhouse, they went through a door into a shed where the wizard looked around and threw the next copper piece on to the wall-plate between the cowhouse and the shed, saying, 'That's all right.' They then retraced their steps back to the gate on to the turnpike road, and crossed the road to a gate opposite. Here Harrison placed another copper piece between the gatepost and the earth. Walking back across the road he then pushed the fourth piece into the earth beside the gatepost next to the orchard. Then, in William's words, 'he commenced to pray, at the same time leaning his head upon his arm, which was then upon the gatepost.' 'He prayed aloud,' recalled William, 'so that I could hear him. I do not remember the words, but it was a prayer in which he referred to the seven wise men, and of which he was one, and it was to free me and the farm from witchcraft.' The praying went on for about five minutes and then Harrison concluded, 'There, you are all right now; no one can pass this gate to do you harm.'

Their final destination was the farmhouse where the last copper piece had to be secreted to ensure complete protection. William introduced Harrison to Harriet, saying he was a dental surgeon of long acquaintance, and then invited him to stay for dinner. The couple gave Harrison a tour of the house, and taking advantage of a moment when Harriet was in her bedroom Harrison told William that the final piece had been secreted. They then went to the sitting room where William drew some beer. Once Harriet had gone into the kitchen Harrison reassured William that 'no person will ever molest you,' and asked for a pen and paper. Harrison wrote some 'hieroglyphical signs' on the paper and, handing it back to William, said, 'If you want to retake the farm, and you put that paper in your pocket, you may then go to Mr. King, and he will let you it; only, you must let me know beforehand when you are going.' The conversation then ceased as Harriet returned from the kitchen.

During dinner Harrison remarked that Harriet looked unwell and William informed him that she had no appetite and was 'never out of the doctor's hands'. Harrison then recommended that if she took certain herbs available at the druggist's she would soon get well. The herbs were a mixture of gentian, juniper berries, valerian, aniseed and a little extract of liquorice.[49] William later followed his advice, though Harriet was loath to take them. After dinner William accompanied the wizard back to the Fox and Grapes where they met Hardcastle and Orrell, and sat drinking until three o'clock. William gave Harrison half a crown as an initial payment for his morning's work and before parting asked if Harrison had drawn up his nativity yet. He had not, but said he would. William next met the wise-man three weeks later when the subject of marital strife first came up.

## William's beliefs

Some readers may find it hard to understand how a man of William's social background, religious upbringing and education could believe so deeply in magic. His financial security meant he had no need to rely on magic as a safety net in times of misfortune. If his crops failed and livestock died, his father would have picked up the bill. If he fell ill, he would have received the best medical treatment in Leeds. To explain his belief in magic and the supernatural we need to explore the popular and religious cultures that he grew up in and shaped his understanding of the world around him.

William may have been brought up and educated in middle-class Methodist society but he would also have known and imbibed the beliefs and attitudes of the local popular culture. In his early years much of his time was spent in the care of the family servant Mary Wood, who was not a Methodist, and who perhaps told him stories and tales of local note and incident. He also had considerable contact with the working classes through his youthful participation in charitable work and teaching, while during his teenage years on the farm he socialised with the labourers. It is likely, then, that he knew and shared some of their beliefs and traditions regarding magic and supernatural beings. Joseph Lawson (1821–1890), a woollen manufacturer and merchant of Pudsey, a township several miles to the west of Leeds, wrote, for example, that in his youth 'Satan, or the devil, was often seen in various forms on his errands of temptation and deception' in and around the area.[50] The Devil was, as William believed, also thought to be responsible for thunder and lightning. According to Lawson, 'the whole atmosphere was supposed to be full of good and bad spirits, on errands of mercy or of mischief.' 'Both young and old,' he said, 'have their lives made miserable by these most horrible superstitions.'[51] William was no exception. He once told his friend John Thompson that he had seen the fairies, or hobs as they were known, reaping in a field one day. But it was ghosts and apparitions that caused most concern to William, and he sometimes asked to be accompanied home after dark for fear of encountering them.

In the district around Leeds there were two particularly frightening supernatural beings that people in William's day feared meeting at night: the barguest and the padfoot. Both took on a variety of guises, though a shaggy black dog with large fiery eyes was the most common. The barguest's favourite haunt was a piece of wasteland between Headingley Hill and Wrangthorn in the north of Leeds, and on the death of local notable people it would call all the dogs in the district to howl and bay in commemoration.[52] The padfoot appeared in the unusual form of a pack of wool, and a rattling of chains was often heard. Sally Dransfield, a carrier from Leeds to Swillington during the mid-nineteenth century claimed to have seen it a number of times rolling along the road or bursting through hedges.[53] In the 1830s Joseph Lawson was personally acquainted with one young man, a 'decent, conscientious person, and very exceptional in his education, being a good reader, writer, and arithmetician for that time,' who was in the habit of seeing the padfoot on dark nights. The man, like William, was also partial to drink and seems to have usually met the padfoot on his way home from the inn. On one occasion he met a woman who walked beside him on the road. She wore a white cap and a bed gown. He was convinced it was his mother, a respected Methodist who had died when he was a few weeks old. He believed the apparition was the work of divine intervention and subsequently became a Methodist preacher.[54]

One of the reasons for the success of Wesleyan and Primitive Methodism was that their preachers and members shared this wider popular belief in a world full of spirit beings and providential visitations – a culture of belief that most nineteenth-century Anglican clergymen denounced and sometimes preached against, accusing Methodism of promoting popular 'superstition'.[55] The founder of Methodism, John Wesley, whose works William would have imbibed in his childhood, was a strong and vocal believer in witches, devils and spirits. His journals are full of instances of supernatural encounters, particularly cases of diabolic possession. For Wesley and his followers the Devil and his minions were an ever-present threat. In October 1739, for example, he prayed over a possessed young woman of Kingswood who had to be held down by two or three people while in her fits. At one point she screamed, 'I am the devil's now. I have given myself to him. His I am. Him I must serve. With him I must go to hell,' and began to pray to Satan. In May 1746 he recorded an 'amazing instance of distress' concerning a young woman suffering a violent fever who drank nothing but water for twenty days, and came to believe the Devil had taken her body and soul. She cursed and blasphemed, tore her clothing to pieces, and everything she swallowed was as fire and brimstone she said.[56]

It was not purely prejudice that led Charlotte Brontë to refer to the 'mad Methodist magazines full of miracles and apparitions and preternatural warnings, ominous dreams, and frenzied fanaticisms.'[57] Although by the mid-nineteenth century Wesleyan Methodist publications had become rather sober, old copies of Wesleyan publications like the *Arminian Magazine* were still part of the Methodist literary diet, and they contained numerous accounts of providential happenings, satanic interventions and spirit possessions. By the 1830s the tone of Wesleyan Methodist preaching had also been toned down somewhat, but there were still those preaching hell fire and damnation. We get a taste of the sort of fiery sermons William would have heard in his youth from those of the Wesleyan Methodist preacher William Dawson (1773–1841), who farmed at Barnbow and was a well-known figure at the markets of Leeds as well as its chapels. He was a tireless preacher, making around 100 preaching journeys a year. It was said of his sermons that 'though sometimes crude, [they] always presented bold, original, startling, and oftentimes beautiful, ideas.' There was a strong emphasis on the physical landscape of hell and the ever present Devil. One of his sermons against sinners brought home to his audience the horrors of Satan's lair: 'at the day of judgement that chain shall be drawn, at white heat, out of the flames of hell, and shall be wrapped round, and round, and ROUND, thy writhing body; burning into thy wretched soul, until, long before the coil is exhausted, its weight shall sink thee under the surface of that burning lake for ever and for ever!'[58]

Yet, whereas William's belief in devils and apparitions may have been largely acceptable to those he mixed with in middle-class Methodist circles, his confidence in Harrison's powers would certainly have not. On this issue there was a yawning gap between popular culture and Methodism. John Wesley despised cunning-folk. An entry in his journal for 24 July 1761 records how, after preaching at Bramley, Yorkshire, a fourteen-year-old boy named Jonas Rushford told him how he and a couple of adult neighbours visited the renowned wise-man of Skipton, Timothy Crowther.[59] They wanted to know the fate of a man who had been missing for twenty days. To divine what had happened Crowther asked Jonas to get into bed with a mirror, and then placed a cover over him and asked him what he saw. At first Jonas saw his mother, but when asked to look for the missing man Jonas saw a vision of how the man had been murdered by two men and thrown into a coal-pit. When, on the following day, Jonas showed his neighbours the spot, the body of the man was found sure enough. To Wesley, the story was 'improbable only, or flatly impossible, when all the circumstances are considered.' 'They that can believe this,' he thought, 'may believe a man's getting into a bottle.'[60]

Why, the reader may ask, was this story of Crowther's success pure fiction, as Wesley put it, when the actions of witches, apparitions and the possessed were largely accepted? It is because cunning-folk were viewed as presumptuous pretenders, who could not have any real powers. If they appeared to achieve magical results it could only be through illusion or the deception of the Devil. This point was explained in detail decades later by the Wesleyan minister James Heaton in a lengthy tract on the evils of such people and the error of consulting them. It is quite likely Heaton (1782–1862) was acquainted with the Doves, as they shared a mutual friend in the preacher John Dungett.[61] The Methodist bookseller and auctioneer John Holmes also sold Heaton's tract in Leeds.

'The black art can wear a white surplice,' Heaton warned, and 'Satan can transform himself into an angel of light, and his ministers, the magicians, can, and often do, appear to be *good men*.' But such cunning-folk went 'far deeper into the dark, occult arts than most medical men dare venture even to look, and are almost deep as hell in science and in guilt. They are *wise* indeed in wisdom from beneath.'[62] It was the application of astrology that particularly aggravated Heaton's religious sensitivities. Astrologers, he reckoned, 'seldom know the evil of their art; it blinds their conscience while it professes to open their eyes,' but their activities were a 'diabolical attack on the sovereignty of God, a treacherous plot against the divine government, counsel, and worship.'[63] As for those who consulted cunning-folk, Heaton admitted that many of them 'do not know, or do not believe, that there is any thing so diabolical, or any thing so wicked in these practices ... Did they know this to be true, they would not be guilty of the sins. But ignorance and unbelief, though they may in some degree palliate the guilt, will by no means justify the sin.'[64]

There were no mitigating circumstances for William. Through his association with Harrison he had mired himself in diabolical sin, and as Methodist preachers warned, once you gave entry to the Devil he dragged you down to the depths of hell.

## In deeper with the wizard

Three weeks after the working of magic at White Well Farm, William managed to lose the written charm Harrison had given him to influence Mr King. He therefore paid a visit to Leeds, leaving his horse at the Black Swan Inn at the bottom of Lowerhead Row and walking to Harrison's house near the South Market. The wizard gave him a replacement charm, and as per his instructions, it was agreed that William would meet King the following Wednesday. William then brought up the subject of his unhappy relations with his wife, but someone entered the consulting room and so Harrison suggested they go to the Old Red Lion for a beer and talk over the matter. The interview lasted only half an hour this time. According to William's account of the conversation, Harrison said it was 'no wonder' he had trouble with his wife, as she was two-faced and always 'illifying' and backbiting him to her friends. 'I then asked him,' recalled William, 'if anything could be done so that we might live happily together, for I had married her for love and nothing else.' Harrison replied, 'That can be done; but it will take some time to work it round.' The wizard nevertheless hinted he could effect some immediate change, saying that William could go home content for he would cause Harriet to greet him with a smile.

William made his way back to the Black Swan. While the ostler was occupied with fetching his horse from the stable he chatted with the ostler's wife. She told him that some sacks had recently been stolen from the yard. William said, 'I know a man, or a wise-man, who can tell you who has stolen them.' Displaying his charitable streak, he wrote down the name of the ostler and the number of stolen sacks and set off on his horse to consult Harrison again as to the identity of the thief. As he passed the Old Red Lion, however, his horse stumbled and he was thrown into the street, dislocating his right arm. The injured William was put to bed at the inn and Orrell sent for Harrison. The wizard offered to set the arm, but William apparently had less faith in his medical skills than in his magical powers and asked instead for the family surgeon George Morley. Morley was unavailable but one of his assistants came and set the arm, and a cab was sent for to take William back to Bramham. Harrison was evidently displeased at the professional slight.

A few days after the accident, Harrison sent word via Hardcastle that the fee for his services to date amounted to half a sovereign. As Hardcastle was going to Leeds to sell some potatoes, William asked that he pay the wizard from the proceeds of the sale. This transaction seemed to have passed smoothly, but the next did not go so well. Hardcastle sold a sample of wheat to the merchants Sutcliffe and Hartley of Bradford, but they failed to pay. Next market day William went into Leeds to meet them but they did not show up, and instead left a message at the New Inn, Vicar Lane, that they would meet him at the following Tuesday market. When William and Hardcastle turned up at the appointed time they were not to be seen and so William once more resorted to Harrison's magic. The wizard said he would cast a spell over Sutcliffe and Hartley to ensure they would be at the Talbot Inn the following Tuesday to pay the money. This time Harriet went with William in their phaeton while Hardcastle rode a cartful of potatoes to the market. The Doves stayed at the Black Swan Inn before going to the Talbot around two o'clock, where they met up with Hardcastle and Harrison. They waited some time but the Bradford merchants once again failed to appear. The three men decided to look for them in other public houses, while Harriet stayed behind complaining of fatigue. They eventually found Hartley in the Ship Inn but he walked off without paying. This disappointing outcome seems to have shaken William's confidence in the wizard, but it was restored before too long thanks to a personal tragedy.

## A predictable death

During the autumn of 1854 Christopher Dove's health rapidly deteriorated. His memory began to fail and his mind was 'drawn into illusory imaginings'.[65] His father's illness preyed strongly on William's mind. One wonders if he was aware and expectant of the annuity of £90 a year his father was to leave him. Several years before his death, Christopher had consulted the Rev. William Lord as to how he should deal with his son in his will. He advised that William was not in a fit state to dispose of any substantial property. Consequently the annuity was left to two trustees, the woollen manufacturer and merchant John Brigg and a family friend George Reinhardt, who were empowered to dispense weekly sums to William and his wife for maintenance and support.

Considering William's increasing dependence on Harrison's guidance, it is no surprise to find that at the end of October he sought out the wizard to discuss his father's health. Harrison told him that his father would not get better, and William then asked, 'Do you know when he'll die?' Harrison replied, 'Between November and February.' In December William met Harrison by chance while drinking in the Old Red Lion. He told Harrison his father was not getting any better, and asked once again whether he could tell him more precisely when he would die. Harrison obligingly informed him that 'he will not live till the 25 December'.

Despite his physical weakness Christopher continued to attend chapel, but on Sunday 17 December his friends dissuaded him from going – an ominous sign for one so devout. He took to his bed with his Bible and a copy of Wesley's sermons. He died aged seventy-one just before midnight on Christmas Eve. His last words to his family were: 'The grace of our Lord Jesus Christ, and the love of God, and the fellowship of the Holy Ghost, be with you all. Amen.'[66] Obituaries were published in the local papers. The *Leeds Mercury* praised him as 'an active and exemplary Christian, ever ready with his purse, his time, and his influence, to extend the kingdom of Christ, and to advance the welfare of man.'[67] The Trustees of the Oxford Place Chapel recorded their sadness at the loss of their 'highly esteemed and beloved brother', praising his 'meekness of deportment and rectitude of principle'. He was buried in the family plot at Oxford Place Chapel; Peter M'Owan later gave the funeral sermon to a large congregation.[68] As Henry Spencer remarked, with the benefit of hindsight, Christopher 'was providentially taken from the evil to come, and spared a mortal anguish'.[69]

William later confessed: 'I rather doubted Harrison's power, but my father's death happening before the 25 December, I was impressed with a strong belief that Harrison was possessed of supernatural power.' In light of the wizard's impressive display of prediction, his views on William's two other 'problems' at this time assumed greater importance. Regarding his marriage, during one pub consultation in November, Harrison apparently told him that his wife would never 'be right' until she had children, and that he should never have married her in the first place. The wizard said the herbs he had prescribed would help her conceive and then things would be better. Regarding the tenancy of White Well Farm, ten days before his father's death William had finally been to see Mr King, who, impervious to the magic of the wizard's charm, refused to extend the tenure. Harrison brushed aside this setback saying, 'Never mind, work your land as usual, he will let you the farm yet; he has a spell upon him; he is an Irishman, and will take a good deal of working upon; but rather than you should miss the farm it will be death to him.'[70]

## A change, but not for the good

Irish blood proved too strong, that, or basic business sense. Although William boasted of making a healthy profit – he told his brother-in-law that he was £700 in pocket – his stewardship of White Well was a financial disaster, wasting an estimated £1500.[71] So in March 1855 William's ill-starred career as a farmer came to an end and the Doves moved to a house in the hamlet of Woodhouse, near Normanton, some nine or ten miles south west of Leeds. Harriet's isolation was alleviated by the arrival of her sister Susan Jenkins, who came to stay with them for five months. William attended the local Wesleyan class meetings, although his mind was not always consumed by pious reflection while there. On one occasion, for no apparent reason, he began to boast to those in class how he was worth £5000 and would make £20,000 before he died. William's religious observance was also no brake on his cruel pranks. On one occasion he fired a gun at the door of his neighbour Sarah Furness as a preaching was taking place.[72]

Relations with Harriet deteriorated further. Their maid, Elizabeth Fisher, the daughter of one of Dove's neighbours Samuel Fisher, a railway porter at Normanton station, observed that the couple 'lived very unhappily'. They still had their moments of childish fun together, as when William pushed her about the place in a wheelbarrow, but in August the couple had a serious row, and with her sister in the house Harriet seems to have felt bolder about persisting with her complaints. Once again

William sought help from Harrison, who said he would remedy the situation and that William should write to him to let him know how things went. Two days later he wrote to say that there was no improvement and he must do something to restore the peace. He gave the letter to Samuel Fisher. Harriet had seen him write the letter, however, and asked Elizabeth to get it from her father's table. Harriet and Elizabeth read its contents, which, according to the maid, contained the request that Harrison 'torment Mrs. Dove while she was at Manchester'. A copy was made for safe keeping, and Harriet placed a blank sheet in the envelope and asked Elizabeth to replace it on her father's table. William had seen the women whispering to each other and with his suspicions aroused, he wrote another letter and posted it himself.

A few days later, William went to Leeds to see Harrison, who expressed his puzzlement at having received the blank letter. William explained what had happened and then, according to William, the wizard uttered the words that would come to haunt him: 'You never will have any happiness until she's out of the way.' 'How do you know that?' asked William. 'Come upstairs, I'll tell you; for I've got your nativity marked out.' Once upstairs Harrison took out a sheet of paper from a drawer and drew a circle and the signs of the zodiac. As William recollected:

> There were also hieroglyphical forms, opposite various figures denoting years, beginning at 27 (my age) and continuing down to 50 or 52. The figures after 27 were 32 repeated twice or three times. He referred to the forms opposite the various figures, and reading from a book my destiny. He said 'Between the age of 27 and 32 everything will go against you, you will have nothing but misfortune' – that at 32 the sun and moon would come in conjunction, (I think conjunction was the word he used), and that then everything would be in my favour; that at 32 years of age I should lose my wife, that at 32 I should marry again, that at 32 I should have a child, and that at 32 I should have an addition to my fortune, and that for my sake he did not care how soon it was here, for until then I should never be a happy man; that after I was 32 everything would go well for a few years.[73]

Harrison also told him how at one point in the future his fortune would be boosted, that at another time he should avoid a lawsuit, and at another he must neither travel by land or water. If all such precautions were taken he would ultimately die respected by all those around him. This was good news, but William was most eager to know more about his future wife. Harrison said she would 'have auburn hair, light complexion, and a good fortune. If you had married a person of this description at first, you would have done well.' Harrison closed the book of destiny, and the two men finished the consultation with a few glasses of ale at the New Cross Inn, one of Harrison's regular drinking haunts situated in Meadow Lane, a few steps from the South Market and about forty yards from 5 North Row. Harrison could see the Inn from his window. William later taunted Harriet, 'I have seen somebody about you, and I know that your days will be ended in February.'[74] Relations were clearly getting to a head and the fate of a walking stick was instrumental.

William had been given the stick, engraved with his initials, by a friend named William Windsor who worked for the auctioneer David Holmes. It was evidently a particularly fine stick and immediately caught the admiring eye of Henry Harrison. William, exhibiting a characteristi-cally generous impulse, gave it him. When he got back home Harriet noticed the stick was missing. William said he had mislaid it in Leeds, but she suspected Harrison had something to do with it. She mentioned her suspicion to William's sister Mary, and her husband Benjamin Marsden decided to pay Harrison a visit. He brought a policeman with him to 5 North Row and demanded the return of the stick, but Harrison refused to hand it over. Marsden then asked William for authority to con-fiscate the stick. He declined and even wrote to Harrison, telling him he must keep the stick as he had given it to him as a gift. Harriet now took up the battle of the stick herself and, accompanied by her sister, went to see Harrison to demand its return, but still Harrison stuck to his stick. The next day, sick of the discord it was causing, William finally gave in and handed Harriet's sister a letter requesting Harrison to give her the stick. The wizard acquiesced and the stick was handed over, albeit with William's initials removed and 'H.H.' put in their place.

During the battle over the stick William's nights were haunted by strange noises. 'The noise was like that caused by breaking of pots,' he recounted, 'and sometimes as if some heavy packaging was rolled across the floor. One night I thought some person was kicking the door, but when I looked at the door there were no marks.' He was so disturbed by them that he gave up attending evening class meetings, saying that he could not leave his wife and servant alone while they plagued the house. The noises reached a crescendo the night after the stick was returned. William believed they were caused by devils sent by Harrison in retribution, and he accused him as much next time they met, though the wizard denied it.

## Talk of separation

By now William and Harriet were sleeping apart. William asked the wizard to put his nocturnal devils to good use by frightening Harriet into sharing his bed, but to no avail. Harriet complained to her mother of the parlous state of their marriage and in October Mrs Jenkins paid a visit to Normanton for a couple of weeks to try to resolve the matter once and for all. Her intention was to have her daughter separate from William and bring her back to Plymouth.

Before the passing of the Matrimonial Causes Act in 1857, obtaining a full divorce allowing both partners to remarry required an Act of Parliament and was very expensive and exceedingly rare. The only real alternative for many troubled middle-class couples like William and Harriet, where adultery had not been committed and no complaint of serious cruelty made, was to obtain a deed of separation drawn up by a solicitor. Such deeds guaranteed the wife financial security by binding the husband to provide her with an allowance of roughly one-third of his annual income. The downside was that the wife would lose the mainten-ance payments if she had sexual relations with any other man. The hus-band, of course, could take a mistress without any adverse consequences. This was just one of the gross gender inequalities embedded in the law of the time, which did not recognise the legal rights of married women at all. The position Harriet could find herself in was movingly described at the time by Caroline Norton, who experienced the separated state and was a prominent campaigner for more just divorce laws: 'Alone. Married to a man's name, but never to know the protection of this nominal hus-band, nor the joys of family, nor the every-day companionship of a real home. Never to feel or show preference for any friend not of her own sex, though tempted, perhaps, by a feeling nobler than passion.'[75]

When the request for a separation was put to William he did not seem bothered whether Harriet left or stayed, but he nevertheless consulted

Harrison on the matter. He advised that if she wanted to go then 'let her go', though when William expressed his desire not to be separated Harrison hedged his bets by adding, 'If she goes, she'll return.' With this win-win scenario in mind William agreed to the separation and his executors agreed to pay her £20 a year from his annuity as part of the settlement. So, one day, William, Harriet and her mother made their way to the office of the lawyer John Hincks, at 7 South Parade, to sort out the paperwork. But things did not go to plan. As they sat in Hincks's office sorting out the details William turned to Harriet and asked if she was still willing to remain with him. Harriet looked at her mother and asked, 'What shall I do?' She replied that she wished her to come home with her. Hincks then interjected, 'Mrs Dove, if you are willing to try your husband again for a day, a week, or a year, I will not charge you anything for making out the papers.' Harriet agreed.[76]

## Notes and references

1 *Leeds Mercury*, 12 August 1856.

2 *Leeds Intelligencer*, 16 August 1856.

3 For a thorough account of cunning-folk in this period see Owen Davies, *Cunning-Folk: Popular Magic in English History* (London, 2003); Owen Davies, *Witchcraft, magic and culture 1736–1951* (Manchester, 1999), pp. 214–29; Owen Davies, *A People Bewitched: Witchcraft and Magic in Nineteenth-Century Somerset* (Bruton, 1999), chs 2 and 3; Owen Davies, 'Cunning-folk in the Medical Market-Place during the Nineteenth Century', *Medical History*, 43 (1999), pp. 55–73; Owen Davies, 'Cunning-folk in England and Wales during the Eighteenth and Nineteenth Centuries', *Rural History*, 8 (1997), pp. 93–109.

4 William White, *Directory and Topography of the Borough of Leeds, Halifax* (Sheffield, 1858), pp. 14, 15 and 28.

5 Cited in the *Leeds Intelligencer*, 16 August 1856. I have been unable to trace the relevant Oddfellows' reports.

6 *Somerset County Herald*, 30 April 1864.

7 *Somerset County Herald*, 3 March 1866.

8 For discussion on these issues see Davies, *A People Bewitched*, ch. 2.

9 *Hull Advertiser*, 24 May 1856. For some other urban examples see Davies, *Witchcraft, magic and culture*, pp. 116, 102; Owen Davies, 'Urbanisation and

the Decline of Witchcraft: An Examination of London', *Journal of Social History*, 30 (1997), pp. 597–617.

10 *The Times*, 7 March and 24 March 1857. See also Susan Hoyle, 'The witch and the detective: mid-Victorian stories and beliefs', in Willem de Blécourt and Owen Davies, *Witchcraft continued: Popular magic in modern Europe* (Manchester, 2004), pp. 56–61; Davies, *Cunning-Folk, passim.*

11 Few of Bridges' papers and notes survive unfortunately, but he summarised his findings in his book *Phrenology Made Practical and Popularly Explained* (fourth edition, London, n.d.), pp. 135–7. For some archival accounts regarding Bridges' lectures see Shropshire Archives Office, 665/3/1076 and 665/3/1077.

12 Bridges, *Phrenology*, p. 124.

13 Bridges, *Phrenology*, p. 136.

14 *Leeds Mercury*, 18 July 1840.

15 The incident was recalled in the *Leeds Times*, 25 October 1856.

16 William White, *Directory of Leeds, Bradford* (Sheffield, 1854), p. 88.

17 *The Times*, 21 July 1856.

18 *Leeds Intelligencer*, 16 August 1856.

19 S.T. Anning, 'Early Medical Education in Leeds', in Beresford and Jones (eds), *Leeds and its Region*, p. 241.

20 See, for example, *Extraordinary Life and Character of Mary Bateman, the Yorkshire Witch* (Leeds, 1809); *The Times*, 26 October 1808.

21 William Wheater, 'Yorkshire Superstitions', *Old Yorkshire*, 4 (1883), pp. 267–8.

22 *Leeds Mercury*, 9 August 1806.

23 *Leeds Mercury*, 9 December 1854.

24 *Leeds Intelligencer*, 8 August 1857.

25 Irvine Loudon, 'The Vile Race of Quacks with which this Country is Infested', in W.F. Bynum and Roy Porter (eds), *Medical Fringe & Medical Orthodoxy 1750–1850* (London, 1987), p. 124.

26 See the censuses; *Pigot and Co.'s Royal National and Commercial Directory* (London and Manchester, 1841), p. 224; Edward Baines, *History, Directory and Gazeteer of the County of York* (Leeds, 1822), p. 41; White, *Directory and Topography of the Borough of Leeds* (1858), p. 65.

27 Hilary Marland, *Medicine and Society in Wakefield and Huddersfield 1780–1870* (Cambridge, 1987), p. 221.

28 Marland, *Medicine and Society*, pp. 222–3.

29  Eric M. Sigsworth and Phillip Swan, 'Para-medical Provision in the West Riding', *Society for the Social History of Medicine Bulletin* 29 (1981), p. 38.

30  Hilary Marland, 'The medical activities of mid-nineteenth-century chemists and druggists, with special reference to Wakefield and Huddersfield', *Medical History* 31 (1987), p. 420. See also Marland, *Medicine and Society*, ch. 6.

31  Figures compiled from Baines, *History, Directory* (1822); William White, *Directory of Leeds, Bradford* (Sheffield, 1854).

32  This is what P.S. Brown found in mid-nineteenth century Bristol; P.S. Brown, 'The vicissitudes of herbalism in late nineteenth- and early twentieth-century Britain', *Medical History*, 29 (1985), pp. 71–93; P.S. Brown, 'Herbalists and medical botanists in mid-nineteenth-century Britain with special reference to Bristol', *Medical History*, 26 (1982), pp. 405–21; Davies, 'Cunning-Folk in the Medical Market-Place', pp. 63–70.

33  *Daily News*, 10 January 1856.

34  *The Lancet*, 63, 1599 (1854), p. 458.

35  'Mr Ward's Defence of Irregular Practitioners', *The Lancet*, 29, 754 (1838), pp. 699–701.

36  *Leeds Mercury*, 12 August 1854; 9 December 1854. The same cure was practised by a West Country cancer-curer later in the century; see F.B. Smith, *The People's Health 1830–1910* (London, [1979] 1990), p. 334.

37  See Lucinda McCray Beier, *Sufferers and Healers: The experience of illness in seventeenth-century England* (London and New York, 1987); Davies, *Cunning-Folk*, p. 107.

38  See Roy Porter, '"I Think Ye Both Quacks": The Controversy between Dr Theodor Myersbach and Dr John Coakley Lettsom', in Bynum and Porter (eds), *Medical Fringe*, pp. 58–61; Irvine Loudon, 'The vile race of quacks with which this country is infested', in Bynum and Porter (eds), *Medical Fringe*, p. 107; Mary Fissell, *Patients, Power, and the Poor in Eighteenth-Century Bristol* (Cambridge, 1991), p. 63.

39  *Olla podrida, from the Hull advertiser and exchange gazette* (Hull, 1800), p. 39.

40  See Porter, '"I Think Ye Both Quacks".'

41  Davies, *Cunning-Folk*, pp. 105–6.

42  William White, *General Directory of the Town, Borough, and Parish of Sheffield* (Sheffield, 1856), p. 250. See also William White, *Gazetteer and General Directory of Sheffield* (Sheffield, 1852), p. 220; White, *Directory and Topography of the Borough of Leeds* (1858), p. 74.

**43** Francis X. King, *The Flying Sorcerer* (Oxford, 1992), p. 41.

**44** See, for example, *Culpeper's English Family Physician* (London, 1792).

**45** White, *Directory of Leeds, Bradford* (1854), p. 278.

**46** *Leeds Intelligencer*, 16 August 1856.

**47** See Christine Hillam, *Brass Plate and Brazen Impudence: Dental Practice in the Provinces, 1755–1855* (Liverpool, 1991); A. Hargreaves, 'Dentistry in the British Isles', *Clio Medica*, 72, 1 (2003), pp. 171–330; J. Menzies Campbell, *Dentistry Then and Now* (Glasgow, 1981); Eric G. Forbes, 'The Professionalisation of Dentistry in the United Kingdom', *Medical History*, 29 (1985), pp. 169–81.

**48** See, for example, his adverts at the back of *An Historical Guide to Leeds* (1858); *Leeds Intelligencer*, 27 January 1855.

**49** *Manchester Guardian*, 13 March 1856.

**50** Joseph Lawson, *Letters to the Young on Progress in Pudsey during the last Sixty Years* (Stanningley, 1887; reprint Firle, 1978), p. 70. For biographical detail on Lawson see Pat Younghusband, 'Joseph Lawson, Pudsey 1821–1890', *Lawson Times*, 5 (1998), pp. 8–10 (available at http://web.onetel.net.uk/~gdlawson/times5.pdf).

**51** Lawson, *Letters*, pp. 68, 69.

**52** William Henderson, *Folk-Lore of the Northern Counties* (London, 1879), pp. 274–5. See also Katherine Briggs, A *Dictionary of Fairies* (London, 1976), pp. 16–17.

**53** Henderson, *Folk-Lore*, pp. 273–4.

**54** Lawson, *Letters*, pp. 69–70.

**55** See Owen Davies, 'Methodism, the Clergy, and the Popular Belief in Witchcraft and Magic', *History*, 82 (1997), pp. 252–65; Davies, *Witchcraft, magic and culture*, pp. 12–16; James Obelkevitch, *Religion and Rural Society: South Lindsey, 1825–75* (Oxford, 1976), pp. 276–312; John Rule, 'Methodism, popular beliefs and village culture in Cornwall, 1800–1850', in R. Storch (ed.), *Popular culture and custom in nineteenth-century England* (London, 1982), pp. 48–70.

**56** Wesley, *Journal*, entries for 23 October 1739; 19 May 1746.

**57** Cited in H.F. Mathews, *Methodism and the Education of the People 1791–1851* (London, 1949), p. 173.

**58** Robert Athow West, *Sermons by the Late Mr William Dawson, of Barnbow, near Leeds. With a sketch of the author* (London and Otley, 1860), pp. xii, xvi.

**59** For information on Crowther see Kathryn C. Smith, 'The Wise Man and his

Community', *Folk Life*, 15 (1977), p. 27; W. Harbutt Dawson, *History of Skipton* (London, 1882), pp. 390–4.

**60** Wesley, *Journal*, 24 July 1761.

**61** See James Heaton, *Memoir of Mr. John Dungett, of Newcastle-upon-Tyne* (London, 1833). Dungett, *Life and Correspondence*, p. 200. For details of Heaton's life and views see Jason Semmens, '"I will not go to the Devil for a Cure": Witchcraft, Demonic Possession, and Spiritual Healing in Nineteenth-Century Devon', *Journal for the Academic Study of Magic*, 2 (2004), pp. 132–55; Jason Semmens, 'The Dock Dæmoniac: Or, a Study of Possession, Dissent, and Healing in Early Nineteenth-Century Plymouth', MA Dissertation, Exeter University, 2001.

**62** James Heaton, *Farther Observations on Demoniac Possession, and Animadversions on Some of the Curious Arts of Superstition* (Frome, 1822), p. 37.

**63** Heaton, *Farther Observations*, pp. 47, 45.

**64** Heaton, *Farther Observations*, p. 88.

**65** M'Owan, 'Memoir of Mr. Christopher Dove', p. 976.

**66** M'Owan, 'Memoir of Mr. Christopher Dove', p. 976.

**67** *Leeds Mercury*, 30 December 1854.

**68** Osborn, *A Man of God*, p. 250.

**69** Spencer, *Men that are gone*, p. 151.

**70** *Leeds Mercury*, 12 August 1856.

**71** *Leeds Intelligencer*, 15 March 1856.

**72** *The Times*, 19 July 1856, p. 12.

**73** *Leeds Mercury*, 12 August 1856.

**74** *Daily News*, 12 March 1856.

**75** J.G. Perkins, *The Life of Mrs Norton* (London, 1909), p. 191; cited in Lawrence Stone, *Road to Divorce: England 1530–1987* (Oxford, 1990), p. 169. On the subject of separation at the time see Stone, *Road to Divorce*, pp. 153–69; Mary Poovey, *Uneven Developments: The Ideological Work of Gender in Mid-Victorian England* (Chicago, 1988).

**76** *The Times*, 19 July; *Leeds Mercury*, 19 July 1856.

# CHAPTER 3

# Poisonous relations

*'If you have poisoned your wife, your conscience will go with you'*

On 21 December 1855 the Doves, along with their servant Elizabeth Fisher, moved to 3 Cardigan Place, Burley, a pleasant rural village of cottages and villas about a mile and a half northwest of Leeds.[1] Mary Wood, the family servant who had looked after William as a child, and her husband John, a cabinet-maker and also the constable of Burley, lived just up the road. Cardigan Place was a small development situated away from the main settlement, next to the railway and near the gasworks and the Perseverance Iron Foundry. The tenants consisted of the families of tradesmen and modest professionals such as railway agents, contractors and clerks. No. 3 had been unoccupied for a while and the previous tenants had abandoned a couple of cats that continued to prowl hungrily around the yard. An irrelevant note of interest it may seem, but those cats soon got on William's nerves and were a link in the chain of events that followed.

The move was meant to provide a new start for the young couple. William had promised to stop drinking and he even made a brief effort to find work. He applied for the job of pay-clerk to the Leeds Board of Guardians, but was unfortunately unsuccessful. Harriet soon struck up a friendship with their neighbour at No. 2, a 28-year-old widow named Jane Whitham. She had been living in Cardigan Place for a couple of years with her two-year-old son. Her first child Clarissa had died in 1852 aged only three and her husband John, an engineer, died shortly after.

She enjoyed Harriet's company but was not best pleased with William as the sound-proofing was none to good and she was frequently disturbed by the noise he made when he stumbled around drunk in the evenings. William was rather taken with her, however, particularly as she fitted rather well the description Harrison had given him of his future wife.

# Poison

On 3 or 4 January William went to the New Cross Inn near the South Market for a drink. He asked Ann Walker, the innkeeper's wife, to fetch Harrison. When the wizard turned up an old copy of *The Times* was produced and he began to read aloud the report of the inquest on a 28-year-old man named John Parsons Cook, which had been held at the Talbot Arms, Rugeley, Staffordshire. Cook had died at the inn unexpectedly on 13 November, having returned from Shrewsbury Racecourse with a gambling acquaintance named William Palmer, a 34-year-old general practitioner.[2] An inquest was called into the unusual death of someone so young, and a chambermaid testified that on the night Cook died Palmer had given him some pills, not long after which Cook experienced excruciating convulsions. They were symptomatic of tetanus, but Cook's body showed no sign of the tell-tale external lacerations of the disease. At the *post mortem* several of Cook's internal organs had been removed and sent to the eminent toxicologist Alfred Swaine Taylor and his colleague Dr Rees at Guy's Hospital. At the inquest Taylor reported that tests for a wide range of poisons had proved negative apart from a small quantity of antimony, which was a common emetic and potentially lethal in large doses. There was little evidence of this in Cook's case, however, and so, based on the chambermaid's account, and the information that Palmer had recently obtained strychnine ostensibly to kill rats, Taylor came to the highly tendentious conclusion that Cook died of strychnine poisoning.

It was this story that Harrison read to William in the New Cross Inn. One passage in the report intrigued William in particular:

> *Dr. Taylor then referred to the other symptoms which are attendant on the result of administration of strychnine, observing that he knew of no other poison that was able to produce convulsions like strychnine. There were poisons which cause paralysis, but he knew of no other which*

*could produce the effects he had heard detailed there except strychnine; and therefore his opinion was that death had been caused from its administration. The only medical difficulty which presents itself was the absence of any proof that the pills contained strychnine, in consequence of none having been discovered in the analysis of the body; but there existed this difference between arsenic and poisons of that kind and strychnine – that, while the former would remain in the body and bear the test of chymical analysis, the latter was so speedily absorbed in the blood that in the course of an hour after administration no chymical test at present known could detect it.*[3]

In short, according to Taylor, a metallic poison like arsenic remained for a long time in the body, and therefore could easily be detected long after death, but an organic substance like strychnine was undetectable in the human body only an hour after ingestion.

After Harrison had finished reading, Dove asked him whether he thought strychnine could be detected, and the wizard replied, 'No, nor yet any other vegetable poison.' Intrigued, William then asked, 'What other vegetable poisons are there that cannot be detected?' 'Digitalis, belladonna, particularly if it was crystalised,' replied the wizard. William asked if Harrison could provide him with strychnine as he wanted to get rid of the cats plaguing his new house. Harrison replied 'No, sir,' and when William asked why not, he said, 'Not for the world.' William then went out of the back door to urinate, and on returning said he would get some elsewhere in that case, and then left. Harrison turned to Ann Walker, the landlady, and wondered, 'What do you think about it?'[4]

The Doves' marriage quickly deteriorated once again and the familiar pattern of rowing and making up continued. After only a month William confided in John Wood that he was very unhappy and believed he and his wife must part. On other occasions, however, the couple would visit the Woods and appear happy together. Relations were certainly not helped by William's lack of employment and the amount of free time he had on his hands. Drinking became his chief way of passing the hours and was the cause of most rows. On 26 January, for example, William received £5 from his trustees and proceeded to spend most of it on alcohol over the next few days. When John Wood visited the couple he was disgusted to see a drunken William stick his arms up his wife's petticoats in his presence. John later cautioned William about spending all his money and not giving any to Harriet. William turned to Harriet and asked, 'Do I owe you anything?' Harriet replied, 'Yes, you owe Mr. Wood one shilling, which you borrowed off him to get drunk with.' In response he went upstairs and came down again with two sovereigns, which he threw on the table. Wood picked them up and handed them to Harriet. Later that evening William moaned to Wood about his wife's behaviour and Wood replied, 'All women talk to their husbands when they get drunk, and you must excuse it.' Although Wood disapproved of William's behaviour he also thought that Harriet was unnecessarily sharp at times, and he upheld the concept of patriarchal control of the house. When Elizabeth once refused to give William some beer on Harriet's orders, Wood interfered and told her to go fetch him some: 'I thought he was the owner, and ought to have the key of his tap.'

Another typical row took place in early February while Mary Wood was visiting. William had asked Elizabeth Fisher for his supper, but she, with Harriet's consent, refused to give it to him. Mary intervened and told Elizabeth to go and get it. William then asked to have some beer with his meal, and once again Elizabeth was tardy in complying. William snapped, said he could not bear it any longer and left the house by the back door. Harriet then ran and locked it. When William returned shortly and tried to get in through the front door he found that also locked. He began to kick it, swearing he would not be locked out of his own home. He was eventually let in and he took his supper into the front room and locked himself in. Mary Wood persuaded him to open the door and Harriet then went in and made up with her husband. The reconciliation did not last long, however. Before he left the front room for the night he began to wind up the clock. Harriet told him to stop, as he would break it. Mary interjected that it was William's clock and he would have to pay for it if he broke it. Harriet snapped back that she should stop interfering. William shouted that he would break up the house and sell up. So ended another of their bickering fights.

On Sunday 10 February William went to George Morley's surgery to get medicine for Harriet. He ran this errand on a regular basis and he was accustomed to stopping a while and smoking a pipe with Morley's pupil John Elletson, who was in charge of the dispensary. While the surgery boy James Peacock prepared Harriet's medicine, William talked to them about the main topic of the day – the ongoing Palmer sensation. Throughout January inquests were held on the exhumed bodies of William Palmer's brother Walter, who had apparently died of apoplexy in August 1855, and his wife Anne Palmer who had apparently died of cholera in September 1854. Alfred Taylor conducted the toxicological analysis in both cases and found prussic acid in organs of the former and suspiciously high quantities of antimony in the latter. The coroner's jury came to a verdict of wilful murder in both cases.

William looked around the dispensary, pointed to a bottle of antimony and said, 'That is what Palmer poisoned his wife with.' Peacock confirmed that it was indeed. William then pointed to a bottle marked strychnia, stating 'They can't test strychnia.' Elletson corrected him, saying that they certainly could and mentioned nitric acid as a test. To prove his point he produced a copy of *Pereira's Materia Medica*, and turned to the relevant page. Peacock chipped in by saying that Morley had detected strychnine in the stomach of a woman who had died at New Road End. After studying closely the entry in *Pereira's Materia Medica* for a quarter of an hour, William suggested that laying strychnine would be a good way of getting rid of the stray cats at Cardigan Place. Elletson agreed and gave him about ten grains wrapped in white foolscap paper with 'poison' written on it.

On returning home Dove went into the kitchen and asked Elizabeth Fisher to get him a plate. Some fish had recently gone missing from the kitchen and he said he thought the cats had taken it. He took some meat, put it on the plate, sliced the meat open and then sprinkled some of the grains in between. He asked Fisher where he should put the deadly meal and she suggested on top of a dog kennel in the corner of the yard. Having done this he boasted to Fisher that he had enough grains to kill six people. He kept the packet of grains in his shaving case on the mantelpiece in his bedroom for safekeeping. A couple of days later he took out a few grains and put them on a piece of cheese, which he placed under Elizabeth's bed. The following morning she found a dead mouse there and threw it into the ash-pit in the yard. A few days after this the meat had gone from the kennel but there were no dead cats. William set out some more strychnine-laced meat and a couple of days later one of the cats was found dead and was also buried in the ash-pit. William returned to the dispensary and reported his initial cat-killing success, and said that the rain had washed away the poison and there was still another cat prowling about the place. Elletson gave him another five grains and also asked for the skin of the cat so that he could turn it into a tobacco pouch. He never received it, for no further cats were found dead. A fact that would later attract suspicion.

## Medicine and strange symptoms

Harriet's health continued to remain delicate after the removal to Leeds; though now they were only a short ride from town, she was regularly visited by the long-serving Dove family doctor George Morley, who lived at 18 Park Place. The son of a Wesleyan minister and a former pupil at Woodhouse Grove School, Morley had initially been apprenticed to a draper, but his natural inquisitiveness and intelligence soon led him to study medicine.[5] By the 1850s he had become a highly respected figure in Leeds, and had recently helped set up a hospital for women and children at 28 East Parade.[6] A colleague recalled that his 'devotion to his patients caused him to exert himself to the serious injury of his health.'[7] He treated Harriet for what he diagnosed as 'functional disorder of her digestive system, and affection of the nerves.' When in early February Harriet complained of pains in her head and side, Morley prescribed regular drafts of two effervescent medicines to improve her digestion. One was an alkaline mixture of carbonate of soda and syrup of lemons the other an acid drink of tartaric acid in water. She also had a liniment consisting of soap and opium to relieve her muscular pains. On 18 February he further prescribed rhubarb pills to aid digestion.

On Tuesday 19 February Elizabeth Fisher fell ill and returned to Normanton. Her mother agreed to take her place but could only arrive on the following Saturday. In the intervening days William and Harriet were left largely on their own. In the absence of a servant William took on some of the household chores in his ample spare time, occupying himself with black-leading the stoves, cleaning the plate and preparing meals for Harriet. His participation in household chores was not unusual as at White Well he used to help the servants with the cooking. In the evenings he occupied himself by knitting an antimacassar. He seemed to like such handiwork, sometimes working together with Harriet, and had recently completed the image of a bird in crotchet. To help out with the domestic work his mother sent along her washerwoman, Mrs Thornhill, on the Wednesday and Friday. On the latter day William chatted with her in the kitchen and confided that he had been to see a 'witch man', who had told him that his wife would not live much longer. He further intimated that he intended to marry Mrs Whitham, but was 'not going to marry her for what she had, as he had a good home of his own.'

On Saturday afternoon William's sister Jane visited and brought a jelly from their mother. Harriet had a spoonful and complained it tasted nasty and bitter. Mrs Fisher had a bit and agreed it was as bitter as aloes. William also had a couple of spoons. Harriet asked William, 'Did you put anything in that jelly?' William replied, 'Yes, I have put some of the medicine in it.' She chided him that it was an unkind thing to do, and began to suck on an orange to remove the taste. She complained that was bitter also and William asked sardonically, 'You don't think I have put anything in the orange?' She said no and then continued to grumble about his jelly-tampering, to which William replied that he had put no more than a tablespoon in it. He then left and spent the rest of the day in Leeds, first collecting his wife's medicine before calling at his mother's in Park Square during the evening.

On Sunday 24 February Harriet seemed well enough, and walked the quarter of a mile to Burley church with Mrs Whitham. The following morning she arose between eight and nine and shared a breakfast of coffee, toast and bacon with William. Then she played the piano a little while. Shortly after, however, she told Ann Fisher that there was a strange sensation in her legs. As the two women began to make the beds she further complained of feeling 'quite curious' and a few minutes later she collapsed in Fisher's arms. Ann carried Harriet to a chair by the bedside and called for William to fetch Mrs Whitham. She arrived at around half past ten, and later recalled how Harriet 'had jerking of the body, and twitchings of the hand. I took hold of her hand, and she grasped it violently. When we got her on to the bed, her feet were stretched out. When any one moved about, or touched her, she was worse. I observed her in this state between two and three hours.' Every time Harriet was touched or cold water was put to her lips the twitching returned. She had pains in her chest and Jane and Ann tried to give her some mint tea, but it only made her sweat profusely.

While the two women tended to Harriet, William went off to Leeds to fetch Morley. He was not in and so his pupil John William Scarth came instead. On the way William asked: 'If my wife dies will there be an inquest?' Scarth replied, 'The coroner's jurisdiction is confined to accidents and sudden deaths.' William persisted with his rather suspicious line of inquiry, asking Scarth whether Morley would request a *post mortem* examination. Scarth thought he probably would. William then expressed his opposition to any such action, saying his family would refuse to give consent, just as had been the case with his father's death. By the time Scarth saw Harriet the muscular contractions were easing off. He prescribed a mixture consisting of spirit of sulphuric ether, ammoniated tincture of valerian and tincture of henbane. Later in the day, around three or four o'clock, Morley came to see Harriet. He found her lying in bed. She was calm, though her arm occasionally twitched. He asked her to explain her symptoms and concluded that she had an attack of hysteria – an unusually severe manifestation of her usual nervous complaint. He did not consider she was seriously ill, and further prescribed a mixture containing spirit of sulphuric ether, ammoniated tincture of valerian, and decoction of aloes. That evening William wrote the following letter to his mother-in-law:

> *My Dear Mother, – I am very sorry to tell you that my wife is very ill indeed. . . . She is entirely prostrate. Mother has been to her. If you would like to see her you had better come by London, and then you can get from London to Leeds for 3s. 6d. Harriet would like to see you, but she thinks of the expense. My dear wife's love to you all at home, and accept the same from*
>     *Your affectionate son,*
>     *William Dove.*

On the Tuesday Harriet was feeling very weak and Morley prescribed more of the same medicine but with an added infusion of gentian, which was used as a tonic to stimulate the stomach. Meanwhile William whiled away the hours at Thomas Outhwaite's dram shop in Lands Lane, drinking gin and cloves. Here he struck up a conversation with a complete stranger, a baker named Henry Rose, and gave him his calling card. William invited him to take a walk together, saying he had something of importance to discuss. He began by telling him about his wife's illness and said that after her death they would have 'a regular jollification'. He told him to look out in the newspapers for notification of her death. The conversation then took an even more unusual turn. William said he 'could not do without a woman', and told Rose that if he knew one that might suit him, would he 'bring her down to his house?' It is likely that William had nothing more in mind than to be introduced to a respectable prospective wife, but Rose thought he was asking him to act as a pimp, and so replied, 'If you take me to be a character of that sort, you are greatly mistaken, and I'll bid you good morning.'

The next morning Whitham paid a visit and found Harriet feeling a little better. Meanwhile William went in to Leeds and called upon Mary Hicks, who lived with her son John, a bookseller, in Upperhead Row. They had become acquainted with the Doves not long after their marriage, but in recent months they had discouraged William from visiting them because of his drinking. Mary also considered him a liar, and disapproved of William's behaving towards Harriet, which was the subject of gossip. Mary reluctantly let William in because he looked tired and distressed, and gave him some bread, meat and water. William told her that he did not expect his wife to recover, and wished her to talk to Harriet about her soul. So Hicks and her sister Maria Killam took tea with Harriet later in the day and were surprised to find her in a cheerful mood, though she had a dead feeling in her feet and jaw, and complained that her medicine made her nauseous. As William accompanied Mary and Maria back to Armley railway station, Mary remarked that Harriet seemed better than she expected, but William replied that he was 'confident she will not get better'.

Morley also came to see Harriet that day and in her presence William repeated that he thought she would not recover. Morley, angry at such a callous and disrespectful comment in front of his patient, called him aside and chastised him, saying that if he had anything to say on the matter he should say it to him alone. William persisted with his opinion and Morley told him to call someone else in if he did not trust his opinion. William said he would consider doing so. When Whitham visited that evening she found Harriet crying because her medicine was very unpleasant. Judging from its content it would, indeed, have tasted unpleasantly bitter. William was there and suggested, 'Then its no use having Mr Morley'. Whitham recommended Dr Hobson instead. Later that evening William paid a visit to Morley's surgery. The doctor was away and so William talked about his wife's illness with Morley's coachman, William Renton. William mimicked the facial contortions and twitchings of his wife's fits and reiterated that she would not get better. Renton told him he should not say such things to sick people as it sometimes made them worse, and then went to tend his horses. About a quarter of an hour later he locked the stable door and, as he crossed the yard to the surgery, he saw that the light in the surgery was suddenly turned down. On entering he found William there alone, putting his hand into his waistcoat pocket. William said, 'I'm going to light my pipe,' and off he went.

On Thursday morning William wrote two letters, one to his mother-in-law and the other to Morley:

*Dear Mother, – We received your kind letter this morning, and in answer to which I am very sorry to say that my dear wife is no better, but worse. Yesterday, at twelve o'clock at noon, she had one of the shocks, and it did not pass off till half-past two, and at a quarter to twelve last night she had another, which did not pass off till a quarter to three. I had just gone to bed when it commenced, but had to get up again. I was up all Monday night till two on Tuesday, and last night till half-past three, all except half an hour. Mrs. Kilham and Mrs Hicks came to see my wife yesterday; they say they intend to come again. There is a widow lady next door who is so kind I do not know what I should do if it was not for her and Mrs. Fisher. I am nearly worn out as it is, but I intend not to complain. When my dear wife was so ill yesterday, she many times wished her mother was here; it is my opinion if she has any more shocks she will sink under them, and I should not like her to die and none of her friends near her; for they might blame me and say that I had not been attentive enough to her, but I will do what I can for her till I drop. H.'s love to all at home, and accept the same yourself from*

    *Your affectionate son,*

    *William Dove*

*P.S. – I know it is an expensive journey; I wish I had money to send you, for you should have it with pleasure. My friends come very little.*

*Dear Sir, – Mrs. Dove tells me she has entire confidence in you, and she thinks it would be going to needless expense to have any one else. Don't be deceived. I have entire confidence. I don't wish to grieve you to-day. Will you be kind enough to speak to Mrs. Dove to-morrow on religion, for she says she wants some person to take her by the hand, for she feels herself a sinner.*

   *I am, dear Sir, yours respectfully,*
      *William Dove.*

In the evening Harriet had another attack of the same symptoms as those on Monday. Morley gave her a draught of Batley's solution of opium and ammoniated tincture of valerian, a commonly prescribed sedative and painkiller.

At eleven the next morning William went to see the Rev. Thomas Sturgeon, vicar of Burley. Harriet had asked Sturgeon to visit her. William apologised for the boldness of the request as they were not members of his congregation, but he said he had heard that he was willing to give spiritual succour to anyone in the parish. Sturgeon knew his father and told William he remembered him as a good and religious man. William agreed that he had been blessed with pious parents and expressed his regret that he did not live up to the light that was in him, and wished he were righteous so that his prayers for his wife might avail. Sturgeon accompanied William back to Cardigan Place and found Harriet lying in bed in a nervous and excitable state. William left the two alone and Sturgeon joined her in prayer and read some Scripture to her, but the interview was short as Harriet had little to say. Sturgeon remarked to William that she did not appear as bad as he feared.

That afternoon Mary Hicks and her sister Maria Killam paid another visit, as they had promised. They talked with the Doves of the forthcoming visit of Harriet's mother, and Maria said they would like to take tea with her if she came. William, who seemed to be in good spirits, replied, 'That you can, and plenty of tea cakes.' He said several times how delighted he was at the prospect of seeing his mother-in-law. He was most affectionate to Harriet in their company, and offered her a biscuit in the shape of a heart saying, 'Here is a heart, my love, take it.' But she answered, 'I cannot eat it, it is too hard.' Mary and Maria saw William give Harriet a glass of her medicine. She complained of the bitterness as usual and asked for a sweet lozenge to kill the taste. William said Morley had made the medicine three times stronger to suppress the fits, and asked Maria to taste it. She found it very disagreeable and bitter, but not greatly so. William then washed and wiped the glass, and rather gratuitously remarked, 'I always wash the glass, the medicine is so very nauseous.' Shortly afterwards he went into the dressing room.

William accompanied Hicks and her sister back to the railway station that evening. As they walked he talked a lot of his wife's wish not to be subjected to a *post mortem*. He mused that he would probably marry again as no one could expect a young man like him to remain single. Hicks replied, 'Nonsense, she is not going to die.' They missed the train and William offered to escort them back to Leeds. They protested politely that he should return to his wife in case of another attack. He replied that she would not have another until half past ten or eleven. A little surprised at such exactitude, Hicks asked, 'Do these attacks come on periodically then?' But William said nothing. He walked them back to town and talked at length about how he was going to give Mrs Whitham a present for her kindness. He thought of buying her a book – one that would cost not less than sixteen or eighteen shillings. On his way back home, at around nine o'clock, he called at Margaret Young's confectionery shop in Burley Road. He asked for some finger biscuits and then, following his usual pattern of conversation, described to her his wife's symptoms and said he didn't think she would live beyond Saturday night.

As William predicted, Harriet had another serious attack after he had returned from the confectioner's. When Ann Fisher was called up to her bedroom to help she found William by her bedside, holding her hand. Her back was arched, her belly was making strange noises, she had difficulty breathing and was unable to speak. Ann remained with her until two o'clock in the morning. When the attack subsided Harriet remarked, 'Oh, dear, I thought it would have been my last, – I thought it was all over with me.' It soon was.

## Last day

The next morning Harriet was in a poor state. She could not at first drink the coffee that Ann made for her. After a nap she felt a little better, and received the Rev. Sturgeon. She told him of the previous night's attack and how she had never experienced such pain in her life. Morley paid a brief visit around eleven o'clock. Jane Whitham visited next, at around half past two, and found Harriet much better. She brought some homemade jelly consisting of cowslip wine and brandy. William was there when she arrived and in the presence of his wife he asked her, with his usual tact, if they did burials at Burley church. She replied no, they did them at Headingley church and at the municipal cemetery. William then left. He went to the Sutcliffe Arms, Burley Road, where he bought a couple of bottles of porter and had a brief chat with the landlady, Sarah Naylor, about his wife's condition, which he described to her as 'spasms of the nerves'.

Jane and Harriet had tea and at half past three Jane gave Harriet two tablespoonfuls of the medicine, which was kept on the washstand. Morley paid a brief visit around four. A bit later Harriet was well enough to get out of bed and eat a mutton chop with toast and two cups of tea. When William returned at half past five, Harriet complained of his being gone so long, and asked him not to go for medicine that night. He was the worse for drink and lay down on the floor to sleep. Ann Fisher told him he would catch a cold so he got up again and dragged himself to bed. Jane left around half past six and on her way out told William that she had given Harriet her medicine. Jane intended to return again the following day but only an hour or so later William requested her to keep Harriet company, as he was shortly going into Leeds to pick up her medicine. She kindly agreed and found Mrs Fisher rubbing Harriet's leg with the opium liniment prescribed by Morley. Jane helped massage the rest of it into her back. Mrs Wood arrived shortly after. About eight o'clock Harriet asked William, 'Will you be kind enough to give me my medicine, love? It is time.' He went to the washstand and poured some out into a wine-glass. After she had drunk it she asked for a mint lozenge as the medicine felt very hot. She also asked for some water, which William gave her. He washed out the medicine glass, repeating the refrain, 'I always wash it out, as it is very nasty stuff.' He then set off to get the medicine and said he would also ask for a nurse. He was in a rather unkempt state, and as he was about to leave Jane enquired, 'Mr Dove you are not going down to Leeds that figure.' To which he replied he certainly was and off he went.

A quarter of an hour later Harriet warned, 'I believe I am going to have another attack.' Then her back arched, her legs stretched out, her head was thrown back and the muscle spasms and twitching began. Jane and Mary each took hold of a hand, and Harriet gripped them so tightly it hurt. Her hands were hot at first but soon became quite cold. Her face became distorted with pain. Her eyes contracted and her teeth clenched.

Jane could hear mucus clogging her throat but it would not come out. She seemed to want to vomit but could not do so. Her breathing was heavy and laboured; she moaned and let out an occasional scream. In the first half an hour she could still talk but with great difficulty. When Mary attempted to rub her legs she called out, 'Oh! Please don't.' She could not bear to be touched; soon after she became insensible. Mary and Jane burned some brown paper under her nose to try and revive her senses but with no success. Every time the spasms seemed to ease off for a few minutes they would return with even greater intensity.

At ten o'clock Jane left to tell Mr Wood to fetch Morley. Shortly after her return William returned home. He took off his coat and was about to rub Harriet's legs, but Jane warned she could not stand it in her present state. On Mary's suggestion he went to fetch Dr Hobson. William ran to Morley's in Leeds, where he found the surgeon waiting for a cab, having already received the message from Wood. William asked him to bring Dr Hobson as well. Morley called on Hobson, and as they waited for him to get ready, William took up the subject that was uppermost in his mind. He said, 'Mr Morley, if my wife should die she has a particular objection to being dissected, and it must not be done.' This he repeated several times in different forms. Morley said he hoped the necessity would not arise as she seemed better that morning. Hobson arrived and they set off for Cardigan Place.

By half past ten Jane could feel Harriet's pulse getting very weak and it appeared to cease altogether at times. Her face began to turn blue and at twenty minutes to eleven she died in great pain. When William arrived with the doctors minutes later and heard they were too late, he threw himself on to the bed next to his dead wife in apparent anguish until Dr Hobson gently led him away. Morley noted that Harriet's face was slightly livid and her final expression was one of anxiety. He talked to Jane and Mary for a few minutes, enquiring as to her condition prior to death, and then left. Ann Fisher accompanied a tearful William to see John Wood and request him to order a coffin-board. Afterwards William said he was going for a walk. He called at Margaret Young's confectionery shop to tell her 'it was all over' for his 'poor wife', and said he would never forget her last look. He then moved on to the Sutcliffe Arms where he sat near the fire and drowned his sorrow with two glasses of ale and some brandy. He returned home drunk an hour or so later and went to bed. Meanwhile

Ann Fisher and Mary proceeded to lay out Harriet's body. *Rigor mortis* did not set in for an unusually long time and the two women found it easy to wash and prepare the body. They finished around two o'clock and retired for the night.

## Mourning

The next morning William went to Leeds. He called on the Hickses at around half past twelve. He knocked at the shop door and shouted out, 'For God's sake, come down, and let me come in.' Mrs Hicks opened a window to see who it was and then called for her son John to open the door. He could tell that William was intoxicated as well as agitated. William exclaimed, 'Oh, poor Harriet's dead; I wish I could weep.' When Mrs Hicks appeared he said, 'Oh, she's gone, she's gone, Mrs Hicks!' He then became conscious that they saw he had been drinking and explained, 'I was obliged to take some brandy to keep my spirits up.' Mrs Hicks asked if anyone was watching over his wife's body, and he replied he was not sure. William pleaded piteously with John to accompany him back home. As they made their way to Cardigan Place John asked William about Harriet's death. William replied, 'Oh, do not allude to it,' adding that he was apprehensive that there might be an inquest. His fears were shortly to be confirmed.

While William was out George Morley had called to discuss the need for a *post mortem*, and took the opportunity to make a close external examination of Harriet's corpse. Morley did not suspect any foul play at this stage, but surgeons were required to report any strange or unexpected deaths to the coroner, and Harriet's final symptoms, as well as her death at such a young age, were certainly strange and unexpected. He was told that William had gone to see his mother, and so he sent a note to Park Square. William sent him the following letter in response:

> *Mr. Morley. – Dear Sir, It is very harrowing to my feelings the idea of one I love being cut open, particularly as she so strictly requested it not to be. Do you cast any blame on me for my conduct during her sickness? If you do so, it is upon your own responsibility. An answer will oblige.*
> *Truly yours,*
> *William Dove.*

Later that day Morley paid a visit to Park Square and explained his request to William's mother. He told her that shortly after Harriet's death he had learned from his staff that William had obtained strychnine from his surgery. From his understanding of Harriet's symptoms on Saturday evening he suspected that strychnine poisoning was the cause and thought, therefore, that she might have ingested some accidentally. A *post mortem* examination was the only way to know.

The next morning, Monday the third, he received the following letter written by Mary and signed by her son:

> *My dear Sir, – I have stated to William what you said relative to the strychnia, and lest you should have any suspicions relative to poison, he begs you will make an examination, and take any one with you that you may think desirable. – Yours respectfully,*
>     Mary Dove
>     William Dove

Harriet's mother and sister arrived in Leeds in the afternoon to hear the terrible news that they were too late.

## Post mortem

The Leeds coroner John Blackburn formally opened an inquest on Harriet's death at the Cardigan Arms, Kirkstall Road, but then immediately adjourned it to await the results of the *post mortem* examination that was taking place at Cardigan Place. It was usual practice at the period to conduct *post mortem* dissections in the death room, even though the circumstances were hardly ideal for such a medical investigation. There was no stone slab on which to work, so as a handbook suggested, the corpse should be placed on either a kitchen table, or on the coffin lid or a door supported on a couple of chairs.[8] This practice generated understandable public health concerns among some in the medical establishment, who posited the scenario of a surgeon going from having his hands covered in necrotic material one hour to tending patients the next.[9]

There were other more general concerns about the conduct of *post mortems*. It was usual practice at this time for *post mortem* dissections to be conducted by local general practitioners, often those who had last treated the patient. They effectively acted as amateur pathologists and many were not sufficiently skilled or knowledgeable enough to detect some of the more subtle signs of disease or poisoning. Furthermore, their relations with the family of the bereaved could compromise the scientific thoroughness of their examinations.[10] There were understandable pressures from families for the dissection to be done speedily, particularly when they were often present in the home when the dissections occurred. Despite Mary's letter, Morley must have felt such pressures from the Doves. When her husband Christopher died Morley had apparently wanted to conduct a *post mortem* examination but Mary refused.

In the case of the examination of Harriet's corpse, however, there would have been no doubts as to Morley's competency. Not only was he an experienced general practitioner but he was also a lecturer in chemistry at the Leeds School of Medicine, and had a particular interest in toxicology.[11] Furthermore, he invited his distinguished colleague Thomas Nunneley to join him. Nunneley, who lived at 22 Park Place, just a few doors away from Morley, was a lecturer on surgery at the Leeds School of Medicine, and an author of books on the structure of the eye and the nature and cure of erysipelas. He was also a pioneer regarding the use of anaesthetics and was one of the first to use the widely used A.C.E. mixture of alcohol, chloroform and ether.[12] More to the point, he had been testing the effects of poisons on animals for many years.

As James Peacock had told William, Harriet was not the first *post mortem* Morley had conducted involving suspected strychnine poisoning. The previous May he and Nunneley had examined the body of a young woman named Ellen Waterhouse. She was a stranger in Leeds and, being refused a bed at a public house, she was destined to spend her first night wandering the streets. She got talking to a poor married man who invited her to share his children's bed for the night. About a quarter to two in the morning the man's wife was awoken to find Ellen in convulsions. These went on for an hour, then eased off, during which time she confessed she had poisoned herself. An hour later she died during another convulsive attack. Two empty packets of 'Battle's Vermin Killer' were found in her pocket. This was a widely available rat poison consisting of strychnine and flour coloured with Prussian blue. There were three grains of strychnine in each packet. Nunnerley conducted a *post mortem* examination thirty hours after her death. As with Harriet, there was scarcely any muscle rigidity. Three days later he and Morley then analysed the stomach contents. Contrary to Taylor's evidence before the Cook inquest, they had no problem at all detecting strychnine by standard tests. In fact they were so successful at extracting the poison that they made a solution for a colleague, who lectured on medical jurisprudence, to demonstrate to students how to test for the poison.

The main results of the morning's dissection of Harriet's body were summarised by Morley as follows:

*External Appearances. – The body was well nourished, moderately plump, and not at all emaciated. There was no wound or abrasion, or mark of injury of any kind, except the traces left by a mustard poultice which had been applied to the back. The face slightly livid, particularly the lips. The teeth and edges of lips covered with dark sores; eyes sunken and dull, and pupils dilated. The countenance had a certain expression of distress not easy to describe. In other parts the skin was natural, presenting only the discoloration usual after death on the depending parts.*

*Internal appearances. The muscles were soft and of a dark colour wherever cut into. The brain was overcharged with blood, and, in addition to this general infiltration and congestion, there were circumscribed patches of a dark colour fitted in the surface of the right hemisphere. When the surface was cut into it was full of sharp points, showing the vessels to be unnaturally full of blood. The veins of the spine were much congested, and the membranes of the spinal chord were more viscid than natural. The substance of the spinal marrow was natural, except that the grey portion on the lower part of the neck was slightly soft. The heart was of a natural size. The muscular substance was soft, and the cavities were empty, but probably the blood had been drawn out in the examination of other parts of the body. . . . The lungs and organs of respiration were unnatural. The lungs and air passage were gorged with dark blood, so that when cut into they had the appearance rather of pulmonary apoplexy – otherwise they were healthy. The engorgement of the lungs and the deep discoloration of the lining of the air tubes were presented in a degree of intensity seldom observed. The thorax presented a little dark serum. The viscera of the abdomen were healthy . . . The liver, kidney, and other parts were all healthy.*

It was a textbook example of a *post mortem* examination: comprehensive, thorough and meticulously recorded. Yet the dissection, not surprisingly, did not reveal any clear signs of strychnine poisoning. That could only be tested in a laboratory. Morley therefore removed the stomach and intestines for further analysis. Finally, Morley and Nunneley would have stitched up the various incisions they had made to ensure the countenance of the body, particularly the head, showed no obvious signs of dissection that would distress her family.

Over the next few days Morley, Nunneley and a junior colleague named John Heaton worked long hours at the School of Medicine, applying various tests on portions of the stomach and its content. They began on the Monday night at ten o'clock and worked right through until dawn. They resumed the next afternoon, had a short interval for tea, and worked late into the night. On the Wednesday they began again at three o'clock in the afternoon, and worked similarly the next day. They finally finished at five o'clock on Friday morning. In his memoir, Heaton remembered 'the intense interest with which, after a long night's work, the concluding processes were conducted, which ended in the detection of the poison.'[13]

Their first task on the Monday night was to create a solution of Harriet's stomach for testing. A portion of the stomach was mixed with distilled water and sulphuric acid. This solution was filtered and carbonate of lime added to neutralise the acid. It was then evaporated. Rectified spirit was added and heated; this solution was then filtered and gently evaporated until a syrupy liquid formed. On this liquid they applied all the tests they had used in the case of Ellen Waterhouse and several more. When they applied nitric acid it turned a tell-tale red, likewise the application of a little acetic acid and then a solution of chloride of gold produced a characteristic yellowish-white precipitate. To another sample they added pure concentrated sulphuric acid, then bichromate of potash. It turned purple, then red, indicating strychnine. But for Morley and Nunneley, just as convincing evidence as these chemical combinations was the simple one of taste – the solution had the characteristic bitterness of strychnine. They also had someone dig up the grey cat that William had poisoned and thrown in the ash-pit, and conduct parallel experiments on it. The results were exactly the same as those for Harriet's stomach.

As the two surgeons toiled night and day in the laboratory William made arrangements for the funeral and received Mrs Jenkins and her daughter. Although they arrived on the Monday, when they called at Cardigan Place William was away, so they returned the next afternoon. On greeting them he shook hands and they took tea together in the back parlour. The conversation began politely but soon became strained due to William's usual lack of tact. As he showed Mrs Jenkins her daughter's wedding ring he mused, 'I can't think but I shall marry again.' She replied, 'I hope you will never put that ring on another woman's finger.' 'If I do,' said William, 'I'll send this ring to you.' He also showed his mother-in-law Harriet's Bible and her bottles of medicine, and asked if she was satisfied that everything was correct. At some point during the afternoon Mary Hicks also came to see the corpse. When she enquired of William why an inquest had been called, he replied, 'Oh, we live in a bad neighbourhood, and we have not lived happily together; but it's all moonshine.' The coroner's jury having been to Cardigan Place to view the corpse either that morning or the previous evening, the coroner sent a letter on the Tuesday afternoon authorising that the body could now be buried. The members of the family went up to Harriet's bedroom to pay their last respects. William kissed her and recited, 'Lord teach us to number our days that we may apply our hearts to wisdom.' The coffin was then closed.

The funeral took place the next day at Burmantofts Cemetery. Beckett Street Cemetery, as it was also known, was opened in 1845 on a sixteen-acre site northeast of the town on a hillside out in the fields dotted with brick kilns and coal pits.[14] It was built in response to the huge demand for burial space resulting from rapid urbanisation. The town's existing Anglican churches and Nonconformist chapels could not cope and so the Town Council secured parliamentary backing for the venture. It was rather unusual though, in that money was raised through the rates rather than being a private initiative run as a commercial venture, as was often the case in early Victorian cities up until the Burial Acts of the 1850s. As was usual, the cemetery was divided between consecrated ground for Church of England and unconsecrated ground for Nonconformists. Each had its own entrance, chapel and staff. So Harriet's funeral procession would have passed out of town along a road through the brick fields, past the impressive House of Recovery, built ten years before to care for those with infectious diseases, past the first entrance into consecrated ground, and then entered through the second set of gates. Although open for less than eleven years the cholera epidemic of 1849 and the poor sanitary conditions in the town meant that it was already filling up rapidly. The cemetery was laid out according to the ability to pay. Grave plots costing several pounds at the top of the hill for the well-to-do and unmarked common graves at the bottom. One imagines that Harriet's final resting place was somewhere at the top of the hill, but we will never know because she was buried in an unmarked grave, presumably to deter sensation-seekers.[15]

After the funeral William called on Morley to see how the analysis was proceeding: 'I wish to know, Mr Morley, what you have found. Have you found poison?' Morley replied that he had not yet completed the analysis. William then asked, 'Do you suspect me of poisoning? Do you think I could be so cruel?' Morley answered that his suspicions were directed towards accidental poisoning. William protested too much: 'Should I have done it openly, if I meant to poison? Should I have come to your surgery for the poison? Should I have talked about it to others?' There was nothing much Morley could say to this outburst, and the conversation ended.[16]

On Thursday morning William and his mother-in-law had a blazing row. It began when she commented to William that she wished she had been present during Harriet's last hours 'to have seen the cause of death'. William responded angrily, shouting at her, 'You have come here with your poor temper, have you? I don't care for you, nor George Reinhardt, or Jane Dove.' Then, 'Why did you wish to be here before your child died?' he demanded. 'You often spoke unkindly to my child,' she replied, 'and caused her to have hysterics.' The implication was clear: Elizabeth thought that William had killed his wife through mental anguish. William countered that what she died from was far more violent than her usual fits. After this heated conversation, William went into Leeds to distribute funeral cards. He called upon an acquaintance, Thomas Glover Frost, who worked at the Victoria Shades coffee house near Wellington Station. William and Harriet used to visit the Shades together and he had found them a loving couple, though when William visited alone he several times complained of having no children and asked Frost what he would do if he was in his place. On this occasion they talked about what he should do now his wife was dead, whether he should stay at Cardigan Place or sell his furniture and move. William inevitably turned the conversation towards the matter of strychnine. He told Frost he was suspected of poisoning Harriet. Frost enquired what strychnine was like, and to demonstrate William took out his snuffbox and placed a small quantity of snuff on the counter, saying that the same amount of strychnine would be enough to poison him. Frost told William, 'If you have poisoned your wife, your conscience will go with you.' William said nothing in reply.

Around half past two he paid a visit to the New Cross Inn, where he handed a funeral card to the landlord. The bar was quiet and the only other customer was a broker called William Storey, who lodged at the Inn. William sat down and had someone fetch Harrison, who arrived five minutes later. After giving Harrison a card, William told him that an inquest had been opened on his wife. Harrison asked why, and William explained that Harriet had died suddenly and Morley knew that there was strychnine in the house. William then asked, 'Can they detect a grain or a grain and a half of strychnia?' Harrison replied, 'Well, you have not been giving your wife some, have you?' William said, 'No, but I got some from Mr Morley's young man, and some may have been spilt, and she might have got some.' Harrison then left as he had to attend a funeral.

The next day the inquest finally resumed at the Scarborough Hotel. Back at Cardigan Place William was preoccupied with thoughts on the subject of poison. At breakfast that morning he said to his mother-in-law, 'Do you know a spoonful of oil of almonds will kill a person. Arsenic you can detect in a body after twenty years; belladonna you cannot; one is a mineral, the other a vegetable.' He then took a small pinch of salt and continued, 'There is a poison like this; in man it can be detected; in woman it cannot.' William appeared calm but by the middle of the after-noon his nerves began to crack. While the coroner was busy questioning witnesses, William once again resorted to the wizard for reassurance. He knocked at 5 North Row at around three o'clock, and was shown in by Elizabeth Brown. 'How will the case go?' he asked Harrison. 'Shall I be imprisoned?' 'It will be a very difficult case,' replied the wise-man, 'but I can work you out.' William said, 'You only say you can; now tell me, will you?' Harrison replied, 'Set yourself altogether at rest. I will.'[17] That evening William was arrested.

# Notes and references

1 The following account is, unless otherwise referenced, pieced together from reports in the *Leeds Intelligencer*, 11, 15 and 22 March 1956; *Leeds Times*, 15 March 1856; *The Times*, 8, 10, 11, 13 and 18 March 1856; *The Times*, 19 and 21 July 1856; *Leeds Mercury*, 17, 19 and 22 July 1856.

2 See *The Times edition of the last hours and execution of W. Palmer the poisoner* (London, 1856); *Illustrated Life and Career of William Palmer of Rugeley* (London, 1856). For analysis of the significance of the case see Ian Burney, 'A Poisoning of No Substance: The Trials of Medico-Legal Proof in Mid-Victorian England', *Journal of British Studies*, 38 (1999), pp. 59–92; Michael Harris, 'Social Diseases? Crime and Medicine in the Victorian Press', in W.F. Bynum, Stephen Lock and Roy Porter (eds), *Medical Journals and Medical Knowledge* (London and New York, 1992), pp. 108–25; Thomas Boyle, *Black Swine in the Sewers of Hampstead: Beneath the Surface of Victorian Sensationalism* (London, 1990), pp. 60–76. See also the excellent website on Palmer by Dave Lewis and Jim Wheeler, http://www.williampalmer.co.uk.

3 *The Times*, 18 December 1855.

4 *Manchester Guardian*, 13 March 1856.

5 Slugg, *Woodhouse Grove School*, pp. 287–8.

6 S.T. Anning, *The History of Medicine in Leeds* (Leeds, 1980), p. 8.

7 T. Wemyss Reid (ed.), *A Memoir of John Deakin Heaton, M.D. of Leeds* (London, 1883), pp. 191–2.

8 Cited in Ian Burney, *Bodies of Evidence: Medicine and the Politics of the English Inquest, 1830–1926* (Baltimore, 2000), p. 121.

9 Burney, *Bodies*, pp. 116–7.

10 See Burney, *Bodies*, p. 115.

11 S.T. Anning and W.K.J. Walls, *A History of the Leeds School of Medicine* (Leeds, 1982), p. 38.

12 Sidney Lee (ed.), *Dictionary of National Biography*, vol. 41 (London, 1895), p. 275; K. Budd, 'Research into anaesthetic by a surgeon: Thomas Nunneley of Leeds', *Proceedings of the History of Anaesthesia Society*, (1994), pp. 9–15.

13 Reid (ed.), *Memoir of John Deakin Heaton*, p. 192.

14 For a detailed history of Beckett Street Cemetery see Sylvia Barnard, *To Prove I'm not Forgot: Living and Dying in a Victorian City* (Manchester, 1990).

**15** Barnard, *To prove I'm not forgot*, p. 159.

**16** *Daily News*, 11 March 1856.

**17** *Leeds Mercury*, 12 August 1856.

# CHAPTER 4

# Dove in the dock

*'... throw off this despotism of public panic and public opinion'*

The manner in which Harriet's inquest was conducted depended considerably on the professional background of the coroner. The position accrued a certain degree of local prestige, particularly after the Births and Deaths Registration Act of 1836, when a body could not be buried without a coroner's order or a registrar's certificate. Coroners did not require any legal or medical training, however, even though they officiated over what was effectively a medico-legal tribunal. As the role of the inquest became increasingly important, a considerable debate developed as to which profession was most suited for the post: lawyers or medical men? It was only in 1840 that the first medically qualified coroner was appointed, namely Thomas Wakley the influential founder of the *Lancet*. The concern was that people were being murdered in such subtle ways as poisoning, drowning and asphyxiation, and through a lack of medical understanding coroners were failing to investigate properly suspicious cases.[1] John Blackburn was one of the vast majority of coroners who came from the legal profession. He was a wealthy solicitor and by 1856 he had been the Leeds borough coroner for nearly twenty years.[2] As his handling of Harriet's inquest showed, his skill was in questioning witnesses. He evidently knew little of medical matters but in this case, and others he presided over, he benefited from the knowledge of the respected members of the town's School of Medicine.

## Inquest

Following Harriet's burial, the inquest reconvened at the Scarborough Hotel, Bishopsgate, Leeds, at ten o'clock on Friday 7 March. The fact that such a serious proceeding as an inquest should have been held in such a public place as the Cardigan Arms or the Scarborough Hotel may seem rather surprising, but drinking establishments were the usual venues at the time. Indeed, as late as 1877 nearly 95 per cent of inquests in Liverpool were still being held in pubs.[3] Inquests represented the last vestige of a long tradition of holding minor judicial proceedings in inns. During the sixteenth and seventeenth centuries church courts were often held there and well into the eighteenth century the petty sessions, presided over by magistrates, were conducted amidst 'the cluttering of Pots, and the noise and ordure of a narrow Room infected with Drinking and a Throng.'[4] Charles Dickens similarly complained about the unseemly 'odour of gin and the smell of tobacco smoke' at inquests. There was also the more serious problem of witnesses whiling away the time before their appearance by downing drinks in the bar.[5] Considering the witnesses scheduled to appear at Harriet's inquest, this was unlikely to be a problem.

It was not the coroner's role to decide whether a crime had been committed but the jury's, which at Harriet's inquest consisted of the following 'highly respectable' men:

*Foreman of the jury: Stephen Whitham, gentleman, Burley.*
*Richard Backhouse, farmer, Burley.*
*Robert Backhouse, farmer, Burley.*
*George Hobson, farmer, Burley.*
*Samuel Myers, butcher, Burley.*
*Samuel Fuller, gardener, Burley.*
*John Dawson, Burley.*
*James William Taylor, merchant, Leeds.*
*George Wright, cloth finisher, Leeds.*
*William Wilks, builder, Leeds.*
*Henry Horsfall, merchant, Leeds.*
*Henry Swain, merchant, Leeds.*
*George Roebuck, merchant, Leeds.*
*John Abbot, cashier, Leeds.*
*Edwin Jordan, merchant, Leeds.*

They were evidently divided between those who lived in Burley and would have known the Whitham family, and members of Leeds' middle class who would have been familiar with the Doves. None of the jurors, however, were meant to have close ties to those concerned in the inquest or involvement in the events leading up to the death. There were fifteen jurors for Harriet's inquest, which was not uncommon. There had to be at least twelve but having several more members enabled inquests to go ahead in the event of the illness of one or two of them. Furthermore it greatly increased the chances of securing the required majority verdict among at least twelve jurors. In the event of twelve members failing to agree jurors could 'be kept without meat, drink, or fire, until they return their verdict,' though it was observed that 'even this may sometimes be ineffectual.'[6] As the 1854 edition of John Jervis's *Practical Treatise on the Office and Duties of Coroners* made clear, the role of the inquest jury was 'to investigate and determine the facts of the case; they are neither to expect, nor should they be bound by, any specific or direct opinion of the Coroner,' except, that was, in questions of law, regarding which they 'ought to show the most respectful deference.'[7] As well as the coroner, coroner's officer, and jury there was one other person in the inquest room with the right to intervene in the proceedings: Joseph Morton Barret. He was an attorney with an office at 13 Albion Street, and was there on William's behalf. It was rather unusual for lawyers representing one of the key parties to participate in the questioning of witnesses. The inquest was not a trial court; it existed to ascertain the cause of death, and therefore there was strictly no need for their presence. This was, at any rate, the opinion of John Blackburn.

Five witnesses were called that day. Jane Whitham was the first in the stand, and provided a detailed account of the condition of Harriet in her final week of life, which was subsequently corroborated by Elizabeth Fisher and Mary Wood. The last witnesses to be heard were the most crucial – the medical experts George Morley and Thomas Nunneley. Under the 1836 Medical Witnesses Act coroners were authorised to pay for the attendance of an appropriate medical witness, usually the doctor who attended the deceased in his or her final days. A second expert witness, like Nunneley, could also be paid in exceptional circumstances with the permission of the Home Office.[8]

While *The Globe*, in a leading article on Harriet's inquest, commented on the 'unusually competent medical witnesses', and the *Morning*

*Advertiser* commended the 'neat and exquisite experiments of Messrs. Nunneley and Morley',[9] in general expert medical witnesses did not have the best of reputations at the time. An article published in the periodical *The Rambler* in 1856 was pretty representative of negative opinion. It moaned how the weighty decisions of juries rested frequently 'on the mode in which some country apothecary states, colours, or distorts the conclusions of his knowledge, or possibly his ignorance.' Even the more elevated hospital professors came in for an ear-bashing, being accused of turning the courtroom and inquest into 'a field for the display of paltry vanity, personal animosity, and over-weening self-esteem.'[10] There was some truth in both these accusations, but medical witnesses found themselves in a difficult and alien situation. As one medical man complained, when doctors had to give evidence, they were 'made to assume more or less of the appearance of partisans – a position derogatory to, and inconsistent with, the dignity and neutrality of science.'[11]

Morley and Nunneley presented a written report of their *post mortem* dissection and the analysis of Harriet's stomach, and were then questioned by the coroner for the benefit of the jury. The most significant part of the questioning on this first day was the following exchange:

> Coroner: *What is your opinion as to the cause of death?*
> Morley: *I cannot refer that to any other cause than the poisonous effects of strychnine, producing the most peculiar convulsions, so closely resembling tetanus.*
> Coroner: *You heard the three witnesses, Mrs Whitham, Mrs Fisher, and Mrs Wood give their evidence, and describe the effects produced upon the deceased during the various attacks. Were there symptoms referable to any other cause than strychnine? Were they referable to any natural cause?*
> Morley: *I cannot refer them to any natural cause – to nothing but the effects of strychnine. There is no other substance, I believe, which will produce these attacks; the disease which most nearly resembles it is tetanus, but there are of course distinctions.*
> Coroner: *The difference between the two –*
> Morley: *Is perceptible and clear.*

Barret attempted to cast some doubt as to the cause of death, first by questioning when Morley had first suspected strychnine poisoning, implying correctly that this was not his first thought. Then he tried to ask about the condition of Harriet's heart, Morley having already stated that he and Nunneley had not deemed it necessary to make a microscopic examination of the heart because they were already sure that strychnine was responsible.

> Barret: *Would it not have been right to have a microscopic examination of the heart, to see if there was disease of the heart?*
> Morley: *There is no room for doubt there. The symptoms and nature of death were utterly unlike what heart disease can produce. Heart disease never did and never could produce them.*
> Nunneley: *It may be a very proper question to ask, but no man possessing a knowledge of disease would put it. You might as well have suggested the examination of the liver or the kidney – it does not admit the possibility of a question.*[12]

After this put down, the coroner proposed adjourning the inquest until Monday, and the jury expressed their agreement. It was now around half past five. Before adjourning, though, Blackburn informed the jury that in light of the day's evidence he had requested William be placed in custody: 'I don't mean to say Mr Dove is implicated, only the fact of his becoming possessed of strychnine, and she having died of strychnine, has caused some suspicion, but not more than that.'

The responsibility for apprehending William rested with the coroner's officer Ottiwell Kell, a former police sergeant probably seconded to the post because of his bronchitis.[13] After arresting William, Kell searched him and found some keys, two metal boxes containing snuff and tobacco and a gold ring. The items were confiscated, including the ring, which William begged him not to take as it belonged to his wife. Kell subsequently went to 3 Cardigan Place and searched the premises for strychnine but without result. He looked in William's razor case but found nothing more than a pair of razors. The next day William was briefly brought before two borough magistrates, John Hope Shaw and Ralph Markland, at the court house. It was necessary for William to be formally remanded in custody for the duration of the inquest, and this had to be sanctioned by at least two sitting magistrates. Ottiwell Kell was present to make *affidavit* that the prisoner was in custody on suspicion of being involved in the unlawful death of his wife. Shaw asked William if he wished to say anything regarding why he should not be remanded, to which he replied that he had nothing to say. He was then remanded until the following Tuesday and taken back to gaol.[14]

The inquest on Monday was conducted in a very different atmosphere to that on Friday. For one thing, the inquest was moved to the more formal surroundings of the Leeds Court House, situated at the junction of Park Row and Infirmary Street, and rather appropriately overlooked by a recently erected statue of Sir Robert Peel.[15] More significantly, it was the first appearance of William before the public. By now reports of the opening day of what was to prove a long inquest had appeared in the local and national press, generating considerable public curiosity. The numbers wishing to seek admittance to the inquest was great and, as the morning's proceedings had been continually interrupted by problems due to overcrowding, it was decided in the afternoon to move proceedings from the council chamber to the larger courtroom with its public gallery.[16]

For the press William was shaping up as the 'new Palmer'. The case had the potential to develop into a great story and so more interest was taken in his appearance than was usual for a defendant at an inquest. A journalist for the *Daily News* described William as 'rather sickly and cadaverous in appearance'.[17] Maybe this was a result of the shock of his first few nights in gaol, or maybe it was just a product of journalistic licence. More sober newspaper reports on subsequent days of the inquest portrayed a rather less ghoulish figure. The *Manchester Guardian* characterised him as 'a slightly-built man, rather above the middle height, of sanguine complexion, and of irregular but not peculiar features.'[18] The *Leeds Times* commented that he looked 'naturally a healthy subject, and free from those physical causes which so frequently operate on persons of lymphatic or bilious temperament.'[19] The *Leeds Intelligencer* painted a more detailed picture:

> his personal appearance is by no means striking. In stature he is about
> 5 feet 7 inches, and his physical development in other respects
> corresponds. He is thin – his features well marked – the nose and cheek
> bones being somewhat prominent, and the expression is quiet and

*rather firm than otherwise. His hair is dark, and his complexion inclines to be florid. His manner is free from restraint, tending at times to an apparent thoughtless indifference and carelessness, but generally, apart from the position in which he is placed, he would strike the observer as a young man whose deportment was prepossessing. There is occasionally observable a peculiar cast of one eye, which, however, is not a permanent defect.*[20]

William sat in a seat below the dock, next to Joseph Barret, and appeared calm and a little detached from the proceedings. Morley was first in the witness box and much of the day was taken up with questions regarding the medicine he prescribed for Harriet and the *post mortem* analysis. Morley's staff, John Elletson, James Peacock and William Scarth, were also examined regarding their conversations with Dove. The session ended with Nunneley and Elizabeth Fisher. As the day progressed Barret's persistent querying of the witnesses' statements got on Blackburn's nerves, and at one point he exasperatedly warned him, 'You must allow me to conduct the inquiry, if not I must prevent your appearing.'[21] The biggest revelation of the day, judging from the newspaper reports, emerged from an exchange regarding Morley's initial thought that Harriet's fits were merely symptomatic of hysteria. Women who were pregnant, Morley commented, were more liable to hysteria. Mr Barret asked, 'Was Mrs Dove pregnant?' Morley replied, 'She was four months gone.'[22] This would have certainly altered both the jury's and public's perception regarding William's position. There were few crimes more heinous than murdering a pregnant wife. Yet puzzlingly there was no reaction from the public gallery at this news. The session was adjourned around six-thirty and it was arranged to recommence at ten o'clock in two days' time.

On Wednesday the court house was again densely packed with over 200 spectators, mostly well-dressed women.[23] William was seated below the dock as at the previous session, while Nunneley and Morley sat next to Blackburn on the magistrate's bench. The jury and reporters were seated around the barristers' table below. Mrs Whitham was first in the stand, and was asked to recount once again Harriet's condition during her last week of life. It was not long into the questioning before Blackburn upbraided Barret again: 'We don't cross-examine here; and I think in a solemn inquiry like this you should not catch at every-thing.'[24] One important point, however, was quickly clarified fairly early on in the proceedings: Harriet was not pregnant. Several journalists, including those from *The Times* and the *Leeds Intelligencer*, misheard Morley's answer, which was given in a scarcely audible tone, and with some journalistic wish-fulfilment thought he said she was pregnant. Following the appearance of the news report of Monday's inquest, Morley contacted the *Intelligencer* to deny the story, and the paper issued an apology a few days later: 'we regret having, under an erroneous impression, given publicity to such a statement.'[25] Otherwise, the morning also saw the re-examination of Mary Wood, Nunneley and Morley, and the questioning of Ann Fisher, William Storey and, most anticipated of all, Henry Harrison, who presented himself as a dentist, but was questioned only briefly as to the conversations he had with William regarding poison.

The session ended early, at around two-thirty, and the inquest was adjourned until Monday because several articles had been found at Cardigan Place that had been sent to Nunneley and Morley for examination. One of the items in question was a piece of carpet from Harriet's bedroom. A few days after Harriet's funeral Mrs Dove had sent Mary Wood and Hannah Paley to clean up Harriet's bedroom. The two women had brought a little spaniel with them and when they entered the room the dog sniffed out a patch of blood on the floor. Neither of them saw it lick the blood but when they left the premises around ten minutes later the dog keeled over and died. The dog and a piece of the bloody carpet were subsequently given to Morley, along with a small piece of bloodstained wood extracted from the bedroom floor by the assiduous Ottiwell Kell.

There were only two witnesses on the final day of the inquest, which began at ten o'clock on Monday 17 March. By now public demand was so great that hundreds of people were denied entry to the courthouse, and there was a considerable police presence to ensure that proceedings were not interrupted by commotions in the public gallery. From the spectators' point of view there was not much to see, but everyone was there to hear the jury's verdict and how William would react. Nunneley and Morley reported that they were unable to detect any strychnine in the bit of carpet, and traces of it they found in the dog were so small as to be doubtful. They concluded that the dog had not died from licking the bloodstained carpet. More successful was their further analysis on

Harriet's stomach, regarding which Morley read out a written statement. He reported that they had given some of the extract from Harriet's stomach to two rabbits, two mice and one guinea pig. All of them subsequently exhibited the symptoms of strychnine poisoning, and all but one of the rabbits died. They then gave ordinary strychnine to a control group of animals to observe if the symptoms were the same. Morley and Nunneley concluded that the results were 'the most complete proof that the death of Mrs Dove was from the poisonous effects of the strychnia, and from no other cause.'[26] Neither the jury nor Barret had any further questions in response to this statement, so Blackburn turned to William and asked, 'William Dove, do you wish to say anything in reply to the charge?' 'I have nothing at all to say,' he replied.

Blackburn now addressed the jury at great length, reviewing the evidence and making clear their purpose and duty. He could not resist also making a critical remark regarding the behaviour of Barret: 'I fear a very erroneous impression prevails relative to the nature of an inquiry like this. It seems to be thought that this is a court where an accused person is on his trial; that a charge is made, and there must of necessity be a defence. Now nothing is more incorrect, or further from the real nature of a coroner's inquest.' He therefore reminded the jury that their duty was to determine the cause of Harriet's death and not the guilt of her husband. Blackburn finished speaking after some two and a half hours, and then directed Ottiwell Kell to escort the jury to another room to consider their verdict. There could not have been much disagreement between the jurors as it took only forty minutes for them to make a decision and return to the court room. Once seated, Blackburn asked, 'Mr Foreman, have you agreed upon a verdict?' Stephen Whitham replied, 'Yes. We find that Harriet Dove has died from the effects of strychnia, wilfully administered by her husband William Dove.' This caused a sensation in court, and when the noise had died down, Blackburn repeated, 'That is a verdict of wilful murder against William Dove?' 'It is,' said Whitham. William showed no emotion at all as he was led away to the cells.

## Poison and the press

To understand the public and media response to the inquest, and William's subsequent trial, it is necessary to consider the preoccupation with poisoning at the time. As Michael Harris put it, 'Poison seeped through the newspapers of the mid-nineteenth century.'[27] This was partly due to the growing sensationalism of a highly competitive press, particularly after the Repeal of Stamp Duty in 1855, but it was also fed by the growth of life insurance. It was certainly newsworthy when working-class people bumped each other off with arsenic, but far more interest, fear and newspaper sales were generated by the growing concern that middle-class men and women were secretly poisoning relatives to collect on insurance policies – which is exactly what Palmer stood accused of doing. Yet the reality was rather different from perception: by any measure, homicidal poisoning remained a rare event. In England and Wales on average between 1839 and 1849, for example, there were only two cases a year concerning attempted homicide or homicide by poisoning, and there was no sudden increase over the next two decades.[28] The Registrar-General's annual report on births, marriages and deaths for 1856 demonstrated this reality.[29] Of the 22,221 bodies on which inquests were held that year only 432 involved poisoning, thirty-eight of which were from Yorkshire. The vast majority of them concerned accidental poisoning or suicide. To put it in further perspective, only three out of eighty-two murder trials in England and Wales that year concerned poisoning. From the coroners' reports it was calculated that out of 105 identifiable causes of death, poisoning was ranked only sixty-ninth in terms of frequency. Nevertheless, William Farr, the Registrar-General, who had long been concerned with the 'problem' of poisoning, placed particular emphasis on it in his report on the 1856 statistics. 'Poisons are the most insidious instruments which assassins can employ' he observed, and the 'increase of subtle poisons lying for sale in the shops, the increase of life insurance, and the immense number of violent deaths in England, demand the observance of all the existing safeguards of life.'[30] The general public was not confronted with such statistics at the time, of course, yet even if the low rate of murders by poisoning had been publicised, the fear would have remained that many more cases went undetected: poisoning was seen as an insidious, undetectable means of murder.

There were a variety of deadly poisons easily available from the druggist's shop.[31] William had mentioned two to his mother-in-law at breakfast, belladonna and oil of almonds. In 1856 one unfortunate man who was in the habit of taking ash-leaf tea was mistakenly supplied by a druggist with belladonna leaves instead, with terrible but not fatal results.[32] Almond oil was widely used in perfumes and confectionary but contained lethal quantities of prussic acid. The range of available poisonous substances was satirised by *Punch* in a sketch called 'The Poison Shop' set in a druggist's. After supplying a young girl with arsenic, the assistant Bottles, turns to his next client:

> *Now Sir, what can I do for you (to a Stranger with his face muffled and his hat over his eyes)?*
> Stranger. – *Thank'oo; I'll wait.*
> Bottles *(to several customers).* – *You for arsenic? – you? – you? – all of you Arsenic? Six Arsenics; and you? Oh! One Corrosive Sublimate.*
> *(Serves them out packets ready made up.) [Exit with the poison]*
> Stranger *(having watched them all out).* – *I want some of the strongest poison you have got.*
> Bottles – *Well, Sir, I think prussic acid will suit you better than any.*
> Stranger. – *That smells, don't it?*
> Bottles. – *Why yes, Sir. Probably Strychnine would answer your purpose?*
> Stranger. – *Is that pretty stiffish?*
> Bottles *(smiling).* – *Oh! Yes, Sir. I should be sorry to take two grains of it.*
> Stranger. – *Let's have half an ounce.*
> Bottles. – *Half an ounce, Sir? (Weighs it out.) What is the next article, Sir?*
> Stranger.– *Nothing.*
> Bottles. – *Allow me to tempt you with a little Belladonna; very killing, Sir, I assure you. Or would you try our Digitalis? I could recommend our Colchicum, Sir.*[33]

Up until 1851 arsenic stole all the headlines. It was perceived as the poison of choice for the working classes. [34] Arsenic was everywhere in early Victorian England. It was widely used as a colouring agent in a huge range of items including fabrics, wallpaper, food wrapping and children's toys. Moreover it was used as a compound in medicines for skin conditions and asthma. By far the greatest quantity sold by druggists, however, was for use as a vermin killer. Its ease of purchase also made it the poison of choice for suicides, while its tasteless and odourless quality made it the ideal tool of the 'secret poisoner'. The prominence given to arsenic poisoning cases led to flurries of correspondence in the press. A letter published in *The Times* in 1845 is representative of many: 'Suicides and murders are so frequently caused by arsenic, which is generally dispensed for the alleged purpose of destroying rats, that I think there ought to be some legislative enactment to prevent the sale of poison for such uses.' Another letter writer agreed and made the observation that 'The very poor can never want poison for any innocent purpose, and the rest of the community can procure the requisite certificate.'[35] Some respectable high street druggists and chemists imposed there own restrictions on sale to avoid any potential involvement in murder trials. In the mid-1840s the Leeds druggist Mr Hall, who had a shop in Briggate, had a policy of not selling arsenic unless he, or his marvellously named assistant Blanshard Ringoose, recognised the customer or he or she was accompanied by a witness.[36]

While the newspapers provided the ammunition and generated the social pressure for the restriction on arsenic, it was the medical profession, as represented at the time by the Provincial Medical and Surgical Association (later the British Medical Association in 1856), and the Pharmaceutical Society, which successfully pressured a government, reluctant to act against its *laissez-faire* principles, to impose legal restrictions. So, in 1851, the Arsenic Act was passed, making it a legal requirement for vendors of arsenic to keep a 'poison book', in which the date of sale, quantity sold and reasons for purchase had to be recorded. Both purchaser and vendor had to sign off the sale. Furthermore, if the purchaser was unknown to the vendor a witness had to be present and also sign. The Arsenic Act by no means stopped the criminal use of arsenic, though it may have helped restrict its usage by the working classes, which was an implicit aim of the Act in the first place. Besides, there were a variety of other poisons easily available. Coroners' returns for the five-year period between 1852 and 1856 showed that of the 401 people who died annually from poisoning, opium, mostly in the form of laudanum, accounted for 125 of cases on average *per annum*. Prussic acid came next, accounting for 34 cases annually – fifteen of which concerned oil of almonds. Arsenic ranked only third, accounting for 27 deaths annually.[37]

While arsenic stole the headlines during the 1840s strychnine remained in the media shadows. It derives from the seeds of the *Nux vomica* tree, a native to Southeast Asia, and has long been used by local tribes to tip their hunting arrows. It excites the central nervous system, particularly the nerves of the spinal cord, which is why one of the characteristics of strychnine poisoning is the spasmodic arching of the back. In this and other respects the symptoms were similar to those of tetanus. Strychnine, like arsenic, was a constituent in rat poisons and was also used in medicine. Its bitterness, like quinine, also made it a common constituent of tonics and 'bitters', which were drunk to improve appetite, cure constipation and reduce the effects of fever. *Nux vomica* and strychnine were also proposed as cures for cholera, paralysis, hay fever, and constipation.[38] The newspapers' lack of interest in strychnine was basically due to the infrequent incidence of its fatal ingestion. At an inquest in 1854 it was observed that poisoning by strychnine was very rare.[39] It certainly was not the poisoner's weapon of choice, presumably because of its strong bitter taste. The few cases that arose resulted either from suicides or tragic mistakes, such as the 1849 trial for manslaughter of John Jones, a respectable druggist and chemist of Romsey, Hampshire. One of his client's prescriptions contained salacine. In Jones's shop there was a shelf where he kept drugs which were seldom required. On it was a bottle of salacine and one of strychnine, which looked similar. While making up the client's prescription he took down and used the wrong bottle. His client died half an hour after taking her medicine.[40]

Strychnine's initial rise to notoriety came from a newspaper scare regarding the adulteration of beer. In March 1852 English newspapers reported on a statement made by the distinguished French chemist Anselme Payen that the French government was concerned by the large quantity of strychnine being manufactured. Investigations revealed that most of it was being shipped across the channel, with the English beer industry allegedly being a primary purchaser. Brewers, the famed Burton brewers in particular, stood accused of using strychnine to give their ales their characteristic bitterness. This not surprisingly caused quite a sensation. Back in 1830 the Burton brewers had acted quickly when the Society for the Diffusion of Useful Knowledge published a book on brewing that had a chapter, entitled 'Illegal Ingredients', which suggested that unscrupulous brewers used *Nux vomica* and the poisonous berries of *Cocculus indicus* (a climbing plant found in Ceylon) to add bitter-ness.[41] The brewers successfully sued the Society for libel on that occasion.[42] In response to the latest calumny, big brewers, such as Bass, Henry Allsopp and Abbott and Sons, launched a flurry of letters to the press, and two respected professors of chemistry, Thomas Graham and August Wilhelm Hofmann, were commissioned to analyse Burton pale ales. They reported that not the slightest trace of strychnine could be found, and that anyway there was no economic sense for brewers to use the poison as it was far more expensive than hops. To produce the necess-ary bitterness they calculated that 16,448 ounces would be required for the 200,000 barrels produced annually at Burton, yet it was estimated that the entire world production of strychnine amounted to under 1,000 ounces.[43]

It was the Cook inquest, though, that was the catalyst for the much more pervasive media panic in 1856. At the end of January the *Illustrated Times* was running adverts headed 'Secret Poisoning, the Prevailing Crime of the Age'. An exceptional double issue of the paper was produced containing a pictorial historical account of the most remarkable cases of poisoning coupled with sensational accounts of the Cook inquest.[44] William Dove was one of the many members of the gen-eral public who debated the details of the inquest in pubs, homes and over shop counters. Public fear was played upon by the *Leader* in an article entitled 'Poisoner in the House', which tingled the spines of its readers. 'If you feel a deadly sensation within, and grow gradually weaker,' it wondered, 'how do you know that you are not poisoned?'[45] The *Manchester Guardian* was not impressed with such scare-mongering journalism. In early February it observed wryly, 'Poisoning cases are in fashion at present. There is one locality so famous for their production, that scarcely a single person has ended his days in or near it for the last three years, whose death has not been attributed to poison.' 'Public atten-tion is on tenter-hooks,' it continued, 'and there is an immense demand for "further particulars".'[46] As the press and public waited eagerly for the trial of Palmer, the inquest on Harriet Dove helped slake the public thirst. Following the outcome and the arrest of William, the *Leeds Times* hoped that 'this startling and horrible case will open the eyes of the Government to the dangers attendant upon an unrestricted sale of poison.'[47] The *Medical Times* could not repress its gloomy view that a 'dreadful epidemic of wickedness ... now overspreads the land like a pestilence.'[48]

It was not only the press who made capital out of the poisoning scares that year. Those opposed to the free market in poisons and drugs also exploited the media interest and popular concern. The most vocal group was not one of the professional medical bodies, however, but one of their fiercest critics – the British College of Health. This organisation was founded by James Morison, one of the most famous and prosperous inventors and vendors of patent medicine in nineteenth-century England.[49] His 'vegetable universal medicines', popularly known as 'Morison's Pills', were promoted by his followers, the Hygeists, and between the late 1820s and the 1870s millions of his pills were sold, many of them through druggists and chemists. For Morison and his followers, his pills, which purportedly 'cleansed the blood', could cure ailments which the medical profession ineffectually treated with toxic substances.

Back in 1851 the Hygeists had paid for advertisements in a variety of newspapers condemning the Arsenic Act for being ineffectual. They wanted the sale of arsenic and other poisons to be outlawed completely. The advert stated that 'poisons belong to a period of priestcraft and witchcraft, and are totally repugnant to this enlightened age.' According to the Hygeists, the only people who had a vested interest in making poisons available were doctors, enabling them to 'carry on their guinea trade and keep the nation in a state of disease and the mind in thraldom.'[50] Five years later, in response to reports on the inquest on Harriet Dove, it revised its advertisement to press its case with renewed vigour:

*MORE POISON – THE LEEDS CASE.*
*People of England. – Where is all this poisoning to stop. Never, until you*
*force parliament to pass a law that all such deadly poisons shall be*
*declared anti-medicinal, and all doctors and others prevented from*
*using or selling them, under pain of transportation for life. The 'Morning*
*Chronicle' of the 10th March is at last speaking out on this question. It*
*says – 'Already have too many prescriptions from the murderous*
*pharmacopoeia attained publicity.' James Morison, the Hygiest, said this*
*thirty years ago, but he was not then heeded, and the consequence has*
*been what we now see; which is not much to be wondered at, when we*

*hear and see Ministers of the Crown and others in parliament puffing off*
*doctors and their Medical Bills, whilst such doctors are the very parties*
*who patronise, and from whom these deadly poisons proceed!*

*Murderers are only imitating the doctors. How, therefore, can you put*
*a stop to poisoning? As we have often said before, if these poisons can*
*do good in any case, then the Hygeium System of James Morison, the*
*Hygeist, must be false. We feel perfectly safe in leaving the question in*
*that way.*

*We are, Fellow Countrymen,*

*THE MEMBERS OF THE BRITISH COLLEGE OF HEALTH,*

*New Road, London, for the Society of Hygeists.*

*March 14, 1856.*

*P.S. Will you for one moment believe that such an infernal poison as*
*strychnine can be given with beneficial results? As to the deaths*
*proceeding from it, of course you hear nothing: the medical diplomas*
*are a safeguard for that.*[51]

The explicit claim of the Hygeists, and the implicit accusation of others, was that the medical profession as well druggists shared some of the culpability for the actions of poisoners.

Blame was flying in all directions but one man was singled out for particular criticism – Alfred Swaine Taylor, the source of the erroneous misconception that strychnine could not be detected in small doses. Taylor was lecturer of chemistry at Guy's Hospital, and author of several books on medical jurisprudence, most influentially his book *On Poisons in relation to medical jurisprudence*, first published in 1848. By the mid-1850s he had generated a considerable public profile as an expert medical witness, particularly with regard to poisoning.[52] Although the press reports of Taylor's performance as an expert witness at the Cook inquest were generally initially favourable, his comments regarding the detection of strychnine soon began to attract criticism.[53] From the medical fraternity there were repeated illustrations that proved Taylor quite wrong. Nunneley and Morley had found small traces in Harriet's stomach hours after death, and had been successful in the case of Ellen Waterhouse the year before. The details of Nunneley's report on the latter was summarised in the *Manchester Guardian* in February 1856, and prefaced with the observation that 'No circumstance has caused more general and more natural alarm than the statement of Dr. Taylor'.[54] In March, John Henry Pepper, lecturer in analytical chemistry at the London Royal Polytechnic Institution, gave a public lecture on strychnine in which he explained several simple tests for the poison.[55] Another critic was J.E.D. Rogers, lecturer on chemistry at St. George's School of Medicine, who wrote to *The Times*, 'I cannot conceive an opinion more dangerous to public safety than that a fatal dose of poison can be so nicely adjusted as to escape discovery after death.' He had conducted numerous experiments on the detection of strychnine and had been able to detect it in a dog that had been buried for twelve months. He ended his letter by asserting, 'of all known poisons there is not one more readily detected in the tissue than strychnine.'[56] Of the newspapers, none was more critical than the radical *Morning Chronicle*, which, in the light of the arrest of William Dove, highlighted the potentially harmful social consequences of Taylor's fatal pronouncement:

> *We are anxious, as far as our influence will reach, to warn against indulging the fatal notion, that there exists any poison of whatever character which may not be summoned from the grave to join in the demand for retributive punishment upon the felon ... Few things can be more startling and appalling to the guilty criminal, than the chemist producing against him the minute crystals of a mineral poison, drawn from the decaying viscera of his victim.*[57]

The *Association Medical Journal* agreed, and congratulated Nunneley and Morley for demonstrating that prospective poisoners could not 'pursue their dreadful tasks with impunity.'[58]

Yet, from what source did William get his interest in and initial understanding of strychnine? Why, from the newspapers. William stood accused of a crime facilitated not only by the free market in poisons and the erroneous advice of Taylor, but also by the publicity the press gave to poisoning and the initial unqualified reporting of Taylor's opinions. Indeed, the government was well aware of the problematic influence of the press in this respect. The passage of the Arsenic Bill in 1851 was deliberately passed with minimal debate to reduce publicity. When the Earl of Carlisle introduced the Bill he observed that poisoning was a preoccupation of 'certain kinds of mind', and he did not want to give ideas to the criminally suggestible.[59] Some of the press were not unaware of their role in influencing copycat criminals. As the *Saturday Review* remarked, the 'newspaper intelligence in everybody's hands and mouth invests murder with another kind of familiarity. It is not therefore only the deep dye of these crimes, but the publicity of the details, which now-a-days is so important.'[60] But the press were not about to start censoring themselves. Their key self-justifying argument still held force – that by reporting the successful trial and punishment of criminals they were acting as a deterrent to others. As one journalist observed, while it was certainly a little disturbing that the British public 'breakfast on railway-collisions, dine on wife-beating, and sup, may be, on a murder,' it was, nevertheless, 'only constant repetition in the daily journals that forces at last the acknowledgement of wholesale crime from the public conscience and voice, and so brings a pressure to bear on legislation.'[61]

As well as the issue of copycat crimes, the newspapers' reporting of inquests was also problematic and potentially prejudicial to the justice system. Jervis could see the benefits of holding secret inquests to prevent tampering of evidence or the influencing of witnesses and juries, yet he also held to the prevalent idea that the press was an instrument of justice, playing an important role in the detection of truth. Yet the press was a dubious holder of the sword of truth. As Richard Altick put it so succinctly, 'The press could speculate, report rumours, assess character, decide guilt untrammelled by law or any canon of journalistic ethics, and at the same time piously assert its single-minded devotion to truth and justice.'[62] By the time a sensational trial came to court the whole country knew pretty much everything about the case along with a good deal of unsubstantiated detail. The potential for jury bias was serious. The *Daily News* pointed out in March, '"Another poisoning case!" the world is crying out. "Another wife-murder!" there are people who have not scrupled to say, before the inquest on Mrs Dove was concluded.'[63] One journalist observed that 'newspaper reports form the sole intellectual training, in all probability, of ten out of every twelve men who pronounce the guilt or innocence of the prisoner at the bar'.[64] If they had read the inquest reports, what chance of a fair trial for William in such an atmosphere?

# Waiting for the assizes

During his days of incarceration as the inquest progressed, William maintained a relaxed demeanour. He chatted cheerfully with his fellow inmates and the gaoler Hugh Barrett. He frequently read out appropriate passages from his pocket Bible, and said his prayers every night before sleeping. Even after hearing the jury's verdict he exhibited no anxiety or distress. After all, he was confident that Harrison's magic would sway the assize jury. He remembered how Harrison had correctly predicted his father's death, and how he had prevented the bailiffs from getting hold of Hardcastle's goods. Comforted by his confidence in the wizard, back at the gaol he had a hearty tea and later a little supper.

The next day he tucked into his lunch with considerable enthusiasm even though that afternoon he was to be taken to York Castle gaol to await the sitting of the summer assizes. Although his appetite was clearly unaffected by his predicament, he was apparently unusually silent during the train journey to York, making no conversation with his escort. On arrival, Hugh Barrett took William to a private holding room at the station. Some refreshment was provided and then at six o'clock he was escorted through the streets to the Castle. The authorities wanted to avoid any publicity and so only the train guard and some of the station officials were informed of his identity. His passage through the streets of York attracted little attention from passers-by, who would have been used to the sight of prisoners being taken from the station to the Castle. Barrett parted company with William in the office of the prison governor Mr Noble. William shook hands with Barrett and gave a cheerful farewell, saying, 'I shall soon be back in Leeds again. Good morning, Mr. Barrett.'[65] A report on his first few days in his new surroundings showed his appetite was still healthy, taking 'an evident relish' in his meals, which were sent in from town by family and friends. Despite his lack of moral rectitude William had never relinquished his faith, and over the previous few years he had continued to attend class meetings, and much of his leisure time in prison was now spent reading the Scriptures and discussing religious matters with his fellow prisoners.[66]

Not long after his incarceration, William's prodigious appetite began to belie his growing anxiety about his predicament. He attempted to make contact with the one person who he believed could extricate him: not his lawyer but his wizard:

*I feel myself very much pained at finding myself in York Castle, a prisoner, particularly as you told me I should not go to prison, where I shall have to remain till the July trials. What is your opinion of my case? Let the jury bring in my case whatever they please, I am not guilty. Will you tell me decidedly from my nativity what will be the result, if you can? I had put entire confidence in you. If you can do anything for me you must. I have never said anything to any one about our conversations at any time. I have retained Sergeant Wilkins for my counsel, and Barret for my lawyer. People tell me that your evidence against me about my asking whether a grain or a grain and a half would be found, told very much against me. Write me all about this; but mind you don't write anything about this in ink; but let it be written in milk or lemon juice, or anything which will show when it is brought to the fire. When you write, don't let them know you have heard from me, as all the letters written by the prisoners, or sent to them, are read, and I have bribed some one to bring this out! Shall I get off in July? Tell me all particulars. If I am, tell me who is to be my next wife?*[67]

He bribed a man named Robinson, an inmate shortly to be freed, to secrete the letter in his clothing and post it once he was in town. Unfortunately, the man was searched before being released and the letter was found and confiscated. William would have to cope without his wizard's guidance.

There were other people to write to, however. On 22 May he sent the following letter to his mother-in-law, who had by then returned to Devon:

*My Dear Mother, – I have often thought about writing to you, but until now my feelings would not allow me. Little did I think, when you and I were conversing together, that I should ever have been in the situation in which I am placed, and particularly so charged with one of the worst crimes, viz., murder, and the victim my own flesh and blood; but, thank God, I can say let the world think what they like, and let the jury bring it in what they may, I am not guilty of the crime laid to my charge. I know nothing about it. I was very much pained at receiving the letter that I did from William, for he plainly said that he thought, – let me denigh it or not, – that I have murdered his sister. I will only say that, as I hope to appear before my Maker and Judge at the last day, I can swear that I am an innocent man. My trial will come on in the fore part of July, but the*

*exact time I do not know, but I will let you know in time if you will deign to answer this and continue a correspondence with me. The counsellors retained for me are Serjeant Wilkins, Mr. Hall, deputy recorder for Leeds, and I think Mr. Overend. I shall be very glad to hear from you or any of my sisters, and also to keep up a regular correspondence with you, and if I get off at the assizes, which I fully expect, if it be agreeable and will come down and see you. Please send your full direction, and give my kind love to my sisters and brothers and all enquiring friends, and accept the same from your affectionate son,*
    *William Dove.*

There was one last person that William decided to reacquaint himself with in his time of need: the Devil. In his youth William had on several occasions pricked himself with a sharp-pointed knife in order to write a pact with the Devil in his own blood, and he had told Harrison on numerous occasions that he had sold his soul to Satan. Now, in early April, a rumour spread about the gaol that William had a knife concealed on his person. Noble sent two officers to search him. A sharp instrument was indeed found, and sewn up in his clothing they also discovered the following letter written in blood:

*Dear Devil, – If you will get me clear at the assizes, and let me have the enjoyment of life, health, wealth, tobacco, beer, more food and better, my wishes granted, and live till I am sixty, come to me and tell me. And remain your faithful servant,*
    *William Dove.*

On the day he wrote it William was in 'a low, desponding, and queer state'. 'I can't describe my feelings,' he said, but he had suicide in mind. The sharp instrument was ready for that purpose. 'I did feel certain that the Devil would come to me that night', he recalled, but there was no untrustworthier master than the Devil, and he failed to appear and claim his soul.

When Barret eventually got to hear about the letter William had written to Harrison he visited William and told him that he would be unable to draw up a proper defence unless he told him everything regarding his dealings with the wizard. William explained his great anxiety as to whether Harrison was his enemy or his friend, whether he was working for him or against him. It was to ensure Harrison's goodwill that he had written in his letter, 'I have never said anything to any one about our conversations'. Barret urged that whether friend or foe the wizard was a dangerous witness and if he was to be cross-examined for the benefit of the defence William must tell him everything about their relationship. William eventually acquiesced and on 21 and 23 June he dictated to Barret a full account of his dealings with the wizard over the previous eighteen months.

## Palmer

As William whiled away the days in York Castle contemplating the Scriptures and writing letters, William Palmer, the man who had first excited his interest in poisons, was on trial for his life at the Old Bailey. One of the most sensational and well-reported murder cases in English history began on 14 May. A special Act of Parliament was required to have the trial moved from the Stafford assizes to the Central Criminal Court in London to ensure that the intense hostility towards Palmer in Rugeley and Stafford did not influence a local jury. Although inquest juries had charged him with the murder of his wife and brother he only stood trial for that of Cook. In March a grand jury at Stafford assizes had found the charge of the wilful murder of Walter Palmer not proven. If the prosecution failed it was intended, however, that he would still be arraigned for the murder of his wife. It was widely rumoured that Palmer had a hand in as many as sixteen deaths in all, including that of his mother-in-law and one of his illegitimate children, though no concrete evidence was ever found for these claims.

As we have seen, Palmer's case had a profound influence on William's actions, and now William's actions were to have an important bearing on Palmer's fate. George Morley, Thomas Nunneley and Jane Whitham were all called as witnesses at Palmer's trial, and their testimony regarding the symptoms of strychnine, as exhibited by Harriet, were of considerable importance considering the dubious legal basis on which Palmer was being tried for poisoning.[68] Whitham and Morley were called by the prosecution along with witnesses of three other cases of accidental strychnine poisoning. Nunneley, however, appeared for the defence, and stated that he did not believe Cook had died from strychnine poisoning, but 'from convulsions, by the combination of symptoms'.[69]

During their testimony Whitham, Nunneley and Morley were instructed to refrain from mentioning the name of the 'lady' whose death from strychnine they had witnessed at various stages, as it was not legal etiquette to mention a trial pending during a trial in progress. Yet the newspaper coverage of Harriet's inquest had ensured that everyone knew that she was the 'lady' in question. Indeed, all pretence of keeping her name out of the proceedings was abandoned by the end of the trial, and in his address to the jury Judge Campbell referred to 'Mrs Dove, whose name had transpired so frequently in the course of the trial that it would be vain to affect any reserve on the subject now.' Campbell went on to observe: 'The case of Mrs Dove is a very important one, because it is a case in which it is beyond all question that death was caused by strychnine, however administered. It is for you to determine how far the symptoms of this unhappy lady correspond with or differ from those of Cook.'[70]

The trial lasted an extraordinary twelve days but it took the jury only one hour and seventeen minutes to reach a verdict that Palmer was guilty of wilful murder. A couple of petitions were sent to the Home Secretary Lord Grey, one of which was from Palmer's clergyman brother, but Palmer was nevertheless hanged at Stafford on 14 June before an enormous crowd estimated as being around 30,000 strong. Before leaving his cell in his last hour of life Palmer insisted, 'I am innocent of poisoning Cook by strychnine.' It was not a denial of murder but a rejection of the charge on which he was convicted.[71] The morbid fascination with all things concerning Palmer continued before, during and after his trial. Tours were conducted of his former house in Rugeley for a shilling. The white pebbles that lined the pathway to its door were taken and sold at the local fair for sixpence each. Hundreds came to see Cook's grave and they snapped off so many bits from the tree that overhung the grave that it was in a sorry state.[72] Such trophy-hunting and obtrusive sensation seeking highlights the wisdom shown by the Jenkinses and the Doves in ensuring that Harriet's grave remained unmarked. Hordes descending on Beckett Street Cemetery were destined to be frustrated and return home trophyless. Nevertheless, those sensation-seekers hungry for more poisonous revelations could at least look forward to the trial of her husband. For months the fate of Dove and Palmer had been entwined. One man had gone to eternity and now the country waited to see if the other would join him.

# The assizes

The pair of London judges appointed to the summer assizes for the Northern Circuit arrived in York around two o'clock on 9 July. They first attended divine service at York Cathedral before officially opening the proceedings. The next day they followed the old custom of breakfasting with the Lord Mayor and afterwards the trials began at the courthouse in York Castle.[73] Sixty-two cases were listed in the assize calendar, including eight prisoners charged with forgery, twelve with assault and robbery, six with burglary and three with cattle stealing. William was one of three prisoners charged with murder, but it was talk of his trial that was on everyone's lips. The walls of the town around the castle were plastered with posters announcing the forthcoming 'Trial of Dove, the Leeds Poisoner'.[74] The *News of the World* anticipated that it would 'rival that of William Palmer in intensity of interest.'[75] The judge assigned to hear the case was Baron George William Wilshere Bramwell (1808–1892).[76] He was new to the Northern Assize Circuit, having been elevated to the position of judge at the beginning of the year. Bramwell had made a considerable name for himself as a highly respected Queen's Counsel, but now he had a new, more public, reputation to build. In legal circles he was perceived to be domineering and uncompromising, and on his appointment as judge *The Times* expressed its confidence that he would let 'no maudlin sentimentality or pseudo-philanthropy interpose between the criminal and that punishment which the law has assigned to his offence.'[77] In a satirical rhyme *Punch* would later warn of the harsh sentences that awaited those who provoked the 'dander of bold Baron B.'[78]

Big public trials like William's, which lasted several days, were expensive affairs, and as ever the lawyers thrived. The total cost of the prosecution alone was estimated to be around £1176.[79] Mr Overend the QC leading the prosecution, rather than the defence as William had first thought, was paid 100 guineas with refreshers of 10 guineas a day, while the rest of his team, Messrs Hardy and Bailey, received seventy and forty-five guineas respectively. The QC for the defence, Mr Bliss, received 70 guineas plus refreshers and consultation fees for the trial, and his team of Serjeant Wilkins and Mr Hall received fifty and forty guineas respectively. On top of these, fees amounting to hundreds of pounds were spent obtaining and looking after the thirty-three witnesses for the prosecution and twenty-four witnesses for the defence. The total cost of the trial was estimated to be not far off £2500 – making it probably the most expensive case that year after Palmer.

The trial began on the morning of Wednesday 16 July.[80] Demand for places was huge. The High Sheriff received ten times more applications for seats than the courtroom could hold. Before eight o'clock in the morning the passages to the court were thronged with people trying to gain admittance. The swarm was so great around the Castle gates that a phalanx of policemen had to elbow their way through, closely followed by a pack of around twenty journalists.[81] At half past eight William, dressed in a black suit, was led into court with twenty or so other prisoners who had already been convicted but had yet to be sentenced. William looked in rude health. He was tanned, had put on twenty or thirty pounds in weight during his time in prison, and evinced an air of cheerful confidence as he chatted with his fellow inmates. By the time Judge Bramwell appeared half an hour later the court was already packed, mostly with well-dressed women. Once the courtroom was settled and quiet the prisoners were called one by one to hear their sentences read out by the judge and were then led away. After an hour only William was left and the trial could begin.

When his name was called, William 'tripped lightly up the steps, and took his position in the dock with that calmness and perfect self-possession which had distinguished him from the first.'[82] He struck an attentive pose, left hand on hip, leaning on the bar with his right elbow, as the clerk of arraigns read out the indictment: 'William Dove, you stand indicted for the wilful murder of Harriet Dove, at Leeds, on the 1st of March last; you are also charged upon the coroner's inquisition with the wilful murder of the said Harriet Dove. Do you plead guilty or not guilty?' William replied in a firm voice, 'Not guilty, my Lord.' Next the jury was sworn in, and William was asked to interject if he objected to any of them. He remained silent as the following names were read out:

*John Balance, of Island, Knottingley, willow merchant.*
*Edwin Brown, of Park Riding, Honley, land surveyor.*
*Thomas Fox, of Old Church, Pontefract, maltster.*
*James Graham, of Hanover Square, Bradford, tea dealer.*
*Edward William Hewitt, of Elmwood Place, Leeds, stuff merchant.*
*Henry Hopkinson, of Birstall, Gomersal, organ builder.*

*John Foster Horsfall, of West Croft Head, Haworth, gentleman.*
*George Lewis, of Sicklinghall, farmer.*
*Joseph Lucas, of Market Place, New Malton, iron-founder.*
*Robert Midgley, of Salterley, Northowram, worsted spinner.*
*Charles Norton, of Corn Market, Pontefract, innkeeper.*
*Richard Harper Smith, of Barthorpe, farmer.*

After the clerk of arraigns had finished repeating to the jury the charge against William the prosecution opened its case.

Overend began by stressing to the jury the importance of clearing their minds of all preconceived ideas regarding the case: 'Rumours have been spread abroad, and various statements have been made with respect to the evidence to be brought before you. Some of you may have conversed on this matter, and come to a conclusion, and formed an opinion whether the prisoner is innocent or guilty.' If they had, he urged, 'you should dismiss that opinion at once from your mind, and come to the consideration of this important question free from prejudice, free from bias.' That said, he moved on to describe the case, with typical prosecutorial exaggeration, as one of 'the most cold-blooded and cruel murders almost known in the history of crime', and attempted to reinforce this claim by explaining to the jury in great detail the nature of strychnine and its effects. He then moved on to give a history of William's married life, remarking that he was at times kind to Harriet but at other times was abusive, brutal and violent. The rest of his opening statement focused on a detailed account of events in the last few weeks of Harriet's life. After around two hours and twenty minutes he summed up by telling the jury:

> *If I leave your mind in reasonable doubt – I ask you to acquit the*
> *prisoner; but if, on the other hand, this evidence should satisfy your*
> *minds, and lead you to the conclusion that she has died from poison,*
> *and that the prisoner has administered that poison, you will be wanting*
> *in your duty to your country, and your duty to God, if you do not find a*
> *verdict of guilty.*

The court adjourned for refreshments and then the first witnesses for the prosecution were called and cross-examined. Elizabeth Fisher, Ann Fisher and Jane Whitham all gave similar testimony to that which they had given at Harriet's inquest. Mrs Thornhill, the charwoman at Cardigan

Place, Sarah Naylor of the Sutcliffe Arms, and the confectioner Margaret Young were also called, though they were not subjected to much questioning. The session came to a close at a quarter to six, and the jury were escorted away by the bailiff, who was given instructions by Bramwell to allow them the opportunity to exercise their legs in the Castle grounds, but that they must not on any account be allowed to converse with anyone.

The second day of the trial began at nine o'clock. The court was packed once again and numerous women were refused entry. William appeared calm and collected as he took his place at the bar. His childhood nurse Mary Wood was first to give evidence and Bliss's questioning of her led to the first protracted debate between the judge, prosecution and defence. It began with Bliss asking Wood whether, in her opinion, William was 'in his right mind'. Overend objected to the question, and Bramwell, after consulting the McNaughten case, which in 1843 had set a precedent regarding the legal status of the insanity defence, ruled that it was a scientific question and therefore 'might be put to a medical man upon conceded facts, but not to an unscientific person, like the witness.' Mr Hall rose to argue that if such witnesses were not allowed to answer the question the jury would unfairly be excluded from hearing important evidence as to William's childhood mental state. Hall had never heard the question being objected to before, to which Overend countered that he had never heard it put. Serjeant Wilkinson politely queried whether Overend was 'conveniently deaf'. Overend insisted that questions of insanity should only be put to men of science, but Bramwell wavered at the defence's offensive and decided, in the spirit of fairness, that as long as Overend did not wish to press the objection, questions regarding insanity could now be put to non-expert witnesses. Overend consulted with his team and decided to waive the objection as long as the defence did not abuse the concession. Bliss resumed his cross-examination of Mary Wood and elicited from her the opinion that as a child William 'was not in his right mind'. Next in the witness stand was Hannah Paley, followed by Mary Hicks – who stated she had no means of judging William's insanity, then Maria Killam, John Wood, Rev. Thomas Sturgeon, John Hicks and Henry Rose.

After Rose came one of the most eagerly anticipated witnesses, Henry Harrison. He began by informing the court: 'I am a dentist. I profess water casting. I have done a little in astrology.' He admitted to knowing William for around twenty months, and that he had been asked to cast his nativity but had not finished it. He recalled his conversation with William in the New Cross Inn about the Palmer case, and also confirmed that he had received a visit from William on the first day of Harriet's inquest when, as Harrison remembered it, he had told William, 'Go back, if you are innocent. What need have you to be frightened? They will not take you.' Under questioning from Bliss he stated: 'I never saw him but twice without being in liquor, and then he was always talking about being haunted by devils and spirits, thunder and lightning. He told me he had sold his soul to the devil, but he thought I had bigger power over the devils than he.' In answer to a question from Bramwell, Harrison replied, 'I did not encourage him to think I could rule devils. It was his own fancy! I told him I could cast his nativity and when I saw the state of his mind I did not finish it.... I thought I could do that for him. I believe in the stars.' Bramwell snorted, 'You do. And you find a great many others do the same thing, I dare say!' Harrison was allowed to leave the witness box after a couple of further innocuous questions from a juror and the judge.

Ann Walker, landlady of the New Cross Inn, her lodger William Storey, and Elizabeth Brown next spent a few minutes each in the witness stand giving evidence as to conversations they overheard between William and Harrison. Harriet's mother and sister testified as to the Dove's marital problems, William's drinking, his wild behaviour, and the nature of Harriet's hysterical fits. Then, after a brief appearance by Ottiwell Kell, the prosecution moved on to the evidence regarding William's purchase of strychnine, with John Elletson, James Peacock, John Scarth, William Renton and their employer George Morley all being called to the stand. As the main expert medical witness for the prosecution, Morley was cross-examined in considerable detail. Bliss suggested that Harriet could have died from a severe hysterical fit rather than poisoning. Morley admitted that all Harriet's symptoms, if taken separately, were 'referable to hysteria, which imitates almost every type of disease, sometimes tetanus.' He had never, however, known a case of hysteria that incorporated all of Harriet's symptoms in her last week of life. The only feasible explanation was the administration of two or three grains of strychnine. Nunneley was called to confirm Morley's medical evidence, and stated that 'Hysteria would not account for those symptoms; as described they are more accordant with strychnia than any other disease.' Several respected surgeons from Leeds and York were called to corroborate the medical evidence. The prosecution also managed to get the renowned toxicologist Professor Robert Christison to testify. Over the years Christison had appeared as a medical witness at many trials in England and Scotland, including that of the notorious body snatcher William Burke (1829), and had also given evidence for the prosecution at Palmer's trial. Under cross-examination by Bliss, Christison conceded that from the accounts of Harriet's attacks, he 'might attribute them to hysteria . . . but I have never seen such a combination of symptoms in my professional life.' As to William's mental state, he said he had heard too little of the case to enable him to form an opinion regarding his insanity one way or another. It was six o'clock by the time the medical witnesses had finished giving testimony. The prosecution had ended its case and the next morning it would be the turn of the defence. Bliss had made little headway with the prosecution witnesses when it came to proving William's insanity, but he may have sowed some doubt in the jury's mind regarding the cause of Harriet's death.

On the third day of the trial the crush in the public gallery was greater than ever and the places were already filled an hour before Judge Bramwell took his seat at nine o'clock. William seemed in good spirits and before being put in the dock enjoyed several pinches of snuff.[83] In his opening address to the jury Bliss took up the theme of prejudice touched upon by Overend at the beginning of the trial: 'Unfortunately this case, and the details of it upon imperfect statements, and on one-sided accounts only, have been carefully and extensively circulated and carried into every family, into the mind of every reader, and into the ear of every hearer in the country. I beg you, before entering upon this case,' he urged, 'to throw off this despotism of public panic and public opinion, so industriously spread in this case.' Bliss flagged up William's drink problem but his defence rested primarily on three strategies. The first was to highlight the possibility that Harriet had been accidentally poisoned. In his experiments on poisoning cats and mice William may have left fatal traces of strychnine around and about the house, which accidentally found their way into Harriet's medicine glass. Or maybe someone out of curiosity opened the paper containing the grains. Being of a light nature 'a slight draft of air would blow it away.' It could, he suggested, have blown into Harriet's food. More convincing was Bliss's second line of defence, the one he had already been pushing, that Harriet died from a violent hysterical attack. Had not Morley initially diagnosed her earlier fits as such? Both of these strategies must have been deliberate smoke-screens to sow doubts in the minds of the jurors, for the third defence argument, and the one that Bliss decided to concentrate on, contradicted the other two, for it acknowledged that William had poisoned his wife, but only in a state of insanity. 'I hope to be able to show you,' he said, 'that this man from his youth upwards laboured under defects of under-standing, that have since developed themselves, and driven him to the commission of the crime with which he is now charged.' Bliss proceeded to give a potted history of Dove's eccentric behaviour throughout his life, and focused on his belief in Harrison's magical powers. When Bliss men-tioned that Harrison had removed from his initial practice in the Dewsbury Road, Bramwell interjected, with good reason, 'Don't mention where to, or you will have foolish people going to him.' William's letter to the Devil was read out and caused a sensation in court. Bliss also pro-duced another letter, written to the prison schoolmaster in June, which read as follows: 'Dear Sir, – I am very uneasy about a rumour which is said to be prevalent respecting me about the town of Leeds, that I am or pretend to be insane. I hope that my conduct while in prison will prove the contrary.' This may have seemed like a counterproductive move by Bliss but with marvellous oxymoronic logic he announced: 'This letter, gentlemen, is in itself evidence that the prisoner was not feigning insan-ity. For it is one of the proofs of insanity that the lunatic declares that he is of perfectly sound mind.'

Bliss concluded an impressive five-hour speech by emphasising William's diabolic pact, concluding, 'if you think it will tend to the repression of crime; if you think that the law requires that a man who believes he has sold his soul to the devil – who, under this dreadful, this impious, this insane delusion, should be hanged at York Castle for an example, I ask you why? – as an example to whom? To the insane? Alas! They are never governed by the example of others.' The jury would have to decided whether William was a man 'accountable for his actions, and executed on the scaffold, or whether he is a man to be confined as a lunatic, as the law in such cases provides.' Although the *Leeds Intelligencer* disagreed with the basis of Bliss's argument it recognised that his speech was 'one of the most splendid forensic efforts which the bar has witnessed for many years'.[84]

The first of the defence witnesses was William's brother-in-law John Sloggett Jenkins. Shortly after marrying Sarah Dove in June 1854 he left Woodhouse Grove and the couple moved to Madras, where John became the headmaster of the Presidential School. Having heard of the death of his sister and arrest of William, he returned to England at his own expense to give evidence. Jenkins expressed his conviction that his brother-in-law was insane: 'I found him invariably incoherent in his ideas – no subject in which there was anything like coherency.' 'I became entirely disgusted with his expressions of insanity,' he stated. As to the cause of his sister's death, Jenkins refused to believe that William had murdered her: 'I and the other members of the family are convinced that her death resulted during an hysteric fit.' Several of William's school-teachers were called next. Richard Hiley said he had reason to suspect that William 'was not "altogether there"': 'Sometimes he had some glimmering of intellect, at others it was only a malformation.' Charles Hanmer, a teacher at Hiley's school, testified that as a child William 'had decided tendencies to insanity.' The Rev. John Manners recollected that his general impression of William was 'that there was something strange, unaccountable, and different in him from other boys.' In the Rev. William Lord's opinion, William 'was not of sound mind.' After these witnesses to William's early life, Aaron Frankish, Jonathan Gibson and several of their labourers were put in the witness stand to testify to William's wild and peculiar behaviour. The third day of the trial concluded with similar evidence being provided by William's servants during his spell at White Well Farm and several people who knew him at Normanton. Joseph Abbott, a Normanton schoolmaster and brewer, recalled, for example, that when he first met Dove 'he told me he had some black potatoes. They were very mealy and good. I disputed it, and said I never heard of such things. Before I had been three minutes in his company I formed an opinion of the state of his mind ... he had not the prudence of ordinary men.' William also once asked him to make his will, in which he wanted to leave his property to his wife for her lifetime, and then be passed on to her friends.[85]

The fourth and final day began with further witnesses for the defence. John Thompson, the Aberford schoolmaster, told Judge Bramwell, 'I knew Dove, and knew him well, and am sure he is not of sound mind – he had a little intelligence – and I think he knew it was wrong to steal, to murder; but I don't know that he knew the commandments.' William had told Thompson about hiring a wizard to put a spell on Mr King, and once asked Thompson if he believed in witchcraft. Thompson replied that he 'did not understand the art'. One day he found William 'practising magic, or something of the sort'. He brought out a plate, a saucer, some gunpowder and a bottle of liquid, twined up a piece of paper and lit it. Expecting an explosion Thompson ran off. John Noble, governor of York Castle, appeared briefly in the stand to report on the confiscation of William's letter to the Devil, and then the last but most controversial witnesses appeared – the insanity experts.

The main medical expert for the defence was Dr Caleb Williams of the Retreat Lunatic Asylum at York. Williams had been present throughout the trial to hear all the evidence, and along with his colleague John Kitching had interviewed Dove several days before to ascertain his state of mind. 'From all I have seen and heard,' he told the court, 'I consider his powers of mind during the fatal week were probably influenced by his notions regarding supernatural agency, and that consequently he was the subject of delusion.' Under cross-examination by Overend, Williams admitted that he had never come across another case in which an insane person patiently committed murder using repeated doses of poison. Dove's actions were certainly not impulsive, but rather 'an uncontrollable propensity to destroy, to give pain, or to take life. This propensity may for a time be a permanent condition of the mind; and this would lead to a constant seeking to accomplish the object. I think that a person, with such a propensity, committing murder, would not know that he was doing wrong.' Williams developed the point further, leading Bramwell to ask: 'If a man nourishes any passion until it becomes uncontrollable, that is moral insanity?' 'It is,' he replied. Dr George Pyemont Smith, proprietor of a Leeds lunatic asylum, agreed with Williams that Dove was insane. He was cautious, though, about whether he was governed by an irresistible propensity when he poisoned Harriet, and considered he had some awareness of right from wrong when he did it, but his insanity rendered him 'utterly regardless of consequences'. Kitching expressed his general agreement with this view. Unlike Williams, though, he thought that Dove's crime was in part an act of impulsive madness: 'We have a

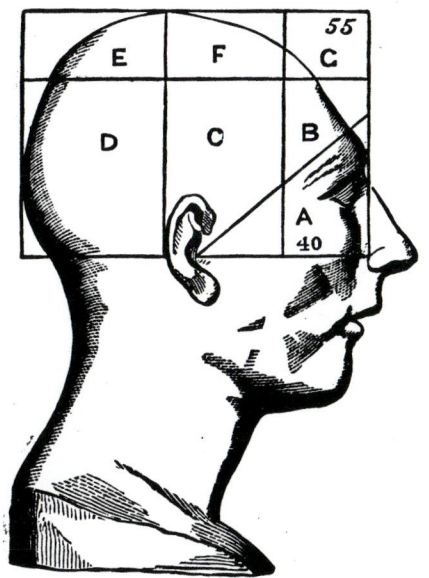

Diagram 29.—Dove.  Reduced.

*William Dove*

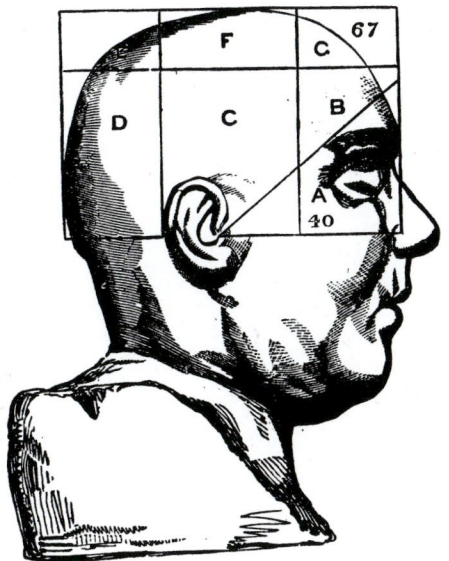

*William Palmer*

**PLATE 1** ◆ *Dove and Palmer compared. Note the same 'basilar phero-metrical' angle of 40 degrees, which Bridges thought common to most murderers.*

From Frederick Bridges, *Phrenology Made Practical and Popularly Explained* (4th edn, London, n.d.).

Diagram 45.—An Illustration of the ideal Head of Christ.

Diagram 57.

James Tunnicliffe, the witch doctor, from a sketch made at his trial. This is a good specimen of the wizard type; it indicates all that is grovelling.

**PLATE 2** ◆ *Jesus and Tunnicliff compared.*

From Frederick Bridges, *Phrenology Made Practical and Popularly Explained* (4th edn, London, n.d.).

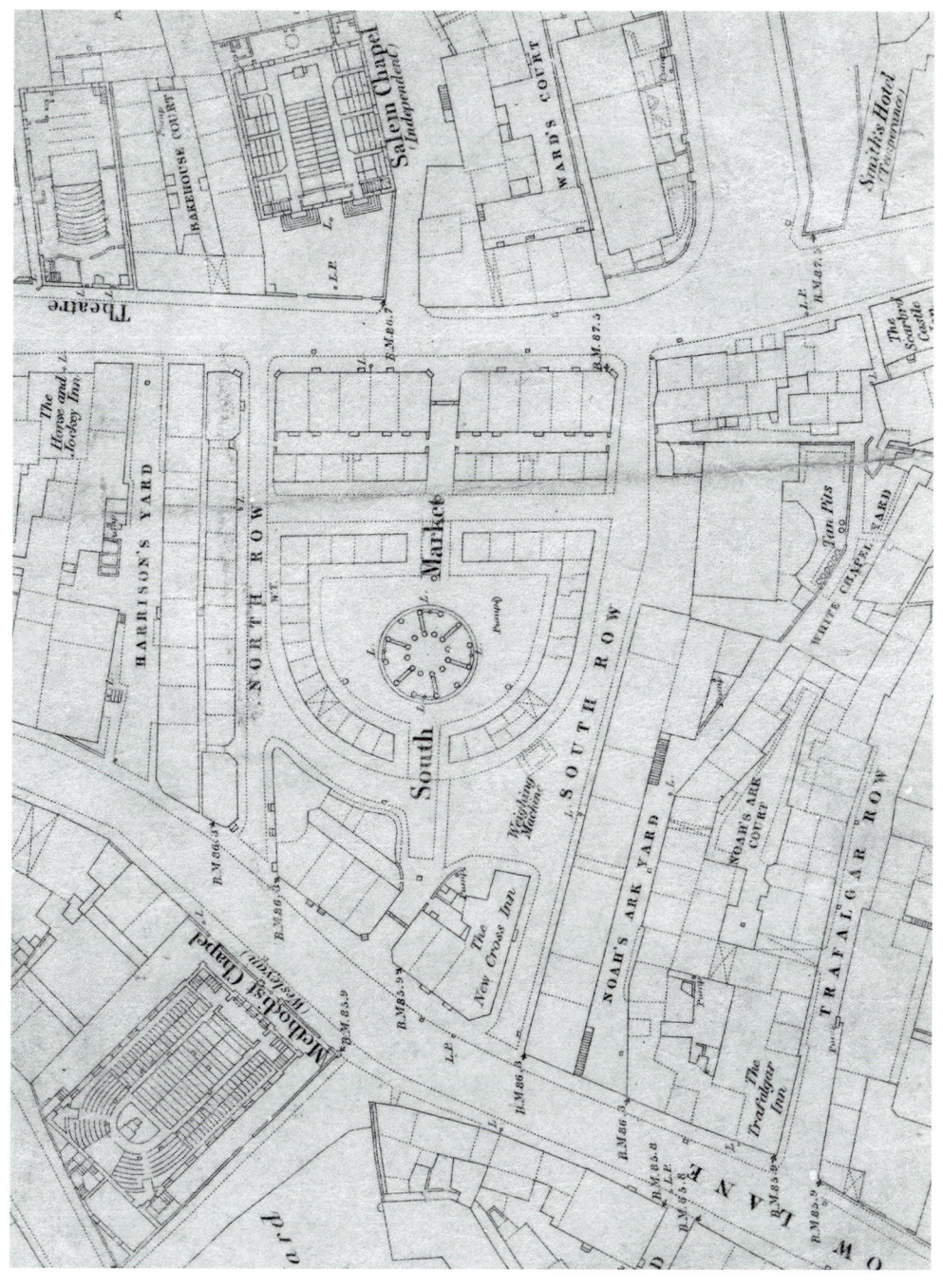

**PLATE 3** ◆ *Plan of the South Market and surrounding area, 1847. The New Cross Inn is clearly marked, as is North Row, where Henry Harrison moved around 1850.*

# THE TWO DOVES:

OR, MEMOIRS OF

## MARGARET AND ANNA DOVE,

LATE OF LEEDS, ENGLAND.

BY PETER M'OWAN.

NEW-YORK:

PUBLISHED BY G. LANE & P. P. SANDFORD,
For the Sunday School Union of the Methodist Episcopal Church,
at the Conference Office, 200 Mulberry-street.

J. Collord, Printer.
1843.

**PLATE 4** ◆ *The Two Doves by Peter M'Owan.*

**PLATE 5** ◆ *Photograph of the rear of nos 23–33 Meadow Lane, 21 May 1900. To the left of the photograph is the back of the New Cross Inn, though by 1900 it was called the South Market Hotel. To its right is the entrance to the South Market. The group of people on the left would have been facing the South Market. Harrison lived a few yards on from the right of the photograph.*

**PLATE 6** ◆ *The judge at William's trial, Baron George William Wilshere Bramwell (1808–1892).*
From Charles Fairfield, *Some Account of George William Wilshere: Baron Bramwell of Hever*
(London, 1898).

**PLATE 7** ◆ *Thomas Wright. Artist, George Frederic Watts*

National Portrait Gallery, London.

**PLATE 8** ◆ *Thomas Nunneley.*

T.H. Barker, *Photographs of Eminent Medical Men* (London, 1867). Wellcome Library, London.

*From a Photograph by W. Willmot, Liverpool*

**PLATE 9** ◆ *Frederick Bridges (d. 1883).*

Frederick Bridges, *Phreno-Physiometrical Characteristics of James Spollin* (London, 1858).
British Library.

# THE LAST MOMENTS AND
# EXECUTION OF WM. DOVE!

## For Poisoning his Wife, by Strychnine at Leeds, on the 1st. of March who was tried at the York Summer Assizes, July 16th, 1856.

### A COPY OF VERSES.

'Hark! the solemn bell was tolling,
A wretch, I do for mercy cry,
My moments on are swiftly rolling,
At York I am condemned to die,
For a crime I never thought of;
I never did on poison look,
Until I read the deeds of Palmer,
Who killed his friend John Parsons Cook.

CHORUS.

I poisoned her I swore to cherish,
I murdered her I vowed to love,
On the scaffold I must perish,
Behold the fate of William Dove

My loving wife was young and virtuous,
But I did was her cruelly,
And for the crimes I have committed,
William Dove must hanged be —
I thrice administered the poison,
Strychnine, I my partner gave,
Pain and anguish she endured,
I sent her to her silent grave.

I saw my virtuous wife to suffer,
I sent her to the silent tomb —
I did my love with poison murder,
When in the midst of youth and bloom :
I thought my troubles all were ended,
When I saw my darling die.
But I could not when unbefriended —
Escape my God's all-seeing eye.

Oh God! have mercy on a sinner,
Look down with pity from above ;
Oh, is there not one spark of mercy,
For the wretched William Dove —
Just, O God, I own my sentence,
And I well deserve to die —
For the deed I have committed,
On York's fatal gallows high

Cursed was the crimes of Palmer,
That has brought me to the tree,
Had Dove not read the deeds of Palmer,
Into my mind had never entered.
Such cruel, base and deadly strife ;
It was the deeds of William Palmer,
Tempted me to slay my wife.

The wretched hangman stands before me,
Death summons me in youth & bloom,
Trembling on York's fatal scaffold :
I am hurried to the tomb.
For William Dove there is no mercy,
There is nothing can me save —
Driven from this world of sorrow,
To a sad untimely grave

Oh, my God, when is thy presence,
How before thee can I stand,
When I know I've thee offended,
And have broken thy commands :
I at the altar vowed to cherish,
And through life my partner love,

Her protect and kindly nourish ;
Sad is the fate of William Dove.

Oh my friends by me take warning,
Lead a sober honest life,
Struggle hard, night, noon and morning
To protect a virtuous wife —
Shun, oh shun, intoxication,
Trust in him who reigns above —
Look at the sad situation,
Of the wretched William Dove.

Chorus.

Trembling on the fatal scaffold,
I, for murder now do stand,
The grave is waiting to receive me,
Sad, unhappy, wretched man.

On the 16th day of July, he was plac'd at the bar ;
Hundreds of people assemble both near and far,
Each seem'd so anxious this wretch for to see,
How awful to say he must die on the tree.
The judge summed up and the jury retir'd,
To consider their verdict and soon it was heard.
That he was guilty most awful is doom?
And he must lie in a murders tomb.

The judge he address him and thus he did say,
You must prepare to die on the tree,
Your days are number'd are your time it is short,
I'd have you to pray sincerely to the Lord.
Now christian consider what is feelings must be,
In the prime of life he must die on the tree,
May he to his maker boudly call,
For to have mercy on his guilty soul.

## A LETTER.

Dear Mother and Sisters.—This comes to take my last farewell of you all, and I hope the melancholy tuation in which I am now placed will be a warning to you all to shun the evil courses that I have followed to you know my own vicious principles have brought to what I now am, as I neither feared God nor an, but I am sincerely sorry for it —and hope that my wretched situation will be a warning to you my ar friends, for justice is the only safeguard of society ad to that protecting power, all must yield obedience that grieves me is my dear Mary, that I did not tend to the good advice you gave me, and that I am ch a great offender, but I hope the Lord will give fortitude under my sufferings. When I awoke is morning, I kneeled down at my bed-side and ked God's pardon—but my Dear Friends I could t say much, for I was soon speechless, I fell down th my face to the ground for near an with tears running down my cheeks. I sighed and groaned and w all my sins, and that without repentance, hell was ady to receive me —I thank God for being so kind such a wretch as me, and pray God that he may ve me at the last hour.

My dear friends, trifle no longer, but pray to God have mercy on you—pray for me, and think it a essing that I am now making myself fit for another orld. I could like each of my friends to have something belonging to me, to keep in remembrance of me my absence, that when they see it, they may think my unhappy fate, which I am about to suffer ; and ay my untimely death be a warning to you all, I send y kind love to all Friends and Relations, and ask ardon of all those I have offended.

*To the Queen's Most Excellent Majesty.*

The humble petition of Mary Dove, the other of William Dove, now in York astle, under sentence of death, having een pronounced guilty of the charge for which he was imprisoned in March last, by most respectable and respected jury, which ry, from the mass of evidence adduced, roving him to be of unsound intellect, recommended him to mercy on that ground.

Your petitioner begs to state that, although the development of his defective intellect in many of his eccentricities was ot personally known to herself, because of er son's frequent absence from home, yet many of them were practised under her own oof and others of an equally conclusive haracter, which have no record in public rint. Permit then the afflicted mother of f William Dove to entreat your majesty to ause the recommendation of the jury to be

carried out, and the life of her son to be spared. Your majesty will easily understand that a mother, so circumstanced, can say but few words. Your petitioner humbly requests that it may please your Majesty to spare the prisoner's life. And your majesty's humble petitioner, as in affection and duty bound, will ever pray.

**MARY DOVE.**

The authorities of York Castle having received official notice from the Home Office. that the Law must take its course in the case of William Dove, found guilty of the murder of his Wife. The Home Secretary having intimated to the deputations that waited upon him, that after consulting with the learned judge who tried the case, he knew nothing to induce him to make any remission of the punishment assigned by the Law to the Criminal.—Consequently the execution will take place on Saturday, the ninth of August,—on Mr. Noble the Governor of the Gaol, accompanied by the Chaplain entering his cell and informing him that the execution would take place at the usual time, he manifested no emotion ; he said that he was quite prepared.

The murderer Dove, is never left by himself for a single moment, two prisoners and a turnkey are constantly with him day and night ; his sleep is trouble—his dreams are frightful—he starts suddenly on his iron bedstead, and stretches out his arms as if imploring for mercy, his body covered with cold damp sweat.—Such is the awful situation of the condemned felon—William Dove who, in a very short space of time will end his days on the scaffold. On Sunday last, what is called the condemned sermon was preached in the chapel of the prison by the Chaplain of the prison, he took his text from Romans,—6th chapter, 23d verse,— " the wages of sin is death."—The minister delivered a most impressive discourse, The prisoner has been visited by his dissonsolate mother and his only sister, the interview was of the most painful description, He has not made any direct confession yet.

The Conduct of Dove since his Conviction.

Last week the Rev. M. Punshon, of Leeds and the Rev. J. Hartley of York, Wesleyan

ministers, had visited Dove in the condemned cell. The have done so, and in addition to those gentlemen, Mr. Murfin, of York, one of the city missionaries, has seen the prisoner, but we believe his demeanour has been much the same as it was last week not only exhibiting any contrition for the grave offence laid to his charge, but not admitting that he had committed any such crimes.

## THE CONFESSION.

York Friday. Afternoon.
The prisoner has fereely admitted to Mr. Wright, that he poisoned his wife, and that for that offence he ought to die. The witnesses the jury the Judge he admits only did their duty, and that his conviction was correct. He is very penitent and resign to his fate.

## EXECUTION.

Saturday, August 9th, 12 a.m.
The execution took place this morning, at 12 o'clock, in front of St. George Field.
At an early hour this morning a large number of persons had assembled, and others were still seen wending their way from the adjacent towns and villages, many of whom were apparently footsore from the distance they had come, and at the time of the execution there could not be less than

twenty thousand assembled.
At six o'clock the criminal was taken from his cell in the centre of the building from the "condemned cell," to be in readiness for the execution. Here he was allowed his breakfast, the chaplain remaining with him, all the time, conversing with him and reminding him of the mercy granted to the penitent criminal crucified with Christ on Calvary. At last the moment came when he must take his farewell of life.
At a few minutes, before twelve o'clock. the Sheriff arrived at the gaol, accompanied by his bailiff and a number of Halbertman. He at once entered the prison and formally demanded the body of the convict for execution, at the door of the cell in which he was then placed.
Dove was now pinioned, and notice was given of the approach of the procession by the appearance of a warder on the scaffold. Shortly after, the Sheriff and officials, bearing wands, appeared on the drop ; they were followed by the Chaplain without his canonicals, (the prisoner has made a confession,) followed by the prisoner, close upon whom was Jackcatch, and a warder of the prison. Dove was at once placed under the fatal beam, and the white cap drawn over his face, and the rope adjusted, the bolt was drawn, which launched the wretched criminal into eternity.

MRS. M. NAPPEY, PRINTER, 17, COPPERGATE, YORK.

**PLATE 10** ◆ *The Last Moments of W.M. Dove*

**PLATE 11** ◆ *Dove in the condemned cell at York Castle.*

**PLATE 12** ◆ *The execution site at York Castle c. 1880s. In the foreground is the open space of St George's Fields where the crowd gathered in front of the scaffold. The doorway to the scaffold can be seen midway up the side of the building in the centre of the photograph.*

man of deficient mental powers; besides that, he is insane; he is liable to do any absurd, cruel, vicious, or irrational action that presented itself to his mind, as his whole life shows. Supposing him to be insane, I should not apply the term "vicious" to him or "malignant".' After further cross-examination of Kitching the case for the defence was closed. The disagreements between the three medical experts had somewhat undermined the insanity strategy that Bliss had painstakingly built up over the previous day and a half.

At twenty minutes past one, after half an hour for refreshments, Overend began his reply, which lasted nearly two hours and twenty minutes. He pointed out to the jury that Bliss had adopted a multiple defence that was 'some proof that he had not much confidence in either.' He criticised the 'grossly exaggerated' testimony provided by the defence witnesses regarding William's strange ideas and wayward behaviour. They had heard from one witness, for instance, that 'he must have been mad, because he said that he had seen black potatoes. Why the High Sheriff, and two of the jury, and he himself, had all seen black potatoes; but, because the witness was ignorant of the existence of black potatoes, therefore the prisoner must be mad.'[86] As to William's boyhood pranks, they were merely 'those which many a boy had played, had been well flogged for, and had subsequently become a good man.' His drinking accounted for other such acts in adulthood. 'He was a cruel boy, but most boys were cruel. They went to dog-fights and bear-baitings, and were ashamed as men of such scenes; so the prisoner had ceased doing many cruel acts as he grew up.' If William had long been insane, Overend asked, why did the Jenkins allow their daughter to marry him? If his mother really thought he was of unsound mind 'would she not have felt it an imperative duty to have appeared in the witness box? Where were his sister, brothers, cousins, friends, – where were they? Were they called? None.' Apart from the fact that William had no surviving brothers Overend was highlighting a crucial weakness in the defence. The absence of William's mother and sisters must have appeared odd to the jury considering his life was at stake. However, the full force of Overend's withering criticism was saved for the medical experts. Regarding Caleb Williams's notion of the 'uncontrollable propensity' of the morally insane, Overend considered that 'a doctrine more dangerous to society never was uttered in a court of justice.' 'How monstrous,' he asked, 'was the theory of Dr Williams, that if a man would only think upon a crime long enough, he would become insane upon it, and not be responsible for his acts.' Overend finished speaking at twenty minutes to four, and then there was a twenty-minute refreshment break, which evidently could not come too soon for William.

What of his behaviour during the trial so far? By all accounts he maintained a remarkably calm and relaxed demeanour throughout. Even more remarkable though was that he seemed more preoccupied with his next meal than with the testimony of friends, acquaintances and doctors. Each day of the trial William would frequently turn to look at the courtroom clock, apparently impatiently awaiting the next interval for refreshments. When the moment arrived 'he always walked quickly out of the dock to the recess behind, and at once pounced upon the basket or bottle in which he knew he would find refreshments.' As one journalist remarked with astonishment, 'he has evidently thought more of when he would be allowed to eat and drink than of the effects of the evidence in sending him to the gallows or otherwise.'[87] Was it another sign of his insanity or was he just confident in a positive outcome?

At four o'clock Bramwell commenced to sum up the case. For six hours he talked, meticulously going over the salient facts for the benefit of the jury. He advised them that they need not worry about the definition of murder for 'if the prisoner administered the poison, he was guilty of murder, unless he was in a state of mind that would render him unconscious.' The defence of insanity, he told them, rested on whether he was aware that what he was doing was wrong. They would have to decide. Bramwell was quite clear what he thought on the matter. He questioned whether those who knew William best, his family and friends, considered him of unsound mind. 'Was not such a belief negatived,' he asked, 'by the facts that he was allowed to go on his travels in America? That a farm was taken for him? That he was allowed to marry a respectable young woman, and go into housekeeping?' During the testimony of the medical witnesses earlier that afternoon Bramwell had been sparing and politely critical in his questioning, he now savaged the views of Williams, Smith and Kitching. 'Experts in madness! Mad doctors! Gentlemen, I will read you the evidence of these medical witnesses – these "experts in madness." – And if you can make sane evidence out of what they say, do so; but I confess it's more than I can do.' Judges had been critical of such medical evidence before, but never so stridently, and his exclamatory comment went down in the annals of medical jurisprudence.[88] After further deconstructing the psychiatrists' arguments he continued: 'If the theory of these gentlemen were true of the prisoner, it would be equally true in the case of every criminal, and form a conclusive reason for liberating every person charged with crime.'

After his tirade against the 'mad doctors' it was disingenuous of Bramwell to subsequently tell the jury that 'he had endeavoured to lay both sides impartially before them; and it was not his duty, as it was not his intention, to indicate any opinion of his own.' They 'must exercise their own judgement; and not let the opinion of the judge have any weight whatsoever.' Why then give his opinion in the first place? As trials became longer, expert witnesses more influential in defence cases, and newspaper reports more extensive during the mid-nineteenth century, judges reacted by becoming more prosecutorial in their summing up. As representatives of elite authority they felt it necessary to impart what they believed to be necessary moral imperatives, values they thought juries might lose sight of under the influence of defence counsels.[89] Nevertheless, juries were capable of negotiating their own moral imperatives and had long proved themselves independent of such judicial influence. They not infrequently gave lesser verdicts than those favoured by judges. Maybe Edward Hewitt and his fellow jurors would do the same.

## The verdict

Following Bliss's 'remarkable speech' the *Leeds Times* reported that it confidently expected that the jury would deliver a 'not guilty' verdict on the grounds of insanity. At five minutes past ten the jury left the courtroom to deliberate. One or two of the members suggested they all engage in a prayer to God to direct them to a just conclusion, the rest of the jurors assented. No lengthy discussion ensued because, as one juror later explained, 'There was but one opinion as to his guilt ... a more unanimous jury it is hardly possible to conceive.'[90] They returned to court after thirty-five minutes and the clerk of arraigns asked: 'Gentlemen of the Jury, have you agreed upon your verdict?' The Foreman Edward Hewitt replied, 'We have.' 'How say you, guilty, or not guilty?' 'Guilty,' he replied, 'but we recommend him to mercy on the ground of defective intellect.' The clerk now turned to William and said, 'William Dove, you have been convicted of the crime of murder; have you anything to say why the sentence of death should not be passed upon you, according to law?' William began to speak but only had time to utter 'I have only to say ...' before the proclamation of 'Silence' was called in preparation for Judge Bramwell's final act.

It was the first time that Bramwell had undertaken the solemn duty of sentencing someone to death and, as he placed the black cap on his head and began to address William, he was visibly affected with emotion and his voice reduced to a whisper at times. 'You have been found guilty of murder', he intoned, 'the most dreadful of all crimes, and it is in your case one of the worst possible description.' The jury, he said, had

> shown a firm determination to do their duty, though, at the same time, they have yielded to their natural impulses in recommending to mercy one upon the state of whose mind there has been so much said. That recommendation shall be forwarded to the proper quarter, and, if acquiesced in, mercy will be extended to you; but be prepared to find it rejected.

He then concluded with the customary words when delivering the death sentence:

> that, for the crime of wilful murder, you be taken hence to the prison from whence you came, and thence to the place of execution, and there hanged by the neck till your body be dead, and that your body be afterwards taken down and buried within the precincts of the prison in which you have been confined after this your conviction. And may the Lord have mercy upon your soul.

For the first time William's face quivered with emotion. It seemed as though he was about to speak out, but after a moment's hesitation he stepped out of the dock and was escorted from the court.

## Notes and references

1 See Mary Beth Emmerichs, '"Getting away with Murder?" Homicide and the Coroners in Nineteenth-Century London', *Social Science History*, 25, 1 (2001), pp. 93–100.

2 Sylvia Barnard, *Viewing the Breathless Corpse: Coroners and Inquests in Victorian Leeds* (Leeds, 2001), p. 12.

3 Cited in Burney, *Bodies of Evidence*, p. 85.

4 Cited in J.A. Sharpe, *Crime in Early Modern England 1550–1750* (London and New York, 1999), p. 126.

5 See Burney, *Bodies of Evidence*, pp. 83–5.

6 John Jervis, *A Practical Treatise on the Office and Duties of Coroners*, 2nd edition (London, 1854), p. 253.

7 Jervis, *Practical Treatise*, p. 256.

8 Burney, *Bodies of Evidence*, pp. 108–9.

9 Cited in *Leeds Intelligencer*, 22 March 1856.

10 'Scientific Evidence: The Trials of Palmer, Dove, &c.', *The Rambler* 18, Old Series (1856), 228, 314. See also Gary Greenwald and Maria Greenwald, 'Medicolegal Progress in Inquests of Felonious Deaths: Westminster 1761–1866', *Journal of Legal Medicine*, 2 (1981), 200–209.

11 George Robinson, *Observations on Some Recent Cases of Poisoning* (Gateshead, 1856), p. 3.

12 *The Times*, 10 March 1856.

13 Barnard, *Viewing the Breathless Corpse*, p. 20.

14 *The Times*, 10 March 1856.

15 White, *Directory and Topography of the Borough of Leeds* (1858), p. 20.

16 *The Times*, 11 March 1856.

17 *Daily News*, 11 March 1856.

18 *Manchester Guardian*, 17 March 1856.

19 *Leeds Times*, 15 March 1856.

20 *Leeds Intelligencer*, 15 March 1856.

21 *The Times*, 11 March 1856.

22 *The Times*, 11 March 1856.

23 *Manchester Guardian*, 13 March 1856.

24 *Leeds Intelligencer*, 15 March 1856.

25 *Leeds Intelligencer*, 15 March 1856.

26 *Weekly Dispatch*, 23 March 1856.

27 Michael Harris, 'Social diseases? Crime and medicine in the Victorian press', in W.F. Bynum, Stephen Lock and Roy Porter (eds), *Medical Journals and Medical Knowledge* (London and New York, 1992), p. 120.

28 Burney, 'Poisoning of No Substance', p. 69, n. 32.

29 Figures extracted from *House of Commons Parliamentary Papers*, vol. 23 (1857–8), pp. 122–3, 131, 197.

30 *Parliamentary Papers*, vol. 23 (1857–8), pp. 196, 198.

31 See Katherine Watson, *Poisoned Lives: English Poisoners and their Victims* (London, 2003).

32 *Daily News*, 10 January 1856.

33 Reprinted in *The Times*, 6 September 1849.

34 See Peter Bartrip, 'A "Pennurth of Arsenic for Rat Poison": The Arsenic Act, 1851 and the Prevention of Secret Poisoning', *Medical History*, 36 (1992), pp. 53–69.

35 *The Times*, 14 January 1845; 15 January 1845.

36 *The Times*, 6 January 1845.

37 *Parliamentary Papers*, vol. 23 (1857–8), p. 201. In nearly 113 cases no specific poisons were mentioned.

38 C.E. Jenkins, 'Treatment of the Malignant Cholera with Strychnine', *The Lancet*, 24, 625 (1835), pp. 657–8; W.C. Clough, 'Cases of paralysis cured by strychnine', *The Lancet*, 29, 757 (1838), pp. 805–6; G.T. Gream, 'On the use of Nux vomica as a remedy in hay-fever', *The Lancet*, 55, 1397 (1850), pp. 692–3; J. Hyde Houghton, 'The use of Nux Vomica in cases of Constipation and Costiveness', *Association Medical Journal*, April 5 (1856), pp. 271–4.

39 *The Times*, 30 November 1854.

40 *The Times*, 8 March 1849.

41 [D. Booth], *The Art of Brewing* (London, 1829).

42 *The Times*, 12 May 1830.

43 Thomas Graham and August Wilhelm Hofmann, *Report upon the alleged adulteration of Pale Ales by strychnine, etc.* (London, 1852). See also Baron Liebig and Justus Liebig, 'Remarks upon the Alleged use of Strychnine in the Manufacture of Bitter Beer or Pale Ale', *The Lancet*, 59, 1501 (1852), pp. 551–2.

44 See, for example, the *Daily News*, 30 January 1856.

45 *Leader*, 15 December 1855; cited in Burney, 'Poisoning of no substance', n. 25.

46 *Manchester Guardian*, 8 February 1856.

47 *Leeds Times*, 22 March 1856.

**48** *Medical Times*, 22 March 1856; cited in Harris, 'Social diseases?' p. 120.

**49** See William H. Helfand, 'James Morison and his Pills', *Transactions of the British Society of the History of Pharmacy*, 1 (1974), pp. 101–35; Smith, *People's Health*, pp. 343–4.

**50** See, for example, *Weekly Dispatch*, 23 March 1851.

**51** See, for example, *Daily News*, 15 March 1856. See also *The Hygeist, or Medical Reformer*, N.S. 20 (1 August 1856), p. 153.

**52** See Noel G. Coley, 'Alfred Swaine Taylor, MD, FRS (1806–1880): Forensic Toxicologist', *Medical History*, 35 (1991), pp. 409–27; Harris, 'Social diseases?' pp. 115–8.

**53** See Burney, 'Poisoning of no substance', pp. 72–5.

**54** *Manchester Guardian*, 4 February 1856.

**55** Reported in the *Leeds Intelligencer*, 15 March 1856. On Pepper see the *DNB*.

**56** *The Times*, 13 June 1856.

**57** Cited *in Leeds Intelligencer*, 22 March 1856.

**58** *Association Medical Journal*, 15 March 1856, p. 216.

**59** Bartripp, 'A "Pennurth of Arsenic"', p. 65.

**60** Cited in Richard Altick, *Evil Encounters: Two Victorian Sensations* (London, 1987), p. 124.

**61** Anon., 'Scientific Evidence: The Trials of Palmer, Dove, &c.', p. 227.

**62** Altick, *Evil Encounters*, p. 28.

**63** *Daily News*, 14 March 1856.

**64** Anon., 'Scientific Evidence: The Trials of Palmer, Dove, &c.', p. 227.

**65** *Leeds Times*, 22 March 1856.

**66** *Leeds Intelligencer*, 15 March 1856.

**67** *Leeds Mercury*, 19 July 1856.

**68** See *The Times*, 19 May 1856.

**69** For a detailed examination of the expert testimony given during the trial see Burney, 'Poisoning of No Substance'.

**70** *The Times*, 27 May 1856.

**71** See Burney's 'Poisoning of no substance' for a detailed analysis of the ramifications of Palmer's statement.

**72** *News of the World*, 15 June 1856.

**73** *The Times*, 12 July 1856.

74  *Leeds Mercury*, 19 July 1856.

75  *News of the World*, 6 July 1856.

76  See Charles Fairfield, *Some Account of George William Wilshere, Baron Bramwell of Hever* (London, 1898); *New DNB*.

77  *The Times*, 7 January 1856.

78  Cited in Edward Manson, *Bramwelliana: Or, Wit and Wisdom of Lord Bramwell* (London, 1892), p. 36.

79  *Leeds Intelligencer*, 26 July 1856. See also William Knipe (ed.), *Criminal Chronology of York Castle* (York, 1867), p. 232.

80  The following account of the trial is based primarily but by no means exclusively on the *Leeds Mercury*, 17, 19 and 22 July 1856; *The Times*, 19 and 21 July 1856.

81  *Liverpool Mercury*, 18 July 1856.

82  *Leeds Mercury*, 17 July 1856.

83  *Liverpool Mercury*, 21 July 1856.

84  *Leeds Intelligencer*, 26 July 1856.

85  *York Herald*, 26 July 1856.

86  There are, indeed, several varieties of black or deep purple potatoes. Perhaps those seen by William were Shetland Black potatoes.

87  *Leeds Times*, 26 July 1856.

88  Joel Eigen, *Unconscious Crime: Mental Absence and Criminal Responsibility in Victorian London* (Baltimore, 2003), p. 127; Roger Smith, *Trial by Medicine: Insanity and Responsibility in Victorian Trials* (Edinburgh, 1981), pp. 136–7.

89  Martin Wiener, 'Judges v. Jurors: Courtroom Tensions in Murder Trials and the Law of Criminal Responsibility in Nineteenth-Century England', in *Law and History Review*, 17, 3 (1999).

90  *Leeds Intelligencer*, 2 August 1856. See also *Leeds Intelligencer*, 26 July 1856.

# CHAPTER 5

· · · · · · · · · · · · · · ·

# Mad or bad?

*'Palmer poisoned Cook to save himself from ruin; Dove poisoned his wife for the sake of poisoning her'*[1]

Was William's crime an act of cold, calculated murder or the impulse of a defective mind? Was he, as the *News of the World* put it, 'mad, or only very wicked?'[2] The jury's verdict had left the question open and in the days that remained before his scheduled execution a debate raged among journalists and the medical and religious fraternity. Considering appeals for mercy were to be made to the Home Secretary and to the Queen, whichever way the public debate swung on the issue could prove influential. The legal issues raised regarding premeditation, mitigation and insanity continue to have as much relevance today.

## Cruelty and murder

'Murder is rife in the land in its most violent and its most insidious forms.' reported a doleful *Times* in early 1856. Its editor thought stern repression was needed to get the situation under control.[3] The perceived poisoning epidemic was one reason for the newspaper's pessimism; the other was the growing concern regarding wife murder, which was, according to one newspaper, 'the blackest crime that could be committed'.[4] William personified both anxieties. As *The Times* observed a few months later, 'Unfortunately, the murder of a wife by her husband is an act not sufficiently rare to produce a deep sensation; but when the crime has been committed by poison, and that poison strychnine, general attention is at once fixed on its details.'[5] The newspaper's pessimism regarding murder was based on media fears rather than reality, as homicide in general had long been in decline.[6] But its observation regarding wife murder did reflect the reality that domestic murders were not decreasing at the same rate as male-on-male homicide. This growing concern over wife murder was not only a response to the poisoning scares and murder statistics but was also, as has recently been argued, more generally an aspect of hardening middle-class attitudes towards male violence against women in mid-Victorian society.[7]

Some thought they saw in William's past the signs of a murderer in the making, that he was a natural born killer. His childhood glee at inflicting pain on animals was highlighted, and the lack of stern parental discipline was suggested by some as a root cause of his continued malicious behaviour later in life. The *Leeds Times* reported that 'he is said to have been so exceedingly favoured by his parents as to have materially and permanently influenced and injured his character.' *The Sun* believed that 'if he had been severely chastised at first, he might not have indulged his malignant passions to such an extent.'[8] The link was obviously made between his youthful sadistic streak and his later treatment of Harriet. The *Saturday Review* described him as a 'man who tortures his wife in his maturity, as he tortured animals.' The *Leeds Intelligencer* considered his actions 'as barbarous and cruel as the imagination can suggest.' 'He beat her, got drunk, swore at her, threatened her life,' stated the *Daily News*. *The Times* painted a lurid picture of him 'becoming every day more brutal and depraved ... calling her opprobrious names, throwing her down, and standing over her with a carving-knife, beating her with his fist.'[9] As *The Times* suggested, his life seemed to fit Hogarth's famous series of engravings *The Four Stages of Cruelty*, which depicts the criminal trajectory of the pauper orphan Tom Nero. In the first stage we see Tom torturing a dog with an arrow. In the second, we find him as a young man beating a horse. In the third we see him being captured, having murdered a young woman. Finally we see him being dissected after execution. Hogarth created the series as a warning to the poor, and his depiction of male working-class brutality born of ignorance and deprivation was still current in mid-Victorian England. Yet poverty and lack of education were no explanation for William's behaviour.

The growing concern at the time about spousal violence and wife beating culminated in the 1854 Act for the Better Prevention of Aggravated Assaults upon Women and Children, which enabled two magistrates to issue swift summary justice. Two years later a failed private member's bill further called for the statutory flogging of wife beaters. Again, the problem was seen to be one pertaining to the working classes, and *The Times* expressed this prejudice when it stated that 'William Dove resembled only those ruffians whose delinquencies are almost daily recorded in the police reports of this capital.'[10] As an analysis of divorce court records reveals, however, upper-class husbands were quite capable of meting out similar levels of brutality.[11] Yet although wife beating was seen to be a working-class problem, it was thought by some that the honour of men in general was being tarnished and required protection as well.[12]

Despite the bolstering of the law regarding assault, the judicial system continued to fail to protect abused wives of all social classes, partly because many women were loath to prosecute their husbands and partly because the patriarchal courts continued to deal leniently with wife beaters. Regarding the former explanation we have already seen how Harriet had sufficient reason to prosecute William following his gun-wielding death threats, but one doubts if she ever entertained such an idea. Public airing of spousal abuse could carry as much social disgrace for the wife as for the husband, and great embarrassment would have been caused not only to the Dove family but also to the Jenkins. As to the courts, in mid-Victorian England the guiding principle that wives were the property of their husbands and therefore should obey and submit to their will was still a pervading influence. Many magistrates, judges and juries upheld the rights of men to deal out a degree of physical punishment to wives like Harriet, who was at times verbally abusive and vindictive towards William and, furthermore, denied him his conjugal rights. One Kent magistrate refused to sentence in wife beating cases until he knew whether or not 'she was a woman whose bad temper gave her husband no peace'. A not untypical outcome was that of a 'gentleman' who stabbed his wife after she threw a hairbrush at him during a row. The man was acquitted on the grounds that she was equally to blame for quarrelling.[13]

Yet for all his disturbing behaviour, from the evidence it is difficult to classify William as a wife beater. Only one witness, the young servant woman Elizabeth Fisher, testified to having seen William strike his wife.

The incident apparently took place at their house in Normanton. Fisher said she entered the sitting room one day to find William standing over Harriet with a rolling pin in one hand and a carving-knife in the other, threatening to kill her. Shortly after Fisher came in he left and when he came back later that night he struck Harriet, though not repeatedly it would seem. If the incident did take place as Fisher testified, then it was out of keeping with his normal pattern of behaviour. He was certainly ver-bally violent, particularly when drunk, and quick to brandish weapons in people's faces, but despite his frightening actions, bragging and animal maiming there is little evidence of him ever physically attacking anyone. The depiction of him 'torturing' and 'beating' Harriet proves to be a news-paper distortion of the facts, an exercise in stereotyping. William was made to fit the mould of the archetypal sadistic wife murderer in order to satisfy the preconceptions and tickle the sensations of readers.

The question remained as to why a man brought up in a wealthy, pious household and with a good education became a cruel boy, an 'uncivilised' husband and ultimately a murderer. Was his behaviour in all three phases really connected? William was no product of a poverty-stricken broken home. There was no physical hardship, no cause for a sense of injustice against the world at large. There were no brutal or absent parents. Although he occasionally grumbled about the cost of Harriet's medical treatment, the financial incentive was generally rejected. Perhaps for love? He was certainly attracted to Whitham and intended to propose to her, but there was little suggestion that his was an overriding passion. It was the lack of obvious motive that led some to conclude that insanity was the only answer.

## The mad doctors

Psychiatry, or alienism as it was known at the time, was pioneered by continental doctors during the late eighteenth and early nineteenth cen-turies. It took several decades for it to become an established if controver-sial branch of medicine in England and, as we have seen, during the mid-Victorian period the derogatory title of 'mad doctor' was still widely applied to its practitioners. The most influential figure in the rise of English psychiatry was the physician and ethnologist James Cowles Prichard (1786–1848).[14] Heavily influenced by the work of pioneering

French alienists like Philippe Pinel and Jean Esquirol, he developed the concept of 'moral insanity', which was introduced by Caleb Williams at Dove's trial. According to Prichard, moral insanity was distinct from the three established categories of insanity: monomania, mania (raving madness), and dementia, all of which were considered to be the consequence of intellectual defects, usually resulting from birth, injury or old age. Moral insanity, however, was rooted in the perversion of the emotional aspects of the mind, and could be triggered in perfectly normal people by the stresses and strains of life and the influence of the social environment. Because moral insanity was not the product of obvious intellectual and physical abnormality it was, as Prichard recognised, a difficult illness to diagnose:

> *Eccentricity of conduct, singular and absurd habits, a propensity to perform the common actions of life in a different way from that usually practised, is a feature in many cases of moral insanity, but can hardly be said to constitute sufficient evidence of its existence. When, however, such phenomena are observed in connexion with a wayward and intractable temper, with a decay of social affections, an aversion to the nearest relatives and friends formerly beloved, – in short, with a change in the moral character of the individual, the case becomes tolerably well marked.*[15]

It is clear from this that Bliss's defence case was based on building up a profile of behaviour that fitted Prichard's criteria. Indeed, Bliss read out a relevant quote from Prichard during the trial, though Bramwell dismissed it as inadmissible evidence. Regarding William's eccentricity the jury was provided with accounts of his orchard antics, views on black potatoes, plough innovations, mowing of unripe crops, animal cruelty, and most important of all his belief in supernatural beings, magic and the wizard Harrison. To fulfil the second half of Prichard's template the court also heard of his unpredictable temper, his volatile relations with his parents, and the mix of affection and emotional cruelty he showed towards Harriet.

After the trial, Caleb Williams's controversial diagnosis that Dove suffered from moral insanity received support from some of his colleagues. In early August, James Davey (1813–95), physician at the New Middlesex Lunatic Asylum, Colney Hatch, gave a lecture to the British Medical

Association arguing that Dove was a classic case of 'moral idiocy'. In such cases, he argued, the insane live a normal life of social interaction until some 'terrible catastrophe' calls attention to them, and then their family or friends have them confined, 'or, if popular prejudice and passion prevail, they are barbarously hanged like dogs.'[16] Several months later Williams also resorted to print to clarify his views and defend publicly his position.[17] Having been on the receiving end of Baron Bramwell's scorn, Williams responded in kind by pointing out the inconsistencies of the trial in particular and the justice system more generally. His main criticism concerned the legal rejection of the idea that there were degrees of insanity and therefore degrees of criminal responsibility. Furthermore, while the courts might deliberate at length on whether a criminal was guilty of murder or manslaughter, they would not even consider that he or she could be partially or temporarily insane.

There was, however, certainly no consensus among psychiatrists as to Dove's moral insanity. Both during and shortly after the trial Forbes Winslow (1810–1874), the owner of several private lunatic asylums, founder of the first English psychiatric journal, the *Journal of Psychological Medicine*, and one of the most well-known and controversial psychiatrists at the time, was unconvinced of the evidence for moral insanity and confessed he felt no sympathy for William and thought he should hang. Yet he had a profound change of heart after an interview with George Morley and Joseph Barret, and after reviewing the evidence again decided that William was no moral idiot but was instead a convincing case of inborn imbecility. In other words his intellect was defective from birth: 'His actions were not merely those of a wicked, vicious, or eccentric man, but they evidently sprung out of a stunted, irregularly developed, congenitally defective, and badly organised brain and mind.' This was essentially a confirmation of the jury's verdict. They had not been convinced of the category of moral insanity but believed William had a defective mind. As a consequence Winslow wrote to Barret that he had no hesitation 'in asserting that it would be a great and fatal mistake and a grave act of inhumanity to hang the wretched man.'[18]

The most vocal alienist arguing against the case for either Dove's moral or intellectual insanity also happened to be the most respected practitioner of psychological medicine, John Charles Bucknill (1817–1897), co-founder of the *Asylum Journal*, which began in 1853, and also superintendent at the Devon County Asylum. There was undoubtedly a degree of professional rivalry in his commentary on the Dove trial. At the time, relations between Bucknill and Winslow were frosty, partly because they were editors of rival professional journals and partly because they represented respectively the public and private wings of the psychiatric trade, which did not always see eye to eye on policy and provision regarding the insane.[19] So Bucknill dismissed Winslow's diagnosis of congenital imbecility, noting quite rightly that it did 'not appear to have presented itself to the defence'. In Bucknill's opinion the planning and cunning of Dove's poisoning strategy made Palmer look like 'a bungler' in comparison. He disregarded Caleb Williams's observation that those 'who are familiar with the conduct and habits of lunatics, well know how artfully they lay their plans, and how steadily and watchfully they carry them out, in order to secure the end they have in view.'[20] As to the case for moral insanity, Bucknill believed that even if 'Dr Prichard's opinions on the subject of moral insanity had been accepted in our courts of law (which they never have been), the case of Dove could not have been made to tally with them.'[21] Bucknill thought there was no evidence that William's crime was the product of an uncharacteristic, uncontrollable impulse. In Bucknill's opinion, if William had 'in an excess of rage shot his wife with the revolving pistol with which he often threatened her and himself, or taken her life in any other sudden and impulsive manner,' then there would have been a more valid case for moral insanity.[22] He expressed his concern that some of his fellow alienists were blurring the boundaries between crime, ignorance and insanity. He agreed the boundaries between them were thin but were nevertheless distinct. 'It is lamentable to see great criminals exculpated,' he wrote to *The Times*, 'on the false assumption that crime is a proof of "morbid mental action".'[23]

The judicial position regarding insanity was formally enshrined in the McNaughtan Rules, drawn up after the trial in 1843 of Daniel McNaughtan, who under the delusion that he was being persecuted by the police, attempted to shoot the Prime Minister Robert Peel, but mistakenly shot dead his private secretary instead. In essence the Rules prescribed that a plea of insanity was relevant only if it could be shown that the defendant was *unable* to understand that his or her crime was wrong at the time of committing it.[24] As Bucknill alluded, there was little place for the concept of moral insanity in the Rules, as the burden of proof primarily rested on evidence of either intellectual defect or mental impairment through physical injury. The case for emotional, impulsive insanity, and 'mental absence', where people were said to have committed crimes during bouts of unconsciousness, were effectively excluded. Nevertheless, as Dove's trial and others at the time show, the Rules were not always adhered to in the courtroom.[25] With the growing influence of alienists as expert witnesses, juries reached verdicts contrary to the sense of the Rules, such as the plea of partial responsibility. As a consequence, there were fears that the very foundation of jurisprudence was under threat. The *Association Medical Journal* remarked, regarding the jurors at William's trial, 'the fashionable doctrine of crime itself being an evidence of unsoundness of mind in the person committing it, may have affected them.' Echoing Bucknill, it warned, 'it seems as though we stand in danger of confounding vice and insanity.'[26]

Alienists were not the only ones debating the link between crime and insanity; phrenologists also had their say. The practitioners of this pseudo-science, which purported to reveal the mental character of individuals based on the shape of their heads, had been a strong influence in early psychiatry as it held out the profound promise of the physiognomic diagnosis of mental disease. Forbes Winslow, for instance, had been an enthusiastic proponent.[27] As with modern psychiatry, phrenology was the product of central European medical thinking. Its founder was the Viennese physician Franz Joseph Gall who developed upon an earlier medical tradition of physiognomy by suggesting the size of different sections of the brain, each of which related to specific aspects of human behaviour and moral character, shaped the contours of the skull as the bones ossified during infant development. Gall's ideas were further developed and popularised across Europe and in America by a former pupil, Johann Gaspar Spurzheim.[28] In England the most influential early promoters of phrenology were an Edinburgh lawyer named George Combe and his younger brother Andrew. The brothers wrote several tracts and papers on the phrenological characteristics of murderers and the links between criminal behaviour and insanity.[29] Their interest in the phrenological identification of the criminally inclined in society was further publicised during the mid-nineteenth century by Frederick Bridges, who we have already encountered in relation to the study of cunning-folk.

Bridges was the son of an architect, builder and inventor of industrial machines of Ardwick, Manchester. For reasons unknown, however, the family fell into poverty when Frederick was a child and so his education was cut short and he had to go to work at a local print works. At the age of fourteen he decided to learn to read and write and his autodidactic thirst for knowledge led him to the works of Gall and Spurzheim. His initial interest in the subject may have been partly linked to the fact that he had stunted growth and, as a consequence, his head was disproportionately large, which led his youthful colleagues to nickname him 'Big Head'.[30] It is also likely that he was taught the skills of phrenological practice at the Manchester Mechanics' Institute, where during the 1830s and 1840s the arts of plaster casting and wax modelling were taught by the phrenologist William Bally. Bally was a well-known figure in Manchester and when his exceptional collection of phrenological busts, including many of murderers, was put on display at the Institute during the Christmas holiday in 1844 tens of thousands came to see them.[31] He suffered for his art, though, due to the toxic components in the coloured wax he used. White wax, for instance, contained lead while yellow wax was coloured with the poisonous pigment chrome yellow.[32] In 1851 the local and national press reported that he was in a parlous state, his hands and arms paralysed and his throat badly ulcerated. A subscription of some £150 was raised for him with the backing of the *Manchester Guardian*. He survived and later achieved further public notice for making a cast of William Palmer's head. Bridges also had that privilege but received more publicity for having being paid £50 by Prime Minister Lord Palmerston for a private phrenological report.[33] He subsequently went on to write several works on phrenology including the successful *Phrenology Made Practical*, in which he expounded his views on the criminally insane and how they should be dealt with by the state.

Despite the close links between phrenology and psychiatry, Bridges was highly critical of Caleb Williams and his ilk. In a letter about Dove, published in the *Liverpool Mercury*, he complained that such 'experts' knew very little of the anatomy and physiognomy of the brain 'in a thoroughly scientific sense', and consequently were mere theorisers.[34] Bridges, by contrast, based his findings on physical analysis. Every murderer he had studied had a malformed head, generally characterised by a 'basilar phreno-metrical' angle of at least 35 degrees, which, without going into detailed explanation, was calculated by measuring the angle roughly between the ear hole, nose and brow ridge. Wise, intelligent and honourable people like George Combe had a lesser angle of around 25 degrees. The greater the angle, so Bridges thought, the greater the 'excess of the animal feelings over the moral qualities'. He calculated Dove as being in the 40 degree category and, more generally, the shape of his head was 'that of a low, vicious, partially mental and moral idiot'. William's conduct since youth was not the result of a diseased brain but from an 'organic defect' which Bridges termed 'idiotic insanity'.[35] Bridges did not dispute that Dove knew what he was doing in poisoning Harriet, but

> he was too low in the reflective organs and the moral sentiments to understand the moral consequences of his actions. The monkey and the dog know when they do wrong, and avoid their master from fear of being punished. But no one for a moment supposes that those animals do so from a knowledge of the moral consequences of their actions. Neither did Dove.[36]

By the 1850s, however, phrenology's intellectual influence was on the wane and Bridges' assessment of Dove was scornfully rubbished by the likes of the editor of the *Leeds Intelligencer*, who concluded there was 'nothing in his external appearance or countenance but what is common to those of the educated middle class man'.[37]

## Madness and the supernatural

In its attempt to gain an insanity plea the defence made much of William's belief in the supernatural, and his attempted pact with the Devil was the trump card. When Caleb Williams interviewed Dove in prison he confided to him that he wrote the letter to the Devil while under satanic influence, leading Williams to conclude that 'as a matter of science, I believe his delusion that he had sold himself to the devil was a genuine one.'[38] Overend, however, believed the Devil's pact was an elaborate ruse, 'a wicked design to feign insanity', which was 'evidence of great cunning in the prisoner.'[39] Bramwell insinuated the same possibility when he pointed out to the jury that in his letter to the Devil William had written 'welth' but crossed it out and added the correct spelling 'wealth'. 'If he had been writing this for the purpose of being found,' pondered the judge, 'he did not know why the prisoner should have corrected his bad spelling. If genuine, it was difficult to suppose that the man who wrote it could be of sound intellect. If not genuine, it would rather lead to the conclusion that he was cunning enough to know what he was about.'[40] Bucknill believed the latter was a distinct possibility, a deliberate attempt to manufacture evidence of insanity. He concluded, however, that even if William sincerely believed in his satanic relations 'it would be no proof of diseased mind.' He observed quite rightly that the belief in the Devil's pact was not uncommon and was perpetuated by the various literary accounts of the infamous Dr Faustus. Consequently he believed that such belief was no mitigation for Dove's actions and thought he 'richly deserved to feel the weight of retributive justice.'[41]

The legend surrounding the early sixteenth-century German magician -astrologer Dr Faust had circulated around England in cheap, simple publications called chapbooks since the late sixteenth century. The story tells how Faust writes a pact with the Devil in his own blood, offering up his soul in return for having all his desires fulfilled for the next twenty-four years. The Devil is as good as his word but on the expiry of the bloody contract he brutally kills Faust. Chapbook accounts of the story, such as *The life and horrible adventures of the celebrated Dr Faustus*, continued to be published in considerable numbers during the first half of the nineteenth-century, and it is likely that it was one of these slim popular volumes that fired up William's youthful imagination rather than the literary interpretations of the story by Christopher Marlow or Goethe.[42] What is certain is that neither the popular nor literary versions of the legend would have been allowed in the Dove household, which no doubt would have heightened its illicit fascination for mischievous boys.[43]

Caleb Williams also believed that Harrison's influence over Dove was 'greater than can be explained by reference to mere credulity and superstition.' According to Williams, 'it must be evident to every impartial and unprejudiced mind' that a man who relied so much upon Harrison's supernatural powers 'did not possess a mind of power sufficient to enable him to judge rightly, or to act correctly.'[44] There was little sympathy in the press or among other alienists for this psychoanalytic diagnosis of magical belief; as Bucknill observed, 'if belief in witchcraft is a proof of insanity, half the population in our rural districts are indubitably insane.'[45] The *Association Medical Journal* agreed that those who held to the notion that 'superstitious' beliefs were indicative of mental illness were obviously ignorant of the large sums paid annually to fortune-tellers and the huge sales of popular divinatory manuals such as *Napoleon's Book of Fate*.[46] An editorial in the *Leeds Intelligencer* furthered the point: 'We cannot allow that his consultations with Harrison afford a proof of insanity, or of anything so nearly approaching to it as to acquit him from the responsibility of crime; for, in that case, every one who consults a "wise man" should be placed in safe keeping, and the result be a most enormous increase of our lunatic asylums.'[47]

Yet within the conceptual framework of mental disease at the time the link between belief in the supernatural and insanity could not be so easily dismissed. Numerous people had, in part, been diagnosed as insane on the basis of expressing such fears. In the Devon Lunatic Asylum run by Bucknill there were inmates such as the woman suffering from 'acute mania', resulting from 'want and distress' brought on by the birth of an illegitimate child, who believed she was tormented by witches, and another who was convinced she was bewitched after the death of a son and the seduction of a daughter.[48] Similar cases could be found among the inmates of the West Riding Asylum at Wakefield during the mid-nineteenth century. Among them were the woman who believed she had power over the 'spirits of the air', and the 48-year-old weaver who said strange visions haunted him at night and that the diabolic smell of brimstone clung to him during the day.[49] Henry Sutherland's study of one hundred women admitted to the asylum between 1860 and 1873 revealed quite a few who had similar 'delusions'. One woman accused herself of being in constant communication with Satan, and another saw devils in the shape of dogs sitting on her bed, which was perhaps less disturbing than the woman who believed her stomach was full of devils that devoured all the food she swallowed, and the inmate who was convinced that spirits lived in her mouth and controlled her speech. There was a woman who claimed she was bewitched and would never get better as a consequence, another who saw the ghost of her dead mother at her bedside. One woman felt her eyes were being drawn to the back of her head by some supernatural force, and that her brain was being sucked out through her ears.[50] Such people were not, of course, incarcerated only for expressing such beliefs. All the asylum inmates mentioned above had other symptoms of mental illness. The weaver, for example, had received a terrible blow to the head prior to being haunted by spirits. The majority also suffered from depression and had suicidal tendencies. Then again, so did William.

## Methodists and madness

'Why such a man was not sent to a lunatic asylum, alas! We cannot say. His father, however, was dead before the insanity came to its worst development.' So thought the Wesleyan Methodist paper *The Watchman*.[51] The Wesleyan community rallied around the reassuring view that William was congenitally insane. The notion of moral insanity and the way in which religion was constructed as one of its categories was understandably uncomfortable for Methodists. That a man brought up in the most devout of religious households, educated in Wesleyan schools and a professed Wesleyan throughout his adult life, could have turned into a calculating murderer was just too unsettling. As the editor of the *Wesleyan Times*, who was evidently personally acquainted with the Doves, commented, the Dove household was 'the last in which one would have looked to find a future murderer'.[52] The cause of his actions must have been the result of insanity beyond the influence of familial and spiritual love.

As we have seen, a number of Wesleyans, including William's brother-in-law and former teachers, were key witnesses for the defence. One retired Wesleyan minister who turned up at York wanting to add his own voice to the chorus was the Rev. John M'Lean, an old friend of the Doves who had taught William at Wesley College. In a letter to George Morley, written shortly after the inquest on Harriet, he expressed the view that 'there was an unmistakeable mixture of the madman and the idiot in him then ... how any respectable female could have ventured to marry him unless greatly improved, I am unable to imagine.' As to his 'aimless, thriftless, vulgar wickedness', M'Lean suspected 'he learned from some wicked companion, or from some servant of his father, just as idiots readily do.'[53] In other words, William's bad behaviour was inspired by his contact with the working classes. M'Lean's testimony would have bolstered John Jenkins's view that his brother-in-law was a congenital idiot, but would have somewhat contradicted the defence argument that William was morally insane. But there was another good reason why

M'Lean's offer was declined. He had, in the previous couple of years, developed what was politely called 'an aberration of intellect', which meant he had to be placed under restraint in an asylum. It would hardly help the defence to have a 'madman' testifying to the insanity of an 'idiot'.

An issue that was not raised by the defence or discussed in the press, for obvious reasons, was the role religion might have played in William's behaviour. Back in the eighteenth century, Methodist 'enthusiasm' had been denounced in some quarters for provoking insanity. The Anglican clergyman and physician William Pargeter (1760–1810) was not alone in railing at what he saw as the pernicious influence the Methodists had on the minds of the poor and ignorant. Their preaching led, he believed, to a rise in madness in whichever parish they 'infested'.[54] 'The doctrines of the Methodists,' he asserted, 'have a greater tendency than those of any other sect, to produce the most deplorable effects on the human understanding.'[55] William Hogarth portrayed a similar view in his famous engraving *Credulity, Superstition and Fanaticism*, which depicts a scene in a Methodist meeting-place as a preacher rants to his congregation; nearby a thermometer rises out of a 'Methodist's brain', with the mercury rising from 'suicide' to 'madness'. During the early nineteenth century foreign psychiatrists further reinforced the perception that evangelical Protestants were particularly prone to insanity. In 1818 William Hallaran, physician at the Cork Lunatic Asylum, observed that although there were ten times as many Catholic inmates as Protestant ones in his asylum, the only cases of mental derangement induced by religious excitement were among Dissenting Protestants.[56] Several decades later a survey of insanity in Demark by Jens Rasmussen Hubertz found that out of every 1000 of the population 9.16 Calvinists were insane or 'idiots', compared to 5.85 Jews and 3.34 Catholics.[57] In France, where psychiatry was strongly anti-clerical, the psychiatrist Jean-Pierre Falret asserted that religious fanaticism was 'the most powerful cause of suicide' and, echoing Pargeter, explained away England's perceived high suicide rate by reference to the rise of Methodism.[58]

Early British alienists were in general agreement that religious enthusiasm could induce moral insanity. Prichard thought that 'a severe, impassioned, and almost imprecatory style of preaching,' which enforced 'the terrors rather than setting forth the hopes and consolations which belong to the Christian religion,' was responsible for some cases of insanity. William Charles Wood was likewise in no doubt that 'vehement preaching' could, in certain individuals, 'give rise to attacks of madness'.[59] William Dawson's preaching, with his vivid descriptions of the torments of hell, springs to mind in this context. But in contrast with and in response to the anticlerical views of the French alienists, the British took exception to the idea that evangelical religion was a major cause of insanity or that Methodism was particularly provocative. There was undoubtedly a religious motivation behind James Cowles Prichard's rebuttal of the emphasis some psychiatrists put on religion. He was, after all, a Unitarian and his parents were Quakers. 'There is no subject connected with the history of insanity,' he remarked, 'on which more crude and ignorant notions are expressed than on what is often termed religious madness.' As to the role of Methodism: 'That none of the preachers of this sect have been deserving of such a censure, I shall not venture to affirm; but in the present time at least, it cannot justly be laid either generally or exclusively to their charge.' He could not, however, resist partially contradicting himself by scoring confessional points, suggesting that Catholicism was 'more favourable to the manifestation of insanity' and that its missionaries were particularly good at sowing madness.[60]

Nevertheless, the evidence from English asylums painted a rather different picture. Many of the patients in the West Riding Asylum were 'troubled with doubt on religious matters'. In 1872, for example, a 30-year-old woman was admitted who raved incoherently on religious subjects. She feared her soul was lost and that 'God would take no more notice of her'. The year before, a 52-year-old-woman was admitted with religious delusions, worrying night and day that she would not reach heaven. Another woman in her sixties was depressed because she had stopped attending a place of worship and as a consequence her soul would be lost.[61] Some had prophetic convictions, such as the woman who believed that a second great flood would shortly destroy the world, and another who prophesied that many sudden deaths would shortly occur in her village.[62] Henry Sutherland concluded that the symptoms of insanity shown by women in his sample were exacerbated by 'extreme religious views'.[63] The link between religion and insanity was a chicken and egg question, and by the mid-Victorian period it would seem that increasingly medical men concurred with Beverley Morris, a physician at the York Medical Dispensary, who suggested, 'Might not many of these cases have been found to have arisen subsequently to the commencement of insanity, and so be a consequence rather than a cause.'[64] In general, though, English psychiatrists seemed rather reluctant to consider the issue in depth.

## The press have their say

A few papers were sympathetic regarding the insanity defence. *The Morning Star*, for instance, concluded that Dove was a 'miserable imbecile', and asked, 'if he is not insane, was ever anybody insane!'[65] The avowed anti-hanging paper the *Morning Advertiser* reached a similar conclusion.[66] Most of the press, however, was stridently anti-alienist. *The Saturday Review* called Caleb Williams's views 'a vile, dastardly, emasculate theory'. It further launched a snobbish attack on the jury, who it suggested 'had but the vaguest notion of the meaning of their own language. "Defective" and "intellect" are just the kind of words which have a charm for shop-keepers, farmers and other half-educated persons.' Such vagueness of thought, it worried, was 'creeping over a large part of our population.'[67] Few papers, though, were as vitriolic as the Liberal *Liverpool Mercury*, which held the rather unusual position of being sympathetic to phrenology but antipathetic to psychiatry: 'We want words to express our indignation and disgust at the scientific coxcombry which thus palters with moral laws and outrages the moral sense of mankind.' Considering the ambiguous decision of the jury, it rather bizarrely thanked them for having made 'a stand against the attempt of these necessarian doctors to poison public morality, paralyse public justice, and destroy the social safe-guards of life.'[68]

The concept being advocated by some psychiatrists, that certain types of criminal behaviour was symptomatic of insanity, was considered outrageous, a negation of the concepts of free will and of the personal responsibility that underpinned civilised society.

The hostile press pushed their counter-arguments using the well-worn technique of extrapolation, distorting the views of those being criticised by extending them to their 'natural conclusion'. Thus *The Times*, referring to the symptoms proffered as indications of Dove's insanity, commented that 'acts of brutality and wanton mischief, an incorrigible

temper, perverseness, maudlin fits in the intervals of drunkenness, superstition, and stupidity might, if necessary, be proved of half the ruffians
who cut the throats and break the ribs of their wives in Whitechapel.'[69]
Yet Caleb Williams, who was the focus of much of the press opprobrium,
never said that such types of behaviour were a general indicator of
mental illness and consequently mitigating circumstances for anti-social
behaviour. What he was suggesting was that they *could* be in *certain* individuals when considered in conjunction with other symptoms as part of
an analysis of 'the peculiar condition and circumstances of the
accused.'[70] As Williams emphasised under cross-examination in court,
he could not determine whether a murderer or rapist was vicious or
insane 'without knowing the history of the individual.'[71]

It is no surprise that press opinions on the insanity plea were not
necessarily based on a balanced and impartial consideration of the evidence. The political and religious views of proprietors and readers also
shaped editorial attitudes, as is evident from the position taken by the
three main Leeds newspapers.[72] The *Leeds Mercury*, edited and owned
by the Congregationalist Edward Baines, was the principal paper of
Dissenting persuasion in the West Riding, and there was no doubt a personal angle to the *Mercury*'s sympathetic position regarding William. The
paper had been run for several decades by his father, Edward Baines, a
Methodist and Whig politician.[73] He and his son would undoubtedly
have been acquainted with the Doves, and both Christopher and his
brother had voted for Baines during his stint as a Member of Parliament
between 1834 and 1841.[74] It is not surprising, then, that the paper followed the Wesleyan position and believed William

> never, from the day of his birth, possessed the ordinary average powers
> of understanding, – that his mind is essentially weak and distorted, –
> and that his, consequently, is not a fit case for capital punishment. We
> are as firmly convinced that the intellect of William Dove is defective, as
> of any fact which has ever come within the sphere of our knowledge.[75]

The rival Liberal paper for the town was the *Leeds Times*, owned by
Frederick Hobson. It had Radical sympathies and unlike the *Leeds
Mercury* was an enthusiastic supporter of social and political reform
beneficial to the working classes. It had no religious affiliations, and some
of its readership was overtly hostile to Methodism. One letter-writer

suggested, for example, that the *Leeds Mercury* and its Methodist audience only defended the insanity plea to save face rather than out of true conviction. 'The truth is, Dove belongs to parents of strong religious principles, and by his being hung great scandal is brought on his numerous friends and the religious body to whom he and his parents belong.'[76] The paper's editor had no time at all for the 'mad-doctors', commenting that 'The public prints are deluged with contributions attempting to prove – but only to the satisfaction of the writers – the insanity of Dove.'[77] One reader wrote in to express his agreement, and in a remark offensive to the poverty-stricken dwellers of central Leeds suggested, 'if "defective intellect" is an extenuation of murder, it would scarcely be safe to walk down Briggate at noon-day.'[78] As to the jury at Dove's trial, the paper roundly condemned their verdict: 'what then but the most illogical reasoning, or the most culpable weakness, could induce them to declare their verdict and retract it in the same breath.'[79]

Being one of the leading Tory newspapers in Yorkshire and a staunch defender of the Church of England, it is hardly surprising that the *Leeds Intelligencer* opposed the *Mercury*'s stance, thereby finding itself in rare agreement with the *Leeds Times*. It joined the 'moral' majority in denouncing psychiatrists who 'indulged in theories which were utterly inconsistent with sound reasoning and criminal jurisprudence.'[80] The paper's views were well encapsulated in a letter it reprinted on the Dove trial by the Rev. George Trevor, a rather controversial high church Anglican Canon of York.[81] Trevor denounced the concept of 'moral madness' as 'either a fraud or a delusion'. Indeed, medical men were the 'least trustworthy on the subject', he believed, for they attached 'an exaggerated value to their own profession.' The true experts in moral diseases were to be found among 'our divines, our moralists, our statesmen, and our gaolers, rather than our doctors. The keeper of a house of correction would be a far better witness to such questions than the keeper of a madhouse.'[82]

## Drink

William Dove's explanation for his crime centred on his belief in Harrison's prediction that his wife would die soon and that his circumstances would subsequently improve. William, it would seem, saw his actions as merely hastening predestined events. As we have seen, most commentators pooh-poohed the idea that William's beliefs in this respect were symptomatic of insanity, but they also generally rejected the idea that he was a criminal genius using 'superstition' as a legal blind in case he was caught; but how else to explain his gullibility regarding Harrison? The *Leeds Intelligencer* tentatively suggested that alcohol was the answer: 'Whenever the "wizard" comes upon the stage we have "drink" produced, and the natural inference is that resort was had to Harrison only when Dove was labouring under the direct or consequent influence of liquor.'[83] The *Association Medical Journal* came to a similar conclusion that William's eccentricities were attributable to *delirium tremens*, and had 'no doubt whatever that his belief in devils and evil spirits only existed whilst in the same deplorable condition.'[84] This was in fact what Henry Harrison had suggested at the assizes. 'From my medical knowledge,' he told the court, 'I know that persons affected with *delirium tremens* always hear noises and see strange sights.'[85]

Drink played a prominent role in manslaughter and murder cases and was widely seen at the time as inextricably linked with crime generally. Although drunkenness was considered a self-willed action and therefore legally no excuse for criminal behaviour, it had, nevertheless, long been quite a successful mitigating plea in homicide trials, with murder charges being reduced to manslaughter and even lighter sentences if there was no evidence of premeditation. By the 1850s, however, juries and judges were becoming increasingly unsympathetic to the argument that violent crimes committed while intoxicated were lesser offences than those committed when sober.[86] William's drunkenness was brought up by several witnesses, and highlighted by Bliss, but the defence made no attempt to claim it as a mitigating circumstance. William had not bludgeoned Harriet to death with a blunt instrument in a drunken rage, but inflicted a premeditated and protracted murder with a silent and insidious weapon. We may see little distinction in terms of culpability between the two types of murder, but juries today do not have to send people to the gallows.

The link William's defence tentatively tried to make was that between his drinking and his alleged madness. Caleb Williams had testified that the 'effect of drink on a lunatic is to make him violent and dangerous. Persons liable to insanity would exhibit a tendency and inclination to drink.'[87] Bliss presumably had in mind the trial a few months earlier of the wife murderer Thomas Corrigan where the defence suggested that he committed the crime while in a delusional state brought on by excessive drinking. This was a distinct plea from that of drunkenness for it implied that *delirium tremens* was not merely an intoxicated condition but one of temporary insanity. Although the jury rejected this plea in Corrigan's case the Home Office later accepted it on the presentation of further medical evidence. It was only towards the end of the century, though, that the DTs became more widely accepted in medical jurisprudence.[88] In William's case drink was also problematic for the defence lawyers in that they wanted to emphasise his moral insanity by citing his eccentric behaviour as symptomatic, yet the jury might consider that same behaviour to be merely the extrovert actions of a drunkard, thus undermining the insanity plea. As a result defence witnesses who mentioned his drinking were also at pains, presumably under instruction, to make clear that he was sober during certain episodes of strange behaviour. John Thompson, the Aberford schoolmaster, for instance, testified to one time finding William lying face down in the White Well farm track that led to the turnpike road, his hands covering his face. Thompson called out to him and asked what the matter was, but Dove made no reply. His eyes were red from weeping. Thompson said he did not think he was drunk at the time. William Tomlinson a labourer at White Well recalled that while out working in the fields one day he was approached by William carrying his shirt and stockings in his hands and told him he was going to leave. When his wife and sister came looking for him he asked Tomlinson to cover him in hay so that they could not find him. Tomlinson thought William was sober at the time.

## Hindsight

Retrospective diagnosis of the mental condition of a person who lived over 150 years ago, and whose behaviour can only be pieced together from fragmentary historical sources, can only be a speculative affair. Yet modern psychiatric research can help us to understand better the unusual actions and ideas of those in the past, whether it be criminals or artists. With regard to William Dove it can also help us contextualise the psychological theories of the time regarding his behaviour, and qualify the hostility directed towards those alienists who linked his crime with insanity. To begin with, though, from a modern perspective we need to discard the term 'moral insanity', if not some of its conceptual aspects. Developments in neuroscience and psychiatry have made such crude and broad categories as 'insanity', 'madness' and 'idiocy' redundant. But they have also fallen out of medical usage due to the negative social connotations they have accrued.

Some mental illnesses can be fairly confidently identified from the historical sources. The persecution complex and hearing of voices symptomatic of schizophrenia, for example, would seem to apply to Daniel McNaughtan. Some of those in the West Riding Asylum, who believed they were persecuted by witches or received communications from supernatural entities, were also likely to be sufferers.[89] William, I would suggest, suffered from the related and less easily identifiable condition of bipolar disorder, or manic depression as it is more popularly known.[90] It is estimated that today between 1 and 1.5 per cent of the population suffer from this condition, and until recently it quite often went undiagnosed even though it had first been clinically recognised and categorised as 'manic-depressive insanity' by Emil Kraepelin at the end of the nineteenth century. The main diagnostic feature of bipolar disorder is the bouts of elated or irritable moods that generally last for a week or more. In these phases sufferers have a decreased need for sleep and are easily distracted. They are excitable and have grandiose schemes and ideas, which are expressed in rapid and desultory speech. Depressive phases engender feelings of apathy, despair and suicidal tendencies. Research suggests that alcohol abuse may exacerbate the development and worsen these symptoms. The disorder usually strikes in the early twenties though some research suggests that earlier onset may be related to other childhood behavioural disorders. Numerous studies confirm that untreated sufferers of bipolar disorder are slightly more likely than the general population to commit homicides and violent crime, particularly those with no apparent motive. Considering the sensitivity of the subject I should stress the words 'untreated' and 'slightly' here.

William's behaviour in adult life fits well with the pattern of bipolar behaviour outlined above: the severe and unpredictable mood swings between tearful despair and thoughts of suicide to hyperactive bursts of energy, eccentricity and violent threats; the bouts of boastful behaviour and exaggeration of his financial worth and prospects; the moments of conversation when he would leap from subject to subject, talking excitedly and sometimes incoherently about his various adventures and ideas. Furthermore, his excessive drinking may have triggered or heightened episodes of the disorder. So maybe Caleb Williams, Winslow and other alienists were right to identify Dove as a sufferer of abnormal mental episodes, though only to a certain extent. Williams tried to shoehorn too many of Dove's behavioural characteristics into his case for insanity. Dove's wayward boyhood behaviour need not be symptomatic of the development of his mental illness in adulthood, but instead be the result of what is now called attention deficit disorder. His belief in the Devil and magic, which exhibited no symptoms of hallucination, paranoia or obsession, can certainly be attributed to his religious and cultural development rather than mental illness. There is also nothing substantive in Dove's life history, as we know it, to suggest, as Winslow and others did, that he suffered from a congenital mental disability.

Even if William suffered from bipolar disorder or some other clinically recognised form of mental illness, it is not axiomatic that his crime was a consequence of his illness. Despite the huge advances in our medical knowledge, juries today face the same dilemma as the jury at William's trial 150 years ago, though they do not have to make life and death decisions any more. The Homicide Act of 1957 may have shifted the emphasis in murder trials from proving 'insanity' to the related Scottish legal plea of 'diminished responsibility', but this hardly made the task of decision making any easier for juries. The McNaughtan Rules continued to apply. How to determine whether defendants knew what they were doing was morally and legally wrong? Greater popular awareness of the nature of mental illness, and the ability of expert witnesses to provide biomedical explanations as well as psychological interpretations, has certainly given juries a more concrete foundation for their decisions. A study of diminished responsibility pleas between 1997 and 2001 shows that, in cases where schizophrenia and other psychotic disorders were clearly proven, the plea of diminished responsibility was nearly always successful. The Law Commission expressed its surprise, however, at the 'relatively high' percentage of depression cases where the plea was also accepted.[91] One wonders if the evidence at William's trial was presented to a modern jury whether they would not also find him of 'diminished responsibility'.

# Notes and references

1  *The Nonconformist*, 23 July 1856.

2  *News of the World*, 27 July 1856.

3  *The Times*, 7 January 1856.

4  *Leeds Intelligencer*, 16 August 1856.

5  *The Times*, 21 July 1856.

6  See J.S. Cockburn, 'Patterns of violence in English society: homicide in Kent 1560–1985', *Past and Present*, 130 (1991) pp. 70–106; James Sharpe, 'The history of violence in England: some observations', *Past and Present*, 108 (1985) pp. 206–15; Lawrence Stone, 'Interpersonal violence in English society, 1300–1980', *Past and Present*, 101 (1983) pp. 22–33; Stone, 'The history of violence in England: a rejoinder', *Past and Present*, 108 (1985) pp. 216–24.

7  Martin J. Wiener, *Men of Blood: Violence, Manliness and Criminal Justice in Victorian England* (Cambridge, 2004).

8  *Leeds Times*, 15 March 1856; *The Sun*, 21 July 1856.

9  *Leeds Intelligencer*, 16 August 1856; *News of the World*, 27 July 1856.

10  *The Times*, 21 July 1856.

11  A. James Hammerton, *Cruelty and Companionship: Conflict in Nineteenth-Century Married Life* (London and New York, 1992), p. 107.

12  Hammerton, *Cruelty and Companionship*, p. 61. On notions of manliness and male honour at this period see, for example, John Tosh, *A Man's Place: Masculinity and the Middle-Class Home in Victorian England* (New Haven and London, 1999).

13  Carolyn A. Conley, *The Unwritten Law: Criminal Justice in Victorian Kent* (Oxford, 1991), pp. 74, 75.

14  On Prichard and his ideas see H.F. Augstein, 'J.C. Prichard's Concept of Moral Insanity – A Medical Theory of the Corruption of Human Nature', *Medical History*, 40 (1996), pp. 311–43; Augstein, *James Cowles Prichard's anthropology: remaking the science of man in early nineteenth-century Britain* (London, 1998). On moral insanity and criminality see Roger Smith, *Trial by Medicine: Insanity and Responsibility in Victorian Trials* (Edinburgh, 1981), pp. 38–40; Joel Peter Eigen, *Witnessing Insanity: Madness and Mad-Doctors in the English Court* (New Haven and London, 1995), pp. 76–81.

15  James Cowles Prichard, *A Treatise on Insanity, and other disorders affecting the mind* (London, 1835), pp. 23–4.

16 Lecture reported in the *Leeds Mercury*, 9 August 1856.

17 Caleb Williams, *Observations*.

18 This view was expressed in a letter to Joseph Barret, printed in several newspapers. See, for example, *Leeds Intelligencer*, 9 August 1856.

19 Winslow described himself as a 'psychological physician' as distinct from an alienist. See Michael Shepherd, 'Psychiatric journals and the evolution of psychological medicine', in W.F. Bynum, Stephen Lock and Roy Porter (eds), *Medical Journals and Medical Knowledge* (London, 1992), pp. 191–4; *New DNB*. In 1856 the title of the *Asylum Journal* was changed to the *Journal of Mental Science*.

20 Williams, *Observations*, p. 6.

21 J.C. Bucknill, 'Plea of Insanity – The Trial of William Dove', *Journal of Mental Science*, 3 (1857), p. 132.

22 Bucknill, 'Plea of Insanity', p. 132–3.

23 *The Times*, 30 August 1856.

24 See Richard Moran, *Knowing Right from Wrong: The Insanity Defense of Daniel McNaughtan* (New York, 1981); Smith, *Trial by Medicine*; Joel Peter Eigen, *Unconscious Crime: Mental Absence and Criminal Responsibility in Victorian London* (Baltimore, 2003).

25 See, for example, Eigen, *Unconscious Crime*, pp. 7–9.

26 *Association Medical Journal*, July 26 1856, pp. 629, 630.

27 Roger Cooter, *The cultural meaning of popular science: Phrenology and the organization of consent in nineteenth-century Britain* (Cambridge, 1984), pp. 31, 32, 43.

28 See Cooter, *The cultural meaning of popular science*; John van Wyhe, *Phrenology and the Origins of Victorian Scientific Naturalism* (Aldershot, 2004). See also Wyhe's excellent website: http://pages.britishlibrary.net/phrenology.

29 For a list of their numerous publications see Roger Cooter, *Phrenology in the British Isles: An Annotated, Historical Bibliography and Index* (Metuchen and London, 1989), pp. 61–81.

30 For an account of his early years see Frederick Bridges, *Phreno-Physiometrical Characteristics of James Spollin, who was tried for the Murder of Mr. George S. Little* (London, 1858), pp. 9–22.

31 Cooter, *Cultural meaning of popular science*, pp. 150, 274, 350 n57.

32 *Manchester Guardian*, 1 March 1851; *The Times*, 25 June 1851.

33 'Professor Bridges' Manipulation of Viscount Palmerston', *Journal of Health and Phrenological Magazine*, 7 (April 1858), pp. 58–9.

**34** *Liverpool Mercury*, 25 July 1856.

**35** Frederick Bridges, *Phrenology Made Practical and Popularly Explained* (4th edn, London, n.d.), p. 55.

**36** Bridges, *Phrenology*, p. 56.

**37** *Leeds Intelligencer*, 16 August 1856.

**38** *Leeds Mercury*, 19 July 1856.

**39** *The Times*, 21 July 1856.

**40** *Leeds Mercury*, 22 July 1856.

**41** Bucknill, 'Plea of Insanity – The Trial of William Dove', 130, 133.

**42** See also the numerous editions of *The Remarkable Life of Dr Faustus* and *The History of Dr Faustus*.

**43** On youthful male fascination with the Devil's pact in the eighteenth century see Soili-Maria Olli, 'The Devil's pact: a male strategy', in Owen Davies and Willem de Blécourt (eds), *Beyond the witch trials: Witchcraft and magic in Enlightenment Europe* (Manchester, 2004), pp. 100–16.

**44** Williams, *Observations*, pp. 18–19. For later legal attempts to link witchcraft and insanity see Davies, *Witchcraft, magic and culture*, pp. 39–44.

**45** Bucknill, 'Plea of Insanity', pp. 133, 134.

**46** *Association Medical Journal*, 16 August 1856, p. 707.

**47** *Leeds Intelligencer*, 16 August 1856.

**48** John Charles Bucknill and Daniel H. Tuke, *A Manual of Psychological Medicine* (London, 1858), pp. 529, 545.

**49** Henry Sutherland, 'Menstrual Irregularities and Insanity', *West Riding Lunatic Asylum Medical Reports*, 2 (1872) p. 67; J. Crichton Browne, 'Cranial Injuries and Mental Diseases', *West Riding Lunatic Asylum Medical Reports*, 2 (1872) p. 134.

**50** Henry Sutherland, 'The Change of Life, and Insanity', *West Riding Lunatic Asylum Medical Reports*, 3 (1873), pp. 299–314.

**51** *The Watchman and Wesleyan Advertiser*, 24 July 1856.

**52** *Wesleyan Times*, 4 August 1856.

**53** Letter printed in *Leeds Intelligencer*, 26 July 1856.

**54** See Jonathan Andrews and Andrew Scull, *Undertaker of the Mind: John Monro and Mad-Doctoring in Eighteenth-Century England* (Berkeley, 2001), pp. 89–93, 301–2; Allan Ingram (ed.), *Patterns of Madness in the Eighteenth Century: A Reader* (Liverpool, 1998), pp. 179–86.

**55** Cited in Ingram (ed.), *Patterns*, p. 182.

56 William Saunders Hallaran, *Practical Observations on Insanity*, 2nd edition (Cork, 1818), p. 32; also cited in Prichard, *Treatise on Insanity*, p. 192.

57 J.R. Hubertz, 'The State of Mental Diseases in Denmark', *Journal of Psychological Medicine*, (1853) p. 441; cited in W. Charles Wood, *Statistics of Insanity; Being a Decennial Report of Bethlehem Hospital from 1846 to 1855 Inclusive* (London, 1856), p. 34.

58 Jean-Pierre Falret, *De l'hypochondrie et du suicide* (Paris, 1822), pp. 77, 104. On early French psychiatry and religion more generally see, for example, Roy Porter, 'Witchcraft and magic in Enlightenment, Romantic and Liberal Thought', in Marijke Gijswijt-Hofstra, Brian Levack and Roy Porter, *Witchcraft and Magic in Europe: The Eighteenth and Nineteenth Centuries* (London, 1999), pp. 266–73; P. Vandermeersch, 'The victory of psychiatry over demonology: The origin of the nineteenth-century myth', *History of Psychiatry*, 2 (1991), pp. 351–63.

59 Prichard, *Treatise on Insanity*, p. 188; Wood, *Statistics of Insanity*, p. 34.

60 Prichard, *Treatise on Insanity*, pp. 187, 188, 198.

61 E. Maziere, 'The Use of Opium in the Treatment of Melancholia', *West Riding Lunatic Asylum Medical Reports*, 2 (1872), pp. 268, 273; Henry Sutherland, 'Arachnoid Cysts', *West Riding Lunatic Asylum Medical Reports*, 1 (1871), p. 223.

62 Charles Henry Mayhew, 'Acute Delirious Melancholia', *West Riding Lunatic Asylum Medical Reports*, 1 (1871), p. 257; Sutherland, 'Change of Life, and Insanity', p. 310.

63 Sutherland, 'Change of Life, and Insanity', p. 310.

64 Beverley R. Morris, *A Theory as to the Proximate Causes of Insanity* (London, 1844), p. 17.

65 Reprinted in *Leeds Intelligencer*, 26 July 1856.

66 *Morning Advertiser*, 7 August 1856. See also letters written to the paper by 'A Physician', 29 July and 7 August 1856.

67 *Saturday Review*, 26 July 1856.

68 *Liverpool Mercury*, 23 July 1856.

69 *The Times*, 21 July 1856.

70 Williams, *Observations*, p. 26.

71 *Leeds Mercury*, 19 July 1856.

72 The following provides a useful guide to the political and religious sympathies of newspapers at the time: Charles Mitchell (ed.), *The Newspaper Press Directory* (London, 1856).

**73** See Edward Baines, *The Life of Edward Baines* (London, 1851).

**74** *Poll Book of the Leeds Borough Election, 1834* (Leeds, 1834); *Poll Book of the Leeds Borough Election, July, 1837* (Leeds, 1837), p. 17. They also voted for the Conservative Beckett political dynasty.

**75** *Leeds Mercury*, 9 August 1856.

**76** *Leeds Times*, 9 August 1856.

**77** *Leeds Times*, 9 August 1856.

**78** *Leeds Times*, 9 August 1856. Briggate was and is the main high street in Leeds.

**79** *Leeds Times*, 26 July 1856.

**80** *Leeds Intelligencer*, 26 July 1856.

**81** See the *New DNB*.

**82** *Leeds Intelligencer*, 9 August 1856.

**83** *Leeds Intelligencer*, 16 August 1856.

**84** *Association Medical Journal*, 26 July 1856, p. 630.

**85** *Leeds Mercury*, 19 July 1856.

**86** See Wiener, *Men of Blood*, pp. 256–70; Martin Wiener, 'Judges v. Jurors'.

**87** *The Times*, 21 July 1856.

**88** Wiener, *Men of Blood*, pp. 272–7; Smith, *Trial by Medicine*, pp. 85–7.

**89** For two likely cases of schizophrenic witch belief see Davies, *A People Bewitched*, p. 54; Davies, *Cunning-Folk*, p. 112.

**90** There is a large literature on the subject. See, for example, Juan José López-Ibor, Hagop S. Akiskal, Mario Maj (eds), *Bipolar Disorder* (New York, 2002); Andreas Marneros and Jules Angst (eds), *Bipolar Disorders: 100 Years after Manic-Depressive Insanity* (Dordrecht, 2000); Nurun N. Shah, Patricia M. Averill and Andrew Shack, 'Mixed versus manic bipolar disorder: A comparison of demographic, symptomatic, and treatment differences', *Psychiatric Quarterly*, 75, 2 (2004), pp. 183–96; Susan C. Sonne and Kathleen T. Brady, 'Bipolar Disorder and alcoholism', *Alcohol Research and Health*, 26, 2 (2002), pp. 103–8. On the link with crime and violence see, for example, Theodore Feldmann, 'Bipolar Disorder and Violence', *Psychiatric Quarterly*, 72, 2 (2001), pp. 119–29; Ellen Hochstedler Steury and Michelle Choinski, '"Normal" Crimes and Mental Disorder: A Two-Group Comparison of Deadly and Dangerous Felonies', *International Journal of Law and Psychiatry*, 18, 2 (1995), pp. 183–207; E. Fuller Torrey, *Out of the Shadows: Confronting America's Mental Illness Crisis* (New York, 1996); Sheilagh Hodgkins, 'The major mental disorders and crime: Stop debating and start treating and preventing', *International Journal of Law and Psychiatry*, 24 (2001), pp. 427–46.

91 *Partial Defences to Murder: Provisional Conclusions on Consultation Paper No. 173* (Law Commission, May 2004), p. 15.

* * * * * * * * * * * * * *

# CHAPTER 6

# Fate

*'. . . if you are determined to go to hell, you shall wade through seas of tears, and over mountains of prayers.'*

## The appeals

'We are asked every day, and almost every hour of the day, "Is this man to be executed?"' commented one York newspaper correspondent. The answer to the question depended on the outcome of a concerted campaign to save William's life. 'The whole of Methodist influence will most probably be put forth,' the *Wesleyan Times* correctly predicted.[1] On Saturday 2 August, Joseph Morton Barret headed a deputation to the Home Office consisting of the Rev. Theophilus Woolmer, who a year later would become governor of the renowned Methodist Kingswood School, and William's trustees George Reinhardt and John Brigg, only to find that George Grey was away in Jersey yachting with Sir Charles Wood. Barret arranged instead to meet with the Under Secretary William Massey on the Monday. On that day Barret laid out all the arguments and new evidence in support of the commutation of William's sentence on the grounds of insanity, and handed over a file of letters, memorials and testimonies confirming William's defective intellect. Among them was a memorial signed by twenty-one Wesleyan acquaintances and friends of William's parents. One of the signatories was Peter M'Owan, and among the others were respected ministers such as Charles Prest, Edward Walker and Robert

Newstead. A memorial on behalf of the people of York contained a modest 800 to 1000 signatures.[2] Massey promised to pass on the dossier and to relay the salient points of Barret's defence to Grey.

Massey also agreed to send several petitions to Buckingham Palace. One of these was from the foreman of the jury at William's trial, Mr Hewett, and ten of his fellow jurors. The remaining juror promised to sign if all the others did but there was insufficient time to get his signature. The petition concluded by praying that 'your Most Gracious Majesty will be pleased to spare the life of the said William Dove.' Another was signed by nineteen dignitaries from Leeds and Bradford including Edward Baines proprietor of the *Leeds Mercury*, George Pyemont Smith, Samuel Smith, the senior surgeon at Leeds Infirmary, the Hebblethwaite brothers, wine merchants, the four-time Leeds mayor John Hope Shaw, and the Clerk of the Peace for Leeds Borough James Richardson. The most moving petition, though, was that written by Mary Dove:

> *Your petitioner begs to state that although the development of his defective intellect in many of his eccentricities was not personally known to herself, because of her son's frequent absence from home, yet many of them were practised under her own eye, and others of an equally conclusive character, which have no record in public print. Permit then the afflicted mother of William Dove to entreat your Majesty to cause the recommendation of the jury to be carried out, and the life of her son to be spared. Your Majesty will easily understand that a mother, so circumstanced, can say but few words.*
>
> *Your petitioner humbly requests that it may please your Majesty to spare the prisoner's life. And your Majesty's humble petitioner, as in affection and duty bound, will ever pray.*
>
> *Mary Dove.[3]*

The next day Barret succeeded in gaining a private audience with Grey and went over the case once more. This was something of a minor victory in itself as Grey had a general policy of not giving interviews to petitioners for royal mercy.[4] The Home Secretary promised to write to him the next morning with his decision. When Barret opened it, he most likely knew the gist of its content already:

> *Sir. – I am directed by Secretary Sir George Grey to acknowledge the receipt of your letter of the 2nd instant, and accompanying papers*

*relative to the case of William Dove, now under sentence of death for
murder, and I am to state to you in reply that, after a careful
consideration of all the facts of the case, Sir George Grey regrets that he
cannot feel it consistent with his duty to recommend a commutation of
the sentence on the ground that the prisoner was not fully conscious of,
and responsible for, the crime of which he has been convicted.*

    *I am Sir,*

      *Your obedient servant,*

        *W. Massey.*

Barret quickly telegraphed Noble the terrible news so that William could
be informed as soon as possible. But his supporters found one last glim-
mer of hope. That evening George Grey was to pass through York on his
way north. When the train stopped at York further petitions were made
to him but he said he had already made his decision and had no time for
further presentations.

## Last days

Up until 1836 it was determined by law that murderers be hanged within
forty-eight hours of their conviction. Since then, it was customary at York
that those sentenced to death at the assizes would not be executed until
two Sundays after the presiding judges had left the city. So William's hanging was set for Saturday 9 August, the usual day of the week for executions
in York so as to ensure a good crowd. There was considerable excitement
during the lengthy build up to the hanging. There had not been an
execution in the city for over three years, and so every aspect of the forthcoming event was followed with great interest. The hanging rope, made by
a local rope-maker, was exhibited at a public house on the Thursday night
before the scheduled execution and attracted a large number of sensation-
seekers who got their cheap thrills from touching it. The plain coffin that
awaited Dove's corpse was made by Mr Taylor, a joiner of Davygate, York.
There was so much interest in his work that crowds descended on his
shop to see its construction. When it was taken to the castle, between nine
and ten in the evening before the day of the execution, a large number of
people gathered along the route to see it pass. Crowds also gathered in St
George's Field to gawp at the place where the scaffold was to be erected.

As the practical preparations for the execution continued, William spent his last days in the cramped confines of the condemned cell in York Castle. John Swallow, a Leeds printer who had been shown the cell a few years before, described it well in his diary as

> *a gloomy apartment for day, being furnished with an iron chair and a stone table. The window is very small and well barred with three thicknesses of iron, which prevents the room being sufficiently lighted for ordinary purposes. A sleeping room adjoins it, in which are two beds, one for the culprit and the other for the Turnkey. Each bed stands on one large stone, another stone is placed in the wall at the head of each bed, and another on the side, thereby rendering it impossible to escape through the walls. The condemned cell appears to be one of the most uncomfortable places one could imagine.*[5]

At least in the last few days William was allowed to have meals provided from the city, sent in by friends and relatives instead of the slop provided by the prison cooks.

Word got out about some of William's eccentric behaviour. On one occasion he had an emotional and tearful meeting with two ministers but as soon as they left the cell he turned to someone else and asked, 'Have you ever had any bottled beetroot?' Another time, on seeing some workmen pass by his cell with some boards, he asked, 'Is that deal? I suppose they'll let me have a bit of deal for my coffin.'[6] Just as William had gossiped about Palmer, so now the public gossiped about him. The press lapped up all they could, whether ill-informed or not. On 2 August, for example, the *Leeds Intelligencer* began an editorial by stating 'We fear that very little real change has taken place in the heart of the wretched criminal.' only to end it with the revision that 'Since writing the above we have received information which somewhat modifies the rumours that have been afloat with respect to the impossibility of making any impression on the unhappy criminal.'

As he whiled away the hours, William, like most condemned men and women, received a stream of visitors to his cell. There were those, such as the Rev. Punshon of Leeds and Mr Morfitt, a York city missionary, who were there fulfilling their task of administering to William's soul, urging him to confess and show penitence. It was these people that *The Times*, in a cruel anti-abolitionist tirade, referred to as the 'crowds of pious people dawdling and twaddling, and snuffling and slobbering' at the condemned cell door.[7] The Rev. William Lord, George Reinhardt and John Brigg also came to have a last consoling word with him. There were three men, however, who were the most frequent and closest of his visitors during his final days. One was Joseph Barret. Another was the Wesleyan minister John Hartley (1819–96), a native of Leeds and long-time friend of William's parents. At the time he was engaged on the York circuit, and in a gesture of goodwill the prison chaplain, the Rev. Sutton, agreed to let his Wesleyan counterpart assume responsibility for providing William with spiritual succour. The other man, who visited him no less than twelve times and became a profound comfort to William in his last days, was the widely admired but now largely forgotten prison philanthropist Thomas Wright.[8]

Born in 1789, and raised in Manchester by humble parents, Wright worked nearly all his life in a local iron foundry, eventually rising to become a foreman. He was a Wesleyan Methodist like his mother, and devoted most of what little spare time he had to helping rehabilitate criminals. He found work for hundreds of people released from prison or returned from penal colonies, and raised funds to pay for over a thousand former convicts to emigrate and start a new life. In December 1847 he began to visit the condemned cells of northern England, and was careful not to present himself as a representative of a religious denomination. In 1852 a subscription was got up in Manchester to raise money to enable Wright to quit his job at the iron foundry and devote all his attention to prison work: £3,248 was donated including a sum from the government, which provided Wright and his large family with a sufficient annual income for the rest of his life. His ability to get through to the condemned is evident from the fact that he was the first missionary to get Palmer on his knees praying, whereas as he was impervious to the exhortations of the prison chaplain.[9]

On the morning of Thursday 7 August, around nine o'clock, Barret arrived from London to give William the news in person that the petitions had failed; there was to be no reprieve and the execution would go ahead at the appointed time. There was no sense of shock or despair. The following letter, written to a fellow prisoner named Edward a few days after his conviction, shows that, once he had given up on being rescued by the wizard or the Devil, William had prepared himself for execution:

*Perhaps you may think that the sentence of death has frightened me,
but, thank God, it has taught me that this life is fleeting, and has caused
me to think of another world, and I rejoice to say that I am prepared
either for life or death. If I had to have my choice I should prefer death,
if it was not for the disgrace that it will be to my family and my dear
mother. Thank God I am happy. I think with pleasure that to-day two
weeks, at half-past twelve o'clock at noon, I shall be in heaven. I shall
be in company with my father, brothers, sisters, and my dear wife, and
my prayer is that you may meet me there.*[10]

William asked Barret to visit him alone that afternoon as he wished to
make a statement. He then attended morning service in the prison chapel
where he heard an appropriate sermon on the heinousness of sin and the
mercy of God towards the repentant sinner delivered to the prisoners by
the Rev. George Steward. William appeared to be profoundly affected by
the clergyman's words and on several occasions wept bitterly, his face in
his hands. Then, around noon, William's mother, his sisters Mary and
Sarah, and his brother-in-law the Rev. John Jenkins visited. It was to be
the last time they would ever see him.

On entering the cell his mother threw her arms around his neck and
sobbed deeply, while his sisters knelt at his feet and cried. Jenkins prayed
as they wept. No words were exchanged until several minutes after his
prayer ended. William's mother then threw herself at his feet and begged
that if he was guilty he would confess and spend his remaining hours of
life making peace with God. William made no such confession there and
then but fell to his knees and prayed for forgiveness with uplifted hands.
His family joined him in further prayer. Then, after several minutes of
silent grief, all four members of the family embraced William and left. In
the intense emotional atmosphere of this final meeting William forgot to
ask the forgiveness of his mother and sisters, and so a messenger was sent
to request his mother to return, but her carriage had already left the castle
grounds.

That afternoon Barret returned to the condemned cell as requested.
His services as an attorney were no longer officially required, but he felt
compassion towards William and resolved to help him in any way he
could in his final hours. William first asked Barret to visit his mother to
ask her to send him word that she forgave him. Then he requested him to

write down and disseminate a full confession of his guilt. As well as himself he implicated two men in his crime: 'Palmer's case first called my attention to strychnia,' he said, 'but I never should have thought of using that or any other poison for the purpose of taking my poor wife's life but for Harrison.' William confessed that the first time he gave strychnine to his wife was on Saturday 23 February, the day when his sister brought the jelly to their home in Cardigan Place. While no one was looking he had put something like an eighth of a grain in the jelly. His wife and servant had tasted it and found it bitter. William also had a couple of spoons but never swallowed it. Seeing that such a small quantity had no effect, that evening while he was at his mother's, having picked up his wife's medicine from Morley's, he took the cork out of one of the bottles and touched the wet end of it with the packet of strychnine he had brought with him. He then put the cork back in the bottle and shook it up. On his way home he threw the remaining strychnine away. 'I cannot tell you the feelings of my mind when I put the strychnia into the jelly and into the mixture,' he remembered. 'I cannot describe them. I did not think at the moment when I put it in as to its effects or consequences.' Yet he pursued his homicidal plan. On a visit to Morley's surgery he stole ten grains of strychnine while no one was looking, and hid them in a paper which he kept in the stable. Over the next few days he dabbed the wet end of the cork of Harriet's medicine bottle in the strychnine, causing Harriet to have a series of excruciating attacks, as already described. Regarding the fatal dose he gave her in a wine glass of medicine on the Saturday night she died, William said, 'it flashed across my mind that I had given her the strychnia, and that she would die from its effects. I was muddled before this, and didn't know what I was doing. When the thoughts of her death crossed my mind, I immediately regretted what I had done, and I believe if Mr Morley had come in at that moment I should have told him what I had given her.' On finding her dead later that night, he recalled, 'I felt my situation immediately after seeing my poor wife's corpse, and I then feared a *post mortem* examination taking place within 24 hours after death, as I understood that Professor Taylor had stated that strychnia could not be detected after that number of hours had expired.' William ended his confession by stating: 'I have only to add that the verdict of the jury was just and correct, and that I freely forgive every person who has been concerned against me, as I hope to be forgiven.'

The next morning William handed to Thomas Wright the following letter:

*Respected Sir, – My time is short – my days are numbered, and soon I shall have to appear before the judgement seat of Christ; but I trust my Judge is my advocate and friend, and that I shall meet his smiles, and be welcomed to mansions in the sky. I can truly say –*
*'I the chief of sinners am,*
*But Jesus died for me.'*
*Oh the consolation derived from this passage. I am saved through fire and by death. Ordinary means God had need, but they failed. He has, therefore, used extraordinary means, and blessed be His holy name. I believe it is in answer to the prayers of my dear mother, and that I shall have reason to bless and praise him through all eternity, that he checked me in my mad career, and adopted this plan to save me.*
*Oh! my dear Sir, accept the thanks of a dying man for the kindness I have experienced at your hands. May that God, who is your Father and my Father, bless you both in this life and that which is to come, and may we meet in heaven, is the prayer of*
*Respected Sir, yours affectionately,*
*William Dove.*

Wright later wrote of William that he 'never met with a more sincere penitent under similar painful circumstances.'[11]

During the day William received several more visitors. The High Sheriff of the County, H.S. Thompson, came to ask William if he had any last requests. William had only one – that no cast was made of his head. He did not want to become a freak show attraction, which had happened to Palmer, a model of whom was then on display in Madame Tussaud's. The Sheriff agreed and William thanked him. Noble had also promised William's family that none of his clothes would leave the castle to ensure that they were not exhibited in one of the local pubs. William later spoke further to Noble of his crime and expressed his abhorrence at what he had done. When Barret visited between five and six he brought with him a letter from his mother and one of his sisters, in which they expressed their tender affection for him and forgave his sins. William in turn handed Barret a letter which expressed his profound thanks for all that he had done for him, and concluded with the statement:

*I would wish to remark that I committed the crime through the instigation of that bad man Henry Harrison, of the South Market, Leeds. Had it not have been for him I never should have been in these circumstances.*

   *I remain, respected Sir,*
      *Yours respectfully,*
         *William Dove.*

## Final hours

Around one o'clock in the morning William lay upon his bed and slept for an hour and a half. On waking he joined Hartley in fervid prayers for an hour or so. At four o'clock Hartley withdrew to rest a little, Wright took his place and the praying continued, William conducting himself in an appropriately solemn and penitent spirit. The omniscient warning of a friend uttered when in his youth played on his mind: 'William, if you are determined to go to hell, you shall wade through seas of tears, and over mountains of prayers.' He wrote these words down in a piece of paper, as though it would make a fitting epitaph.

   The day dawned overcast and heavy clouds threatened rain as workmen began erecting the scaffold in the governor's garden, which faced Tower Street and St George's Fields. The scaffold had not been used for three years and so the day before the dismantled beams and joints had been inspected to ensure they were fit for their purpose. It was not unknown for scaffolds to break during a hanging, much to the embarrassment of the authorities and the agony of the hanged. The workmen went about their task as quietly as possible, but townsfolk on their way to work could hardly ignore what they were doing. By the time the scaffold was finished a crowd of around one hundred had gathered, mostly local boys and young men, though some hardy individuals from Leeds, who had walked all night to witness the hanging, lay exhausted on the floor against some iron railings. Around nine o'clock a light rain began to fall.

   Meanwhile, at ten minutes to six, just before the grave-digger began his solemn task, William was taken from the condemned cell, across the castle yard to the Waiting Female Witnesses' room located near the execution ground, the windows of which looked out upon the scaffold. Escorted by Noble and Wright, he walked with a firm step and calm demeanour. He was dressed in a second-best black suit, the clothes he wore during the trial having been taken away by friends. Once in the room he began praying once more and then at half past seven he ate his last meal, a simple breakfast of cocoa or coffee and cake. He appeared rather cheerful, and whiled away the next few hours reading and writing letters. One was on matters unconnected with his crime, which he handed over to Barret to use at his discretion. Another was to his prison friend Edward, and its contents help us to understand William's calm demeanour on that last morning: 'Dear Edward, I, as a dying man, beseech you to meet me in heaven. I am going there. I have not the least doubt in the case. "Prepare to meet thy God." I am firmly convinced that if I had not yielded and struggled as I did do last night, that I should have been lost, lost, lost for ever.'[12]

As the first heavily-loaded trains of the morning began to arrive from Leeds, Sheffield, Bradford, Hull and other towns in the region, the crowds in front of the gallows began to swell. People from surrounding villages arrived on horseback, in carriages and on foot. A group of employees from Farnley's Iron Works near Pudsey organised a workers' outing and borrowed one of the company wagons to get to York. By half past eleven the area was packed but there was none of the hurly-burly fair-ground atmosphere, petty crime and drunkenness that characterised some public executions. Indeed, the *Leeds Mercury* went so far as to say 'that a more orderly assemblage we never saw at an execution.'[13] It was just as well: twelve years before at least twelve people had been trampled to death during a hanging at Nottingham.[14] Meanwhile, back in Leeds special prayer meetings were beginning at Oxford Place Chapel and Brunswick Chapel, attended by many of the town's leading Wesleyans. William's mother and the rest of his family were not present; they had left for another part of the country to avoid public attention.

At twenty minutes to twelve the under-sheriff, W. Gray, arrived at the castle to make the customary demand for the condemned man to be brought out for execution. At seven minutes to twelve William was led into the adjoining press room where he was introduced to the hangman who proceeded to pinion his arms. As he did so, Barret held William's hand and asked him if there was anything in the statement he had made on Thursday that he wished to change. 'Not a word; it is strictly true,' he replied. A couple of minutes later he was ready to meet his death, but before making his final steps to the scaffold he turned to Barret and said, 'Tell my poor mother I die happy.'

At the head of the solemn procession were two ceremonial javelin men, then William and Mr Wright, and behind them the Rev. Hartley, Gray, Noble, George Reinhardt and Mr Pashley, a castle officer. As they passed through the grand jury room and then along a dreary passage leading to the scaffold, Hartley read portions of the burial service of the Church of England, followed by an extemporaneous prayer in which William joined in. At one minute to twelve William stepped out on to the hanging platform. Throughout the morning he had remained remarkably calm and composed, and while the rain poured down he maintained his dignified demeanour as a hushed crowd, estimated at between ten and twenty thousand people, stared expectantly up at him. William shook hands with Hartley, Noble, Wright, Reinhardt and Pashley, and as the castle clock tolled twelve the hangman stepped forward and began to prepare him for the drop. He placed the white cap over William's head, adjusted the rope around his neck, and tied his legs together. William remained in an attitude of prayer with his hands clasped. The hangman then stepped to one side and withdrew the bolt. William's body fell. There was a heavy thud, and in the first few seconds he jerked wildly, his fingers extended to their utmost and his legs convulsively drew up to his chest. After a minute or so the body relaxed, his legs dropped and his hands resumed their clasped position.

His corpse was left hanging in the rain for another hour and then cut down. When the executioner's cap was removed William's final expression remained unusually composed in contrast with the usual contorted features of the hanged. His body was laid out in a coffin in a room adjacent to the gallows where it was waited upon by Gray, Barret, Reinhardt, the gaol medical officers, and Noble and his son who had been a schoolfellow of William's. There was one other man present who William had never met while alive – Frederick Bridges. Having followed the Dove case to its conclusion in the newspapers, Bridges had written to Gray requesting to be allowed to take a cast of William's head after death, and was informed that it was indeed permitted to take casts of those executed at York. Bridges had consequently arrived in York on the Wednesday and had his equipment sent to the castle in preparation. He was greatly disappointed to be told on Friday evening that the High

Sheriff, following William's wishes, had decided to deny him access. Likewise on the Saturday morning Charles Tilney, a Leeds surveyor, was turned away when he applied to take a cast. Bridges was more persistent than Tilney and managed to negotiate at least to take measurements for his phrenological analysis. So while Barret, Reinhardt and the others looked on, Bridges got to work with his tape measures, callipers and gutta percha, and thereby constructed an accurate sketch of Dove's head. Once Bridges had finished, the hanging rope was placed in the coffin to ensure that it was not taken away, cut into pieces and sold as mementoes, and then the coffin lid was finally nailed down.

At three o'clock William was buried in the murderer's plot below the window of the condemned cell. As with his wife, there was nothing to mark his last resting place. For a while after, though, a bust of his head was displayed along with those of other sensational murderers, including William Palmer, at Bridges' Phrenological Institute in Mount Pleasant. Fading posters pasted on walls in York were a lasting reminder of his trial and execution:

> *Cursed was the crimes of Palmer,*
> *That has brought me to the tree.*
> *Had Dove not read the deeds of Palmer,*
> *For murder he'd not hanged be –*
> *Into my mind had never entered*
> *Such cruel, base and deadly strife;*
> *It was the deeds of William Palmer,*
> *Tempted me to slay my wife.*
> *The wretched hangman stands before me,*
> *Death summons me in youth & bloom,*
> *Trembling on York's fatal scaffold;*
> *I am hurried to the tomb.*
> *For William Dove there is no mercy,*
> *There is nothing can save me –*
> *Driven from this world of sorrow,*
> *To a sad untimely grave.*[15]

# Who hanged Dove?

Prior to the execution of William the last person hanged at York was Henry Dobson, a 24-year-old cabinet-maker from Wakefield, who brutally murdered a young woman he lived with named Catherine Sheardon.[16] He was despatched on 9 April in front of a crowd of around 5000 by the well-known figure of Nathaniel Howard. Although highly experienced, having officiated since 1840, he carried out Dobson's execution in an embarrassingly bungled fashion, with Dobson struggling on the end of the rope for several minutes. The castle authorities knew that Howard was old, infirm and unfit to carry out the job and had apparently appointed a new executioner, but the night before Dobson was to hang the appointee was persuaded by his friends not to take on the post.[17] Howard was drafted in at the last minute, which might explain why he did such a bad job. He was swiftly dismissed after Dobson's execution and died not long after on 22 April 1853, aged seventy-three.[18]

If the famous Newgate executioner William Calcraft had been available he would most likely have been employed to hang William, but he was busy at Lewes, Sussex, executing the murderer Murdock before a crowd of some 1500–2000 people of the 'usual class'.[19] Calcraft was a celebrity in Victorian England, executing his office from 1829 to 1874.[20] He was a shoemaker by trade but the occupation of hangman proved more profitable, earning him around £50 a year towards the end of his career. He received a guinea for each Newgate execution and was allowed to perform his duties elsewhere in the country for around £10 a time. It was perhaps for the best that Calcraft was unable to hang William, as despite his long career he was not renowned for his skill, and a number of his victims experienced a minute or two of agony before dying. Part of the reason for this was due to his inclination for a short drop, which meant that the force of gravity was not always sufficient. The use of short ropes was, in fact, the norm at the time, partly because it reduced the risk of the rope getting entangled with the victim during the drop, partly to ensure the rope did not snap or the scaffold break under the pressure. The short drop also prevented the even more unseemly spectacle of the head being pulled apart from the body, an instance of which happened when long drops became standard later in the century. Such an obscene spectacle was, by then, hidden from public view.[21] Yet the short drop could produce scenes of equal horror, as was graphically emphasised by Calcraft's bungling of the execution of William Bousfield at Newgate on 31 March 1856. As soon as Calcraft drew the bolt he hurriedly left the scaffold and entered back into the prison, unaware that Bousfield had survived the drop and had managed to pull himself up and hook his legs on to the side of the scaffold. A turnkey pushed him off, but three more times Bousfield managed to regain his foothold on the scaffold. Finally the prison chaplain demanded that Calcraft return and finish the job, which he did by grabbing hold of the suspended Bousfield and using his weight to eventually finish the process of strangulation. The Sheriffs of London and Middlesex had to write a report on the shameful affair, in which the excuse was offered in mitigation that Calcraft had been unnerved by threatening letters.[22]

As the above experience indicates, the post of executioner was not one that enjoyed huge public compassion. Bungled hangings led to crowds of thousands booing and jeering. Threats were also occasionally made against them by the friends or sympathisers of the condemned. When travelling on duty they were sometimes denied lodgings. The Scottish hangman John Murdoch, who also conducted hangings in Carlisle and Newcastle, avoided this problem by staying in prisons while on business.[23] Why do the job then? There always seemed to be at least a handful of people ready to take on the post whenever Calcraft was unable to oblige or when a provincial hangman retired. When, in 1851, the newspapers reported that Calcraft was unable to execute Maria Clarke at Ipswich, and that the governor may have to perform the duty, the county gaol received ten applications for the post. One asked to be paid £20 for the job.[24] The financial incentive was presumably a prime motive. It was certainly the case initially for Calcraft. His shoemaking business was doing badly and he was making a few extra shillings selling pies round the Newgate scaffold to feed his family before he applied for the post.[25] However, other hangmen at the time often did not receive as much as Calcraft. When John Murdoch retired in 1851 at the age of eighty-four, he was in an impecunious state and had to be supplied with a monthly dole by the Corporation of Glasgow.[26] The early nineteenth-century York hangman William Curry spent his last years in the workhouse.[27]

The lure of public notoriety was also undoubtedly attractive to some. Calcraft, although described as a mild-mannered, unassuming man, clearly enjoyed the public attention despite the occasional death threat.

He dressed rather theatrically and played to the audience. A report on his inspection of the scaffold prior to one execution observed: 'His entrée was hailed with a kind of familiar but suppressed hum of recognition from those in front of the gallows, which was returned by a slight bow and a smile of strange and sinister character.'[28] George Smith, the man who hanged William Palmer at Stafford, exploited his notoriety and participated in a macabre public entertainment got up at the Wilmslow Races in September 1856. The event, organised by a pub landlord named John Fletcher, consisted of the mock hanging of an effigy of Palmer on a purpose-built scaffold. A company of 'trained officials' went through the ceremony of hanging Palmer twice each morning of the races. Admission was one shilling sixpence.[29]

The York hangmen had an even more obvious incentive than money and fame, as by tradition they were usually drawn from among the inmates of the prison and given the prospect of a pardon.[30] The notorious William Curry, executioner from 1802 to 1835, was a recidivist sheep-rustler who had his death sentence commuted in 1793 and spent seven years in prison hulks on the Thames. On his release he returned to Yorkshire where in 1801 he was once again sentenced to death for sheep stealing. His sentence was once again commuted and he took on the post of hangman while serving out the rest of his prison sentence.[31] Curry's successor, a man named Coates, was also a convict, though Nat Howard apparently was not. To maintain tradition, however, he wore prison dress at his first execution.[32]

So, with Howard long gone and Calcraft busy, the York prison authorities had to advertise for a hangman and there was no shortage of applicants. The orthography of the following letter from one caused some amusement in the press:

> To the High Sheriff York Castle. York City.
> Dear Sir Seeing in The Paper you advertise for a Hangman i Will Engage With you. My age is 22 years Height 5ft 8 inches Weight 13 st 6lbs Agent to the Ensurance Company London It is From several Friends in Leeds That i Hang the Convict Laying at York Castle Mr Dove answer will oblidge.

Further mirth was caused by another applicant, a convict, who explained that he was applying for the post because he 'wanted to earn an honest living.'[33]

When the name of William's executioner was revealed by several Yorkshire newspapers after the hanging, it appeared that the castle authorities had kept with tradition. The man identified was Thomas Askren, a former flour dealer, farmer, butcher, cattle jobber and assistant overseer of the poor of Maltby, currently languishing in York debtors' prison. Described as a man 'without money and without friends', hanging was the only means he could think of to pay off his debts.[34] He received £5 for the execution of William as well as a customary gratuity of half a sovereign each from W. Gray and Joseph Barret.[35] Yet Askren indignantly denied he was the hangman and penned letters to several Yorkshire newspapers threatening libel suits if they did not publicly retract their assertions. To the *Leeds Mercury* he complained: 'My impression has always been, that great pains were taken by newspaper editors to get accurate information from trustworthy sources; but that impression is altogether obliterated, and I shall look on the press in future with a suspicious eye, knowing that journalists are easily imposed upon.'[36] He concluded by referring the press to Mr Noble to quash the rumour. Noble kept quiet on the issue, however, not wanting to generate further publicity regarding William's execution. The policy backfired as the debate intensified. A letter was sent to the *Manchester Daily Examiner and Times*, purportedly from Mr Pears, the York Castle schoolmaster, asserting that Askren was not the hangman.[37] Pears, however, denied being its author. Something fishy was going on and the smell seemed to be coming from Askren's direction.

Askren's aggressive public denials caused quite a rumpus in the debtors' prison. He broke a stick over the shoulders of one fellow debtor who pointed him out as the hangman. A couple of inmates responded by writing to the press. James Finlinson confirmed to the *Leeds Mercury* that Askren was the executioner. 'It is not from any animosity to the man that I trouble you with this letter,' he wrote, 'but from a sense of duty to myself and brother debtors.' There was a postscript: 'I may add that from half-past ten to a quarter-past twelve, on the 9th instant, Askren was nowhere to be found; we suspected him, and one of our number saw him draw the bolt.' Another debtor, William Jackson, who was one of the sources who had unmasked Askren in the first place, asserted that Askren had been identified 'by the declarations of the officials of York Castle, and by several other parties who witnessed the execution, and who have seen the hang-man.'[38] He finished his letter by asking, 'I trust that, in justice to myself and other debtors, you will give publicity to the above, and not forget, at the same time, that there is nothing too mean for a man to do or say, who will lend himself to be a hangman.'[39] It was because of this negative view of the position that Askren evidently wished to dissociate himself from the rumours, but posterity reveals that he was as big a liar as he was a debtor. A couple of decades later an anonymous pamphleteer recalled that Askren became 'a man shunned and despised, and often liable to insults and desperate encounters in public company.'[40] Then again he was hardly popular before he became a hangman.

## Why did William hang?

William was one of thirty-one people convicted of murder that year. He was, however, one of only sixteen who hanged for the crime.[41] Why him? Why was he not among the fifteen who escaped the ultimate punishment? First of all he was unfortunate in having been tried in Baron Bramwell's court. Bramwell subsequently proved to be a scornful sceptic of psychiatric evidence and a tough hanging judge, and it was with good reason that the pro-hanging *Times* had welcomed his appointment to the Bench.[42] The Secretary of State, George Grey, was likewise a staunch defender of execution who remained untouched by the many petitions he received, considering them to be unrepresentative of public feeling. He complained of their 'stereotyped' nature and dismissed them as largely the work of a small group of tiresome abolitionists.[43] So for all the effort made on behalf of William and others there is little evidence that petitions and memorials had much impact. There were few stronger representations made than those for the sparing of John Murdock. They included memorials from the jury, who recommended mercy on the grounds that they did not believe Murdock had intended to kill the gaoler. A group of Sussex magistrates were unusually motivated to petition the Home Secretary, and a memorial from the people of Lewes included between 150 and 160 'influential persons', including six clergymen.[44] They were all to no avail and Murdock swung two days before William.

It certainly appears that 1856 was a defining year in which press influence on government law and order policies became embarrassingly evident.[45] As well as the strychnine scare and newspaper outrage over successful insanity pleas, there were two other major press-generated panics that year. The first concerned the 'ticket-of-leave' system, which gave a licensed remission for good behaviour to transported convicts and those who served their period of transportation in British gaols. The system had been formalised in the Penal Servitude Act of 1853 and the press had initially welcomed the idea. In 1856, however, the perceived wave of crime sweeping the country was being blamed on hordes of marauding ticket-of-leave men, and the government was heavily criticised for what was now seen as a reckless penal policy. A year later newspaper pressure led to a tightening up of the system.[46] It was ticket-of-leave men who were thought to be largely responsible for a supposed wave of garrottings or muggings in 1856. Towards the end of the year the press panic was pressuring judges into handing down harsher sentences than usual for such crimes, and when the panic was revived by the press in 1862 it forced the government into passing hasty legislation.[47]

In response to the press, and by his own inclination, the Home Secretary was little inclined towards showing mercy. He gave reprieves only on the strong advocacy of judges or at the request of the queen. Victoria occasionally exercised her royal prerogative, most notably in the spring of 1856, when she apparently ordered the reprieve of two young female murderers.[48] One was Celestina Somner, of Islington, wife of a German engraver, convicted of slitting the throat of her ten-year-old daughter Celestina Christmas.[49] The other was Elizabeth Anne Harris, of Uxbridge, who had drowned two of her illegitimate children, aged five and two and a half, in a canal.[50] Neither denied her crimes. Harris's commutation was apparently a matter of compassion, the many petitions to the queen having provided a very sad account of her poverty-stricken life. She had been abandoned by the fathers of her children and shortly before committing murder she and her children had been inmates in Uxbridge workhouse. Somner by contrast came from a respectable background though, once again, she was ill-treated by her husband. Her commutation was effected by the granting of a certificate of insanity by the Home Secretary, even though the same grounds for mitigation had been dismissed by the assize jury.[51]

As the above examples suggest, the reasons for commutation usually rested on two factors: gender and insanity. Regarding the former, the reprieves of Somner and Harris generated considerable debate about the morality of the public execution of women. 'To the popular question, "whom shall we hang?" there is a disposition in many quarters to answer, "No more women",' wrote one letter writer.[52] It was suggested by some that, in Somner's case, her good looks may have helped swing the issue. This is certainly a possibility. It was clearly distressing to male aesthetic sensitivities to see a pretty face hanging contorted on the gallows, and the perceived likelihood of young women screaming in their final minutes was an upsetting prospect. In his long career Calcraft only once seemed to express compassion for his victims, and that was after the hanging, at Bristol in April 1849, of the attractive nineteen-year-old servant Sarah Harriet Thomas, who killed her cruel and abusive mistress with a stone.[53] 'I never felt so much compunction as I did yesterday,' he confessed. 'She was, in my opinion, one of the prettiest and most intellectual girls I have met with in any society.'[54] One correspondent to the papers in 1856 had no time for such wishy-washy sentiments. There had to be complete gender equality when it came to the death penalty: 'If we may not hang a pretty woman, why execute a handsome man?'[55]

The press began to talk of precedents being set. After Somner's and Harris's reprieve surely no women could be executed? But they could. Elizabeth Martha Brown's capital conviction came too soon after the commutation of Somner's and Harris's sentences to save her life. She had been condemned at the Dorchester assize in August for murdering her husband. He was an unfaithful and abusive man who, when she confronted him about his adultery when he was in an inebriated state, beat her repeatedly with a whalebone whip. In response she took a hatchet and hacked him to death. Thomas Hardy was a witness at her execution and the sight profoundly affected him. Her story was partly the inspiration for *Tess of the D'Urbervilles*.[56] A petition was got up on Brown's behalf by abolitionists, one of whom toured round the local villages collecting signatures, but George Grey was not to be swayed again.

With all the talk of women no longer being hanged, Brown's execution appears as a cold, deliberate reaffirmation of the law to ensure no precedent was created. S.C. Malan, the vicar of Broadwindsor, who knew Brown and felt no pity for her, commended the Home Secretary for 'wisely' taking the opportunity to show that the case of Somner 'was no precedent to follow.'[57] What Brown's execution succeeded in highlighting, though, was the unreasonable, arbitrary application of capital punishment. There was no substantive reason why Brown should die when Somners and Harris did not. A correspondent to *The Times* questioned, 'Did our Home Secretary think the murder of a husband during a violent quarrel a crime of a deeper hue than the murder of a daughter in the most calm and deliberate manner? If we are to have capital punishments, let there be no partiality.'[58] A century and half ago *The Sun* was a vaguely respectable broadsheet but, in trying to understand Somner's reprieve and Brown's hanging, its anti-German rhetoric was just as evident as in its modern tabloid incarnation. It complained that, for the Home Office, having a German husband seemed 'sufficient to protect any woman from the penal consequences of their crimes.' It was symptomatic of the 'extraordinary favouritism displayed towards Germans in high quarters.'[59]

If Martha Brown was unfortunate to have committed murder not long after the reprieve of Somner, so William was unfortunate to have poisoned Harriet soon after the reprieves of Thomas Corrigan and Charles Westron. We see a similar pattern of Home Office decision making in the rejection. In late December 1855 Corrigan, an alcoholic, aged twenty-nine, stabbed his wife Louisa to death while in a drunken rage. Following his conviction eleven jurors signed a petition for mercy on his behalf, just as they did for William. Members of his wife's family also sent a memorial. A petition with 2340 signatures, gathered with the help of Corrigan's lodge of the Ancient Order of Foresters, was presented to the Home Secretary by the Member of Parliament T. Milner Gibson.[60] The substance of the petitions was that Corrigan's act was committed during a bout of insanity brought on by *delirium tremens*. The argument did not seem to move George Grey. Corrigan resigned himself to death, but while workmen were busy putting barriers in place around the scaffold in late February, a last-minute reprieve was granted. On the recommendation of Justice Wightman, who evidently was more open than some of his colleagues to medical witnesses,[61] Grey ordered his sentence be commuted to transportation for life. Corrigan later became a Christian missionary preaching against the evils of drink.[62] A couple of weeks after Corrigan killed his wife, Charles Westron, the twenty-five-year-old son of a Somerset distiller shot dead his solicitor George Waugh in Bedford Row, London, over a dispute about money.[63] Although quite wealthy, Westron did not have an easy upbringing. He was born with a deformed spine, his father committed suicide in 1852, and there were symptoms of mental illness. The jury took some heed of the medical evidence, giving their verdict as guilty of wilful murder, but as a foretaste of William's case they recommended him 'to mercy because in his case we find there were strong predispositions to insanity'. Wightman was once again the presiding judge and in light of the jury's decision abstained from passing sentence of death. He once again consulted with Grey, and Westron's sentence was commuted to confinement in Bethlem asylum.

In both instances the newspapers reacted to the decisions of Grey and Wightman with a mix of bafflement and outrage. *The Times* found the suddenness of Grey's *volte-face* regarding Corrigan quite extraordinary, particularly as there was no doubt as to his guilt. The *Daily News* openly criticised Wightman for not taking the opportunity of repressing at once the notion that a mere 'predisposition to insanity' ought to 'excuse from punishment'. For the *News of the World*, the outcome of the Westron trial was 'the climax of this folly of the age'.[64] With Corrigan and Westron in mind, *The Sun* warned darkly that 'Dove's acquittal on the score of insanity might cause the murders of many innocent persons, and the necessity of similar trials in other parts of the country.'[65] The Home Office had been warned.

## The execution debate

As the above discussion indicates, William's execution happened at a time when fundamental changes were afoot in the English penal system, particularly with regard to the issue of execution. The abolitionist movement, motivated by both social and religious considerations, had been active for several decades, though it was split into two main camps: those against public hanging and those who wanted to abolish capital punishment altogether. During the 1840s the call for an end to hanging had received support from such high-profile figures as Charles Dickens and the philosopher John Stuart Mill, though by the mid-1850s they had reversed their position somewhat, becoming low-profile advocates for private execution.[66] In 1856, however, the debate over the hanging of women, the reprieves of Corrigan and Westron, along with the huge media interest in the trial of William Palmer, reinvigorated both wings of the abolitionist campaign. On 9 May the Bishop of Oxford rose in the House of Lords to call for the appointment of a select committee to examine the current practice of capital punishment, and so the Lords' Committee on Capital Punishment came into being and commenced work on 27 May, hearing testimonies from numerous witnesses from the police force, judiciary, clergy and politics. It would seem the majority were in favour of private hanging, and the weight of such witnesses persuaded the Committee, in its report on 7 July, to call for an end to public execution, suggesting that it did not have any apparent deterrent effect on criminals, and may indeed glorify their reputations. It recommended that hangings be carried out within prison walls and that a black flag be hoisted to inform the public that an execution had just occurred. [67]

Following on so soon from the Palmer trial and the House of Lords Committee, Dove's execution induced a further bout of soul-searching among the middle classes. Referring to the petitions that had been made on William's behalf, an anonymous correspondent to the *Leeds Mercury* opined, 'if such exertions are to be made on so slender a pretext, to save the life of a man who has notoriously been a bad son, a bad husband, and a bad subject, is it not time that the punishment of death should be abolished!'[68] The Liberal *York Herald* published an abolitionist editorial observing that 'experience has shown that the practice has a certain tendency to harden the hearts of that class of people, for whose moral instruction it is said to be intended.'[69] Caleb Williams hoped, 'It is surely not too much to indulge a confident hope that long ere the close of the present century the hanging of lunatics and the burning of witches shall be alike matters of history.'[70]

The Wesleyan Methodists, in particular, were forced to state more publicly their position regarding the Christian morality of execution. The clergy of the Church of England had been engaged in high-profile debates espousing both sides of the argument. The Quakers had been at the forefront of the abolition campaign, and the Unitarians and other Nonconformist groups were also sympathetic. In Response to the Dove trial one of their main newspapers, *The Nonconformist*, stated categorically that 'punishment of death ought to be abolished'.[71] In contrast the various Methodist denominations had remained remarkably quiet on the issue, even though they had long been zealous in carrying out missionary work among the condemned.[72] The execution of one of their own, however, could not pass without some comment. A significant group of Wesleyans had, as we have seen, rallied on behalf of William's reprieve, but the Methodist press adopted a questioning but ultimately pro-hanging position. They concentrated on the issues of insanity and the doubtful morality of public execution. 'Does justice vindicate itself by the strangulation of persons of "defective intellect"?' asked the Wesleyan paper *The Watchman*. In its view, public execution served no deterrent or moral function 'upon the crowd who might assemble round the scaf-fold, no salutary impression could be produced by the last convulsive agonies of a man who was known to have been all his life to some extent insane.'[73] Indeed, the *Leeds Mercury* worried that William's execution would 'furnish to the opponents of the punishment of death a most powerful illustration of one of their stock arguments – the danger of hanging a man who is not morally responsible for his actions.'[74] The views of Thomas Wright can be taken as representative of the Methodist position at the time. Although he believed that William's execution was 'decidedly wrong' on the grounds of defective intellect, he was no aboli-tionist.[75] While he had an 'intense horror and disgust' of public execu-tions and the behaviour of the scaffold crowd, believing they had 'a most injurious effect upon the minds of the young', he nevertheless considered execution a just and moral punishment. He supported private executions under certain conditions. 'Let all the prisoners witness the execution,' he suggested. 'This, I think, might be attended with beneficial results.'[76]

As to what should replace execution as the ultimate deterrent, Dove's trial provoked some ideas. For one Leeds letter writer, who signed him-self or herself 'MERCY', the solution was transportation.[77] The problem was that by 1856 opportunities for sending convicts to the colonies had reduced significantly. Transportation to Tasmania had stopped three years before, and moves were afoot to end the use of Western Australia as a penal colony.[78] In the light of this, new destinations were suggested. Archibald Alison a Glasgow magistrate had recommended during his appearance before a Special Committee of the House of Commons on the 'ticket-of-leave' system, that one of the Hebridean islands should be bought by the government and turned into a penal colony. 'MERCY' was not so sure about the Hebrides: 'I should prefer an island further off, and with a better climate and soil. There is little doubt a convict colony might support itself.' Another Leeds letter writer, who objected to hanging on the principle that it was insufficient punishment, had no time for such namby-pamby solutions. He believed that Dove, and other murderers, 'ought to be put in an iron cage and exhibited to the public in every market town in England, flogged repeatedly, and finally sent into one of the numerous mines to dig for coal, lead, or iron, as the case may be, according to the district in which the crime is committed.'[79] Fortunately this idea remained the perverted fantasy of its author and the Scottish Isles were not turned into penal colonies. The solution to the problem was already in development with a programme of prison-building, and with it the birth of the modern British penal system. Nevertheless, public executions continued until 1868, and it would take the state and the Church of England another 113 years to accept the moral, humanitarian and legal arguments against execution.

## Notes and references

1  *Wesleyan Times*, 4 August 1856.

2  *York Herald*, 2 August 1856.

3  *Leeds Mercury*, 9 August 1856.

4  Roger Chadwick, *Bureaucratic Mercy: The Home Office and the Treatment of Capital Cases in Victorian England* (New York and London, 1992), p. 207.

5  Sally Walker (ed.), 'The Diary of John Swallow', http://Leedsindexers.co.uk/articles.

6  *The Nonconformist*, 6 August 1856.

7  *The Times*, 23 January 1856.

8  See Thomas Wright McDermid, *The Life of T. Wright, of Manchester, the prison philanthropist* (Manchester, 1876).

9  McDermid, *Life of T. Wright*, p. 47; *The Times*, 7 June 1856.

10  *York Herald*, 26 July 1856.

11  Reprinted in the *Leeds Mercury*, 9 August 1856.

12  *York Herald*, 16 August 1856.

13  *Leeds Mercury*, 12 August 1856. For discussion on the scaffold crowd see V.A.C. Gattrell, *The Hanging Tree: Execution and the English People 1770–1868* (Oxford, 1994), ch. 2.

14  David D. Cooper, *The Lesson of the Scaffold: The Public Execution Controversy in Victorian England* (London, 1974), pp. 20–21.

15  *The Last Moments and Execution of Wm. Dove!* (York, 1856).

16  See *The Times*, 21 and 22 February 1853; 19 March 1853.

17  *Leeds Mercury*, 9 August 1856.

18  William Knipe (ed.), *Criminal Chronology of York Castle* (York, 1867), p. 232; *Leeds Intelligencer*, 26 July 1856.

19  *The Times*, 6 August 1856.

20  For general histories of Calcraft see Geoffrey Abbott, *William Calcraft: Executioner Extra-ordinaire!* (St Albans, 2004); James Bland, *The Common Hangman* (Whitecroft, 2000), ch. 20; Horace Bleackley, *The Hangmen of England* (London, 1929), pp. 207–29.

21  See Gattrell, *The Hanging Tree*, pp. 51–4.

22  *The Times*, 1 April 1856; *The Times*, 7 April 1856.

23  *The Times*, 28 March 1856.

24  *Ipswich Express*; cited in the *Daily News*, 23 April 1851.

25  *Life and Recollections of Calcraft the Hangman* (London, c.1880), pp. 7–8.

26  *The Times*, 28 March 1856.

27  Bland, *Common Hangman*, p. 111.

28  *Morning Herald*, 23 February 1864; cited in Cooper, *Lesson of the Scaffold*, p. 18.

29  *The Times*, 12 September 1856. The head of the effigy was apparently a cast of Palmer's head borrowed from someone in Liverpool – presumably Frederick Bridges.

30  Bland, *Common Hangman*, p. 9.

31  Bland, *Common Hangman*, ch. 13.

32  Bland, *Common Hangman*, pp. 112, 167.

33  See, for example, *Leeds Mercury*, 9 August 1856; *The Times* 11 August 1856.

34  *The Times*, 3 September 1864.

35  *York Herald*, 16 August 1856. Contemporary sources, including his own correspondence to the press, give his name as Askren not Askern as cited in later newspaper reports and modern sources such as Bland, *Common Hangman*.

36  *Leeds Mercury*, 19 August 1856; *Leeds Times*, 16 August 1856.

37  *Manchester Examiner and Times*, 14 August 1856.

38  *Leeds Mercury*, 19 August 1856.

39  *Leeds Mercury*, 19 August 1856.

**40** *The Heroes of the Guillotine* (London, *c.* 1868; reprinted 1975).

**41** House of Commons Parliamentary Papers, 23 (1857–8), p. 197.

**42** *The Times*, 7 January 1856. For discussion of some of his later judgments in wife murder trials see Michael J. Weiner, 'The Sad Story of George Hall: Adultery, Murder, and the Politics of Mercy in mid-Victorian England', *Social History*, 24, 2 (1999), pp. 185–6.

**43** Cooper, *Lesson of the Scaffold*, pp. 114–5.

**44** *The Times*, 6 August 1856.

**45** For a broader perspective on the power of the press in this context see Rob Sindall, *Street Violence in the Nineteenth Century: Media Panic or Real Danger?* (Leicester, 1990).

**46** See Peter Bartrip, 'Public opinion and law enforcement: The ticket-of-leave scares in mid-Victorian Britain', in V. Bailey (ed.), *Policing and Punishment in Nineteenth-Century Britain* (London, 1982).

**47** R. Sindall, 'The London Garrotting Panics of 1856 and 1862', *Social History*, 12, 3 (1987), pp. 351–9.

**48** *The Times*, 23 April 1856.

**49** See *Daily News*, 19 February, 20 February and 8 March 1856.

**50** See *Daily News*, 22 February 1856.

**51** See Smith, *Trial by Medicine*, pp. 154–5.

**52** *Weekly Dispatch*, 18 May 1856.

**53** For the trial and execution see *The Times*, 5 April and 21 April 1849.

**54** Cited in Bleackley, *Hangmen of England*, p. 219.

**55** *Weekly Dispatch*, 18 May 1856.

**56** Beth Kalikoff, 'The Execution of Tess d'Urberville at Wintonchester', in William B. Thesing (ed.), *Execution and the British Experience from the 17th to the 20th Century* (Jefferson and London, 1990), pp. 111–121; Kalikoff, *Murder and Moral Decay in Victorian Popular Literature* (Ann Arbor, 1986). See also the book of 'faction', Nicola Thorne's *My Name is Martha Brown* (London, 2000).

**57** *The Times*, 28 August 1856.

**58** *The Times*, 13 August 1856.

**59** *The Sun*, 13 August 1856.

**60** *Daily News*, 25 February 1856; *Weekly Dispatch*, 24 February 1856.

**61** See, Eigen, *Unconscious Crime*, pp. 125–6.

**62** Smith, *Trial by Medicine*, p. 87.

**63** *News of the World*, 20 January 1856.

**64** *The Times*, 25 February; *Daily News*, 9 February 1856; *News of the World*, 17 February 1856.

**65** *The Sun*, 21 July 1856.

**66** Cooper, *Lessons of the Scaffold*, pp. 80–88; Cooper, 'Public Executions in Victorian England: A Reform Adrift', in Thesing (ed.), *Executions*, pp. 152–3; Harry Potter, *Hanging in Judgement: Religion and the Death Penalty in England* (London, 1993), pp. 66–7, 78–9.

**67** See Cooper, *Lessons of the Scaffold*, ch. 5; Potter, *Hanging in Judgement*, ch. 7.

**68** *Leeds Mercury*, 16 August 1856.

**69** *York Herald*, 9 August 1856.

**70** Williams, *Observations*, p. 11.

**71** *The Nonconformist*, 23 July 1856.

**72** Gatrell, *Hanging Tree*, pp. 378–80; Potter, *Hanging in Judgement*, p. 25.

**73** *The Watchman*, 24 July 1856.

**74** *Leeds Mercury*, 9 August 1856.

**75** *Leeds Mercury*, 9 August 1856.

**76** McDermid, *Life of Thomas Wright*, pp. 49–50.

**77** *Leeds Mercury*, 16 August 1856.

**78** See Charles Bateson, *The Convict Ships, 1787–1868* (Glasgow, 1959); Alan Frederick Hattersley, *The Convict Crisis and the Growth of Unity: Resistance to Transportation in South Africa and Australia, 1848–1853* (Pietermaritzburg, 1965); Robert Hughes, *The Fatal Shore: A History of the Transportation of Convicts to Australia* (London, 1987).

**79** *Leeds Times*, 9 August 1856.

# CHAPTER 7

# Hunting Harrison down

*'Sin calls out its ministers'*

The newspapers of the period had a penchant for making parallels between the scenarios and characters in sensational trials and those in well-known novels and plays.[1] The case of Dove and Harrison, however, stumped most of the papers. *The Times* opined that 'Nowhere in the range of fiction is there a story more strange and terrible.' The *Western Flying Post* echoed the sentiment: 'This miserable story of folly and of crime goes beyond the boundaries even of fiction.' The *Leeds Times* thought 'a stranger story than his never passed human lips.'[2] What the papers did not know at the time was that the story was not yet over and was soon to get even stranger.

## Cursing the wizards

Following William's execution the national and local press turned its attention to Harrison, who was labelled as 'Dove's evil genius' by one paper.[3] The debate about the availability of poisons generated by Harriet's inquest was now replaced by a chorus of journalistic concern regarding the ubiquity and pernicious activities of cunning-folk. The existence of people like Harrison was widely portrayed as a poor reflection on the current state of the nation. As a *News of the World* columnist opined:

> is it not humiliating to know that, in spite of all the intellectual
> advancement of which we are prone to boast in this later day, there are

*still amongst us men, and those not wholly uneducated, who are*
*capable of surrendering their reason and of weakly falling victims to arts*
*so low and despicable as those of Harrison.*[4]

'How is it that such men as Harrison are still plying their nefarious trade among us?' *The Times* also wondered. 'Does England still, with its boasted enlightenment, furnish enough of ignorance to support such imposture?'[5] It was a question pondered by the press nationwide, and the answer was invariably yes. Under the heading 'Superstition in 1856' the *Examiner* cautioned:

> *Let it not be supposed that Dove's superstition is an extraordinary*
> *example. There are thousands and thousands who still believe in*
> *witchcraft, spells, charms, astrology, &c. And this superstition is not*
> *confined to the rural districts, though in them it is doubtless most*
> *prevalent, but some of it is yet to be found in towns, and, as we see in*
> *the instance before us, even in such a place as Leeds.*[6]

The Leeds newspapers were particularly sensitive to any inference that their town and its environs were a hotbed of 'superstitious credulity'.[7] They would not have liked an editorial in the Somerset and Dorset paper the *Western Flying Post*, which commented, 'Our readers are perhaps aware that this is not the first time that Leeds has been the scene of conjuring and fortune-telling,' and proceeded to give a brief account of Mary Bateman.[8] It was reports like these that led the *Leeds Times* to worry that the 'wizard-revelations' were becoming 'a considerable nuisance. Our great manufacturing centres in the North of England are not generally considered to be enveloped in the grossest mental ignorance and stupidity.'[9] In a similar vein, the editor of the *Leeds Intelligencer* pointed out that Leeds was no worse than anywhere else: 'Notwithstanding the sneer of *The Times*, we are afraid that, if the whole truth could be known, other counties are as culpable as Yorkshire in this respect, and that there is scarcely a large town in which some impostor does not derive much profit by deluding the credulous.'[10] *The Observer* agreed: 'it is notorious that in many parts of the country there are still persons who call themselves wizards.'[11]

In his last letter to Barret, William had laid the blame for his actions squarely at Harrison's door. Yet, despite their utter loathing for Harrison and his ilk, the press were generally unsympathetic to the view that Harrison was partially culpable for William's deed. 'Harrison may be a quack,' said the *News of the World*, 'but Dove was a brutal scoundrel, anxious to whitewash himself, and any imputation against another having this object ought to be treated with contempt.' The *Saturday Review* was less outspoken but expressed a similar sentiment: 'Dove was as much responsible for Harrison as Harrison for Dove. Sin calls out its ministers.'[12] Yet there was a general consensus that wizards encouraged not only immorality but criminality and, therefore, in light of the Dove affair, something had to be done about Harrison and his ilk. The newspapers felt they were already doing their bit by 'watching and fearlessly exposing at all times dangerous empirics of the Harrison school.'[13] The onus was on the legislators and educators to act.

A good education obviously had not prevented William from succumbing to the lure of a wizard and, as we have seen, other explanations were put forward in his particular case, but most of those who kept cunning-folk and fortune-tellers in business were perceived to be uneducated and ignorant. Therefore the editor of the *Leeds Intelligencer* opined:

> *We do not suppose that the existing Government will take any notice of a matter so nearly affecting the interests of so large a portion of the community as the dupes of this vile system, but we commend the subject to the careful consideration of the educated classes, and ask them to consider whether or not it is their duty to endeavour, by an improved system of education, even though it be a state education, to place their fellow beings in a position that shall not leave them at the mercy of such as the consulting adviser of William Dove.*[14]

The *News of the World* thought that further legal measures beyond the Vagrancy Act and the Witchcraft Act would also be required, suggesting that 'a severe criminal procedure against both the duper and the dupe, varying with age and circumstance, would decidedly diminish the evil.'[15] This suggestion was far more radical than the paper probably realised. Throughout the whole period of the witch trials from 1563 to 1736, when the practices of cunning-folk were prosecutable under the same harsh laws as those against witches, the act of *consulting* cunning-folk was never made a criminal offence. Considering the large numbers of clients of cunning-folk and fortune-tellers the *Leeds Times* reached a more realistic and fatalistic conclusion: 'to think of the entire extinction of such locusts – it's far too much to expect.'[16]

## Harrison fights back

Harrison knew well the calumnies being heaped upon him by the local and national press. He could have remained silent but instead he decided to launch a public counter-offensive by writing the following letter to the *Leeds Mercury*:

> Gentlemen, – I take it for granted that you are sufficiently honourable to allow me a little space in your influential journal to set myself right with the public on the subject of the day, relative to the late Wm. Dove.
>
> Had you, Gentlemen, been in full possession of one-half the facts of the case, you would not have written such severe strictures against my character and profession as you have done; I know you better, but I blame you for being too hasty in the matter.
>
> A more scandalous, unsatisfactory, and impudent statement never appeared in print, than that which came out in your Tuesday's impression. It appears to me, and to hundreds more in this town, that Dove's villanous habit of lying followed him even to his prison, and to the scaffold! I tell you, Gentlemen, and can give you ample proof of the truth of my assertion, that not one-tenth part of Dove's statement in his prison is true. I have uniformly wished him to behave well to his wife, and to go home and use kind conciliating language to her, and 'she would then meet him with a smile.' And he admits that.
>
> The statement made by Dove in June should have been in the hearing of Hardcastle, who declares that all he, Dove, says, is a tissue of lies that can be very soon refuted.
>
> Gentlemen, if the conductors of the press knew half as much about me as they should do in a case of this nature, they would forbear to treat me in the manner they are doing.
>
> I have been the means of lifting up out of a sick bed numbers who are living in and about Leeds, and who would be glad to meet any of my traducers in court to prove that I have cured men of the dropsy and other complaints which the faculty, numbers of them, had abandoned as incurable; and as you, Gentlemen, for my credit, and equally honourable

to yourselves as public instructors, declare that I, Henry Harrison, would have been 'horrified' at the very thought of Dove resorting to poison to get rid of his wife – a most amiable and lovely woman, too good for such a wretch as him, who has, I am sure, died with a lie in his mouth, and lived in the midst of sinful dissipation and folly.

I always told Dove that he never would be happy with his wife until she should bring him some children, and that it would be much better that he should separate from her if he could not live agreeable with her; that it was no credit to him to be continually tormenting a woman who could not yield him those blessings which nature forbad her to give, viz., a half dozen children, which he, Dove, pretended to long for.

Gentlemen, it will be of no use me attempting to deny any one particular statement made by that profligate and unfeeling criminal, as I declare to you, upon my honour, that there is scarcely a sentence of it true; and what is true, is told in such a raving incoherent manner, that the public, aye, the public, have seen the folly of publishing it, and that same discerning public declare 'that the document ought not to have been put into print.'

Gentlemen, I know that you have been imposed upon by the 'made up tales' for Dove's defence; your better nature has given way to the bland remarks of the 'Mad Doctors' who have been 'charmed' and bound with a 'spell' of some colour and shape best known to themselves; but all were not agreed!

No, Gentlemen, neither are all the people of Leeds agreed about your 'leader' of Tuesday last, and think it very hard upon one whom you yourselves declare 'that I should have been horrified with the idea of Dove poisoning his wife!'

Gentlemen, the conductors of the press are not all England, and the people now-a-days are too shrewd to be led away by such foolish and wicked statements as those made in York Castle to Mr. Barret.

The Judge who tried the case told Sir G. Grey 'that Dove was legally guilty, and morally responsible' for the crime of murdering his poor innocent wife.

If I had no better patients and friends than Wm. Dove to requite me for my advice, I should have been a poor man myself.

Gentlemen, both I and Hardcastle declare, upon our honour, that that tale about the 'five coppers' being thrown about the barn to put a 'spell' upon King, and thereby cause him to re-let the farm to Dove, was a pure burlesque upon the simpleton, made out by some wag in the neighbourhood, who found Dove but too credulous to believe anything or anybody who could play upon his foolish imagination and 'selfish propensities.'

God help any man who may have 'dealings' with such an 'evil one' as the late profligate William Dove. I lost pounds by him in time and money, and he would never own that he was under any obligations for advice, either from me or any one else. I trust that no such men as Dove will ever enter my door again to ask me for either advice or assistance under any such domestic troubles as brought Dove to the gallows. The more I am known the less influence will the press have in trying to put me down. It may have a contrary effect! What I have done professionally cannot be depreciated by the gentlemen of the press, because the recipients of relief administered by my skill will never cease to express their gratitude for what I have done for them while they live!!! Only last night, and on Saturday night, the subject was canvassed over in my favour by scores of gentlemen in different parts of Leeds, and sent to me for my satisfaction and comfort.

Gentlemen, I am preparing for the press a something which will alter your opinion, and the opinions of those of the London press as well, I hope, and something which will prove to my countrymen that Henry Harrison is and will continue to be not an impostor, but a real benefactor of his species!

Gentlemen, I commit this letter to your care, and hope to see it in the columns of the Leeds Mercury of to-morrow's impression, and am, Gentlemen, yours gratefully, for the notice you have taken of me – it will do me good.

Hen. Harrison.

Leeds, Aug. 18$^{th}$, 1856.

Postscript. – Dove declares that 'he had not seen me from January to the 6th of March;' then he says 'that he met me in my warehouse opposite my house, and that was in February,' and there 'I promised to make him some belladonna!!' How any reliance can be placed upon such statements is, to me, and to hundreds in Leeds, a complete mystery!!!

Gentlemen, I solemnly declare that I never saw Dove from the first

*week in January to the 6th of March, as he says, so that you see Dove*
*convicts himself! And surely, gentlemen, after such statements, and*
*many others of the same kind, you, on calm reflection, will see that I am*
*an injured man until they are refuted, and your well-known impartiality*
*will do that in a case of this nature.*

*I was bred and born in Boar-lane, and was never two miles out of*
*Leeds, to live my life, as a resident. I never had any occasion to*
*advertise, as the cures I make recommend themselves.*

*Dove declares that he never gave his wife the strychnia for the*
*purpose of taking away her life!! He said he was 'muddled' in his brain*
*before giving her that deadly poison!!*

The press were not yet fully aware that this *tour de force* of bluster and
self-justification contained several bare-faced lies. As we have seen, he
did advertise and he had lived outside Leeds. Even without this knowledge the letter not surprisingly received short shrift from the press. Its
recipient, the *Leeds Mercury*, weighed up the conflicting statements and
concluded: 'On the one side we have DOVE's reluctant statement to his
own professional adviser; on the other HARRISON'S denial "upon his
honour." We prefer the former.' Other papers responded with despising
mockery. The *York Herald* expressed its disgust at 'the impudence of the
"wizard",' and as to his assertions of honour, 'forsooth! – The honour of
a wizard!!!' The *Leeds Times* described the letter as an act of coolly kicking 'the carcass of his victim.' 'Is every herb doctor now to kick up his
heels against that moral barrier from imposition and crime?' its editor
asked. 'Put on your armour, ye flowers of literary chivalry, for the ass has
loudly brayed out a challenge to the lion!'[17]

# Rape[18]

The braying ass's business survived and probably even thrived from the
adverse exposure given to him during the Dove trial. Bad press was often
good news to such people. In early August he was apparently boasting
that the publicity would be worth £100 to him.[19] He was even ironically
championed by *Punch*. When *Raphael's Prophetic Almanac* was published in October, it contained a criticism of the wizard. 'Raphael'
believed that if Dove had, instead of consulting Harrison, been to 'a tal-

ented and judicious professor of the science, he would doubtless have been saved from the fearful consequences of the awful crime of which he had been found guilty.' *Punch*, which was an arch critic of astrological almanacs, responded: 'We would not stand this, were we Harrison. If he does not come to town and kick Raphael, he has no pluck.'[20] A week later, on 1 November, *Punch* issued an update as to Harrison's evident lack of pluck under the title 'A Wizard Vindicated: Mr Punch, last week, invited Mr Harrison, the Wizard of Leeds, to come to London and kick Mr Raphael, the Wizard of Walworth. It is due to the former to state that his abstaining from performing this act of justice has been caused by a circumstance over which he has no control.'[21] Something adverse had obviously befallen Harrison, something that Raphael failed to foresee.

The cause of Harrison's trouble was an attractive twenty-year-old servant named Eliza Croft. She was one of seven children of William Croft, a nail-maker, and his wife Maria, who lived in Pontefract Lane. Eliza had been in service in and around Leeds since the age of eight and grew up away from her parents. The family were poor, and even in periods between jobs she was usually unable to stay at the family home because with all the young children there was no room in their small lodgings. In early 1854 she was hired as a servant at the Brown Cow in Meadow Lane. She stayed there for about a year and a half. About a month before she left she became friendly with a man named John Stephenson, who lodged in Brown Cow Yard and worked at the Gasworks in Meadow Lane. Stephenson was married with two children but had abandoned his wife after three years, and then taken up with a prostitute for a while. The budding relationship between Eliza and John was interrupted when Eliza went to work at the Ship Inn in Dewsbury. She had to leave after a couple of months, however, because of a bad cold that developed into a mild case of pleurisy, a common problem in the heavily polluted atmosphere of such towns. For once she was able to stay with her parents for five weeks while being treated as an out-patient at the Leeds Dispensary. In mid-July she started work as a house servant at the New Cross Inn, which had recently been taken over by Benjamin Shores and his wife. Eliza had presumably been employed at the Leeds hiring fair that traditionally took place on 11 July. It was a day when the town was thronged with young men and women lining the streets, as employers, particularly farmers from the outlying villages, strode up and down inspecting and choosing the servants they would hire for the next year. Once settled at the New Cross Inn, Eliza recommenced trysting with Stephenson, who was now living in Benyon's Court. The relationship was going well but then in August Stephenson stopped coming to see her. He explained his absence by the fact that he had to do night shifts at the gas works on alternate months and August was one of those months. Nevertheless, Eliza was worried that he was losing interest in her and having heard of other people consulting Henry Harrison on affairs of the heart, she decided to pay him a visit.

One Friday evening in early September, around nine o'clock, she walked round the corner to 5 North Row and knocked at the door. Harrison answered and invited her up to his consulting room. She told the wizard about John Stephenson and asked him to divine whether Stephenson would come and see her again. Harrison gave her a glass like a magnifying glass to look through and asked her what she saw. Eliza saw something but could not make it out, and told Harrison she was 'no scholar'. Harrison took the glass and looked into it. Eliza asked him what it was she had seen, and he replied 'affection.' This was a good sign but Harrison said he would need to work on Stephenson and told her to come again in three weeks' time. The interview lasted about ten minutes and she paid sixpence.

Three weeks later Eliza went to consult Harrison again as Stephenson had still not appeared. It was during this consultation that Harrison suggested that if she had sex with him he would be able to draw the young man back to her. Eliza rejected the suggestion and got up to leave. She was about to go downstairs when Harrison grabbed her by the waist and repeated that if she wanted her sweetheart she must give herself to him. Eliza shook him off and went home. Nevertheless, her concern about losing Stephenson made her visit Harrison several more times to see if there were any further developments and each time Harrison proposed sex. She asked instead how much it would cost to restore Stephenson's affections, and the wizard suggested five shillings. Eliza did not have enough so she went to borrow half-a-crown from an acquaintance, a dressmaker named Hannah Wilson who lived in Meadow Lane.

On Friday 17 October Eliza went to see how Harrison had got on with her five shillings-worth of magic. Unusually the back door at 5 North Row was locked, as Elizabeth Brown was at her son's grocery shop down the road. Eliza knocked and Harrison came down and opened the door after having finished with a male client. She followed him upstairs and told him that she still had not seen Stephenson. Harrison replied, 'No, he cannot come until I have connection with you.' As she turned to go downstairs Harrison once again took her round the waist and told her it was no use being so bashful. Then, according to Eliza, he pushed her against the door and raped her, telling her that if she said anything he would bewitch her. Harrison then saw Eliza out and locked the door again. Elizabeth Brown's servant, a niece named Eliza Tate, was downstairs all this time and saw Croft go upstairs with Harrison but heard no commotion. Not long after the alleged rape took place Harrison left the house and Tate went up to his room to clean the windows. She saw something on the floor next to Harrison's desk which made her suspicious. The 'something', described as 'dirt' in the newspapers, was not there before Croft arrived.

'Dirt' was a euphemism for semen, but whether Tate used the term in court is questionable. The newspapers may not have been prudish about providing graphic details of violence and *post mortems* but they certainly were about describing the act of sex. Court records sometimes more accurately reflect the sexually explicit language used by witnesses. In the local court records of the Lancashire town of Rawenstall for 1873, for example, the magistrates' clerk at a prosecution for sexual assault recorded the testimony of one Aaron Elton, who recalled his acquaintance James Hayle boasting how 'he did it twice without pulling out.'[22] The semen on Harrison's floor was presumably the result of Harrison doing just the opposite – withdrawing before ejaculation, the most common means of birth control at the time. As we shall see he had cause to be careful.

When Elizabeth Brown returned home from her son's shop, Tate pointed out the 'dirt' on Harrison's floor and explained that it appeared after Croft had visited. That night, around eleven o'clock, Brown confronted Harrison while he was having a drink at the Nag's Head in Hunslet Lane. She told him 'she had had some dirt to clean away in the room, and that she did not like to see such things in her house, and she should discharge Eliza Croft from coming again.' Harrison did not deny it and merely replied that she 'talked like a foolish woman.' When he returned home that night they had 'further words.'

Eliza Croft, meanwhile, had said nothing to anyone about what had happened, but gossip was already spreading. Harrison boasted to his drinking companions of having had sex with her. On Saturday night a Mrs Philliskirk told Rosanna Shores, wife of the landlord of the New Cross Inn, that something had happened between Eliza and Harrison. She at once spoke to Eliza about it and subsequently dismissed her. In distress Eliza went to Hannah Wilson and said 'there was something which she wanted to tell her but dared not.' It was only on the Wednesday that she finally told Hannah everything. Hannah urged her to make an official complaint against Harrison, and that evening, around seven o'clock, she accompanied Eliza to the police office, where Superintendent James took down details of her complaint and sent police constables Patrick Byrne and Ephraim Williamson to arrest Harrison. They found him drinking at the Nag's Head and took him into custody. Eliza was still in the police office when Harrison was brought in, and in her presence he was charged with obtaining money from her on two occasions for telling her fortune; Harrison admitted she had given him sixpence the first time but denied she had given him five shillings, claiming instead that she had given him half-a-crown in payment for a bottle of medicine for a disease from which she was suffering. Eliza denied this, and then James charged Harrison with the far more serious crime of rape. At this Harrison turned to Eliza and asked whether he 'had not had improper intercourse with her three times.' Croft asserted, 'No, only once.' Harrison was taken to the cells under the courthouse to await a hearing before the magistrates' Bench.

Burne and Williamson then accompanied Eliza to 5 North Row and asked her to show them where Harrison kept his fortune-telling equipment. She pointed to a low desk in the room. When the policemen searched it they found two egg-shaped glass globes, some old books on astrology, a manuscript account book relating to his customers, and another containing the names 'Malkin', 'Palmer' and 'Dove' and other entries the policemen could not understand. There was also a printing block used to produce blank horoscopes. They also found several hundred business cards containing the following excruciating verse:

*Lines on Astrology and Watercasting, addressed to Dr. Harrison, No.5, North-row, South-market, Meadow-lane, Leeds. By a Gentleman.*
 *Prince of Astrologers! For thee*

*Lies ope the Book of Destiny.*
*Kingdoms and states, to thy keen eye,*
*Their future history supply.*
*And all the stars that at our birth,*
*Are set to rule our fate on earth,*
*Thou can'st interpret, and aright*
*Translate the language of their light*
*Descended from a line of Seers,*
*Prophets for near two hundred years.*
*Rare are thy gifts the sick to cure,*
*Life, love, and fortune to insure.*
*This do I know: for it was mine,*
*To call upon thy Art divine,*
*To own its use, its influence feel,*
*And prove indeed that it was real.*
*From a sick bed, raised up I cry*
*To others. – "Wherefore will ye die?"*
*Though useless other treatment be,*
*Try, ere too late, Astrology.*
*To Dr. Harrison, tell your pains,*
*And while th' auspicious planet reigns,*
*He will relieve, revive, restore,*
*And you shall bless him evermore.*

*Dr. Harrison, the great Yorkshire Astrologer and Water-caster, may be consulted at all hours of the day, at residence, No. 5, North-row, South-market, Meadow-lane, Leeds.*

The purpose of the egg-shaped globes became clear when Harrison was asked to empty his pockets. He pulled out a small flat piece of glass with a man painted on it, but before handing it over he attempted to scratch it off. It appears that Harrison would secrete the painted glass under the globe before asking female clients to look into it. The clients would then see the image of a handsome man – their future husband. It was a very old trick. Back in the late seventeenth century the physician John Webster, a staunch critic of cunning-folk, referred to those who 'had artificial glasses, where into they would convey little pictures.'[23]

# Sex and magic

As we shall find later, Harrison was quite capable of committing rape, but in this instance magic becomes a complicating factor in interpreting what took place in his consulting room. The question is one of whether Harrison physically forced Eliza or whether he used psychological coercion, playing on her yearning for the affections of Stephenson and her fear of his magic powers to induce her to have intercourse. This act of what could be described as consenting rape was not unique to Harrison; there is evidence of other cunning-folk using the same ploy to force clients into complying with their sexual demands. A Cornish contemporary of Harrison's, the bisexual cunning-man James Thomas, generated considerable notoriety for suggesting that male clients would have to sleep with him in order for his magic to work. A formal complaint was once made against him by one William Paynter after Thomas said he would have to commit what was described as a 'disgraceful offence' with him in order to cure his wife of witchcraft. Thomas fled the county to avoid prosecution.[24]

Yet the most graphic and tragic example of such sex magic took place back in Leeds a few months before Eliza first went to see Harrison. The culprit was Isaac Rushworth and his victim a 25-year-old woman named Ritty Littlewood. Ritty lived in Sheffield with her elderly father Thomas, a cordwainer by trade. At the age of twenty she had a child but its father absconded not long after. She was not a particularly healthy woman and for some time had been consulting local doctors but to no avail. A neighbour advised her to go to Leeds and see Isaac Rushworth in the Dewsbury Road. So in the spring of 1856 Ritty and her father travelled the thirty-five miles to Leeds. Rushworth ruled her planet and discovered that she was bewitched. He gave her some pills but she did not improve, and in June they requested him to visit them in Sheffield. When Rushworth came he told the Littlewoods that they would never prosper unless they moved nearer to Leeds so that he could attend to them more frequently. They did as he desired and went to live in West Ardsley, a village between Leeds, Dewsbury and Wakefield. As good as his word, Rushworth visited them frequently, supplying Ritty with medicine for palpitation of the heart. It was also here that he first suggested that she would never get better unless he had 'connexion' with her. He said he knew as much because he had ruled her planet but, like Eliza, Ritty resisted his repeated requests for sex.

On the suggestion of Rushworth, Ritty moved to East Ardsley, where Rushworth finally had his way. She had gone to consult him at his house and while there he gave her some treacle parkin laced with something that stupefied her and made her ill. According to Ritty, it was only in this state that she agreed to sex, though she subsequently slept with Rushworth on numerous occasions. Her situation was made all the more vulnerable by her father's death from 'natural decay' on Christmas Day. He was seventy-four. By early 1857 it was obvious that Ritty was pregnant and so on 2 February Rushworth, not wanting to be burdened with any responsibility, brought with him some 'seeds of paradise'. He told her they would make her miscarry and directed her to stew them in a pot and drink the infusion just as if she were drinking tea. Seed of paradise was another name for cardamom, a decoction of which was a known abortifacient.[25] It was, nevertheless, an unusual choice, as there were other far more common and cheaper herbal alternatives used at the time, particularly pennyroyal and savin (juniper).[26] Anyway, the seeds of paradise proved to be effective and on 26 March she gave premature birth to a baby boy. No doctor or midwife was in attendance and after ten minutes the child died.

Throughout their association Rushworth had maintained that Ritty was the victim of witchcraft and she paid considerable sums of money for medicine and charms to counter the spell upon her. On one occasion he came to her lodgings with a bullock's heart and some shoemaker's awls. He burned the heart as an act of sympathetic magic to inflict pain on the witch, and told Ritty to place the awls under her pillow, in her pocket and around the house to keep away her enemies. Another time he sent her two charms written on parchment, for which she paid the considerable sum of £5 – roughly the equivalent of seven weeks' wages for a labourer at the time. One was to ward off witchcraft while the other would 'get her a young man'. No young man was drawn to her door, however, and not long after the abortion Rushworth stopped visiting. He had had his sexual pleasure, defrauded her of a large amount of money, and now he discarded her. In retaliation she reported him to the police. He was arrested, his premises searched, and a great number of books on fortune-telling and astrology confiscated. He was subsequently tried at the York summer assizes on 14 July for procuring abortion and sentenced to eighteen months' imprisonment with hard labour.

Ritty's disappointment and despair were not resolved by this outcome. Prior to his trial Rushworth had managed to have a message conveyed to Ritty that if he suffered any harm he would send devils to torment her, just as William Dove believed Harrison had done to him. Furthermore, he intimated that if he should die in prison his ghost would haunt her night and day for the rest of her life. When, during the trial, one of the jurymen twice fainted it seemed to her that Rushworth's ominous threats were coming true. Following the verdict she suffered a violent fit during which she gouged her face and neck with her fingernails. She had to be physically restrained and a couple of days later the poor woman, who in the space of a year had moved twice, lost her father, been drugged, had an abortion and been abandoned, was admitted to the West Riding asylum in a state of insanity.[27]

## In the dock

Harrison did not have long to wait in the police lock-up. His trial for rape and fortune-telling began at the Leeds Courthouse on Thursday 23 October. The sitting magistrates were the prosperous cloth manufacturer and future mayor Darnton Lupton and J. Ellershaw. Harrison's defence was conducted by Francis Ferns, who would later act on behalf of Alfred Broughton.

Eliza Croft was first to give evidence and was cross-examined by Ferns. Hannah Wilson was next to testify and confirmed she had lent half-a-crown to Eliza and that she had confided in her about what had happened at Harrison's. Superintendent James recounted events in the police office on the Wednesday evening. The only other witness giving evidence that day was a local constable named John Braithwaite who had been friends with Harrison for some twenty years. He testified to having met Harrison in the Nag's Head on the Saturday morning after the alleged rape took place. Braithwaite asked Harrison about the row he had had with Brown in the pub the previous night. 'Is there anything fresh this morning?' he enquired. Harrison replied that 'He had plenty of fresh tongue' from Brown, and explained how she 'suspected that something was not right from what she had seen upstairs, after the New Cross girl had been.' The court session came to a close when Ferns asked for an adjournment of the trial until the following Monday to give sufficient time to collect evidence that would cast doubt on Eliza's testimony. He then requested that bail be granted and that Harrison was prepared to pay any amount – a sign of his financial prosperity. The magistrates refused, however, though they did allow him to remain in the courthouse lock-up rather than be removed to Armley Gaol.

By Monday word had spread around Leeds that the notorious Wizard of the South Market was on trial. The crowds that gathered at the courthouse were the largest for years, greater even than those that gathered for the inquest on Harriet Dove. The public gallery was packed, principally with women, while hundreds milled around outside. The atmosphere was decidedly anti-Harrison. It was not only the general public who were attracted by the appearance of the wizard; the two presiding magistrates were joined on the bench by the mayor and five other magistrates including Ralph Markland. Joseph Morton Barret chose to act on behalf of the prosecution. There was a real sense of anticipation that Harrison was going to get his come-uppance. Yet Harrison still had his supporters. A man called Robert Wells got up a collection to support his case, though how much was raised is unknown beyond the one shilling donated by Braithwaite's wife.

Ferns's defence strategy was two-pronged. First he tried to cast aspersions on Eliza's character in order to undermine her assertion that she had not consented to have sex with Harrison. Emma Ward, landlady of the Brown Cow, was called to testify that she had dismissed Eliza because of her habit of going out in the evenings. To taint Eliza by association, evidence was provided about Stephenson having lived with a prostitute. Ferns also quizzed Eliza as to whether she had been dismissed from service at the Black Bear for being 'too familiar' with the landlady's husband, an insinuation she strenuously denied. To counter these aspersions Barret had assembled his own character witnesses. A warehouseman named William Lister testified that Eliza had lodged with his wife in York Road for three years and her conduct had been good. Rosanna Shores confirmed that she saw nothing wrong in Eliza's conduct or character up until when she was informed of what had taken place with Harrison. Ferns's second line of defence was to highlight an obvious discrepancy in Eliza's account of when the alleged rape took place. Throughout the trial so far Eliza had said the rape occurred around six or seven in the evening. This was contradicted by the testimony of Eliza Tate who said Eliza had visited around twenty minutes to twelve in the morning. More importantly Harrison had witnesses to the fact that he was away from home all afternoon and evening. Friday was usually Harrison's day off and so at a quarter to one he and William Midgley, landlord of the Nag's Head, had decided to go to Colton Common for the afternoon. On the way they stopped off at the Weaver's Arms in Mill Street, and the landlord George Turner joined the party. The three men moved on to the Woodman's Inn where they had another glass of ale. They arrived at Colton around half-past two. On their way home in the evening they stopped at the Weaver's Arms sometime after seven and stayed drinking until nine o'clock before ending the pub crawl back at the Nag's Head.

For the prosecution Barret concentrated on the charge of fortune-telling, which suggests he had some reservations regarding the rape charge. He brought in medical evidence to cast doubt on Harrison's claim that Eliza had paid him five shillings for medicine rather than for magical services. Considering who was in the dock, one can imagine that Barret had little problem recruiting the services of Thomas Nunneley and another surgeon William Nicholson Price to give Eliza a medical examination. Nunneley appeared in court to state that there was 'not the least appearance of disease'. When Ferns cross-examined him, he tried to shift the focus of the medical testimony in his client's favour. He asked whether there were any physical signs of a struggle, which might have been expected in a case of rape. Nunneley responded that he did not find any bruising, only a slight swelling.

Why Eliza decided to lie about the time of the alleged rape is unclear but after hearing the testimony of Tate and Turner, Mr Barr the court clerk repeatedly asked whether she was sure it took place around seven o'clock:

> Mr Barr: *Are you quite certain this happened on the night of Friday, or might it, from any doubt you have upon your mind, have happened at any other period of that day?*
>
> *No answer.*
>
> Mr Barr: *Can you speak with certainty about it, or may there be some doubt of it?*

Croft: *I am certain I saw him at seven o'clock.*
Mr Ferns: *You saw him at seven – speak the truth woman.*
Mr Barr: *But did this happen at seven?*
Croft: *When he took the liberty with me was in the day time, but
    I saw him at seven in the night.*

Eliza turned pale and trembled as she made the confession and there was a collective gasp from the public gallery.

Eliza Tate was next to give evidence and then Croft returned to the witness stand and was subjected to further questioning by Barr and Ferns, during which she reaffirmed that the alleged rape had taken place during the day. After this Lupton suggested the court should adjourn until Thursday. Confident that the rape charge would be overturned, Ferns saw no reason for an adjournment, but Lupton disagreed: 'We think there is a strong case, and the manner in which Croft has given her evidence only shows the lamentable amount of ignorance amongst the female part of the community.' As Harrison then got up to say a word to Ferns someone shouted 'Put him down', and when he was removed from dock there was a loud hissing from the women in the gallery, followed by loud cheers and laughing from the rest. There was also some animosity towards Brown. Many of those in the gallery knew she was more than just Harrison's house-keeper, and that she was complicit in his affairs. She was being disingenuous when she stated that, 'Sometimes young people went to visit him, but she did not know for what purpose. Some went for medicine, some for tooth powder, but for what, or whether for any other purpose she did not know.'[28] When in evidence she had said she was never present when he was engaged in fortune-telling there was a loud exclamation of disagreement from the gallery. At the end of the day's proceedings a considerable number of people lingered around the railings of the courthouse yard waiting for her and her niece to emerge. As the two women made their way home to North Row a hostile crowd formed around them but they received no physical abuse.

The final session of the trial began at ten o'clock on Thursday morning. The public gallery was again densely crowded, but less excited than on the Monday, perhaps because only one witness was questioned. Ferns had Rosanna Shores recalled to the witness box. He had been digging around for dirt on the various witnesses and had received information that Rosanna was not legally the wife of Benjamin Shores, that she was in fact married to a Mr Atkinson. Ferns hoped to further stain Eliza's reputation by casting doubt on the reliability of Rosanna as a character witness. She denied the allegation and insisted she was married to Shores, but despite repeated demands from Ferns refused to say when or where she was married. She clearly had something to hide, but the court clerk agreed with Barret that Ferns's line of questioning was not material to the case and so the examination came to an end.

Before Ferns rose to sum up for the defence, Barret addressed the magistrates' bench and said that on consideration of all the evidence given on Monday he would ask them to withdraw the charge of rape. He recommended instead that Harrison be charged under the Aggravated Assaults Act of 1854, which as we have seen was intended to bolster the protection of women and children from physical abuse. The charge of fortune-telling under the Vagrancy Act of 1824 remained. Barret's decision to drop the rape charge was based on pragmatic legal considerations. Eliza's lie about the timing of the alleged assault hardly helped her case, but there was also the observation that no one heard any sounds of struggle despite the soundproofing being so poor in the North Row that coughing and the ticking of clocks could be heard from one house to another. There was also the fact that she continued to consult Harrison alone in his room after he had already made sexual advances. Barret wanted to see Harrison punished for who he was and did not want to see him get off lightly by seeing a rape charge dropped. In the circumstances, a lesser charge stood more chance of succeeding.

Eliza's decision to make a complaint of rape and Barret's courtroom decision making has to be understood within the context of the legal interpretation of rape at the time. Legal attitudes were certainly changing during the second half of the nineteenth century, and with the ending of the mandatory death penalty for rapists in 1841 conviction rates rose significantly as juries were freed from sanctioning the ultimate penalty. Yet long-held misogynistic attitudes regarding female sexuality and sexual assault were still institutionalised. Some early nineteenth-century legal texts expressed caution in prosecuting rape because it was thought that some women desired force before consenting to sex.[29] Even towards the end of the century doctors such as the gynaecologist Charles Routh could opine that regarding women who made accusations of sexual assault,

'Except upon the strongest corroborating evidence, the presumption is
that they are liars, plausible liars, cunning liars.'[30] Furthermore, at a time
when drunkenness was still sometimes seen as an extenuating rather
than an aggravating circumstance with regard to male criminal intent,[31]
it was still considered by some as an act of culpability if ascribed to rape
victims. At the end of a trial in 1856 concerning the gang rape of a married middle-aged woman after she had gone into a Northampton public
house for a gin, the judge, Justice Willes, informed the jury, 'some doubts
were entertained whether the offence of rape could be committed upon
the person of a woman who had rendered herself perfectly insensible by
drink so as to be unable to give any signs of resistance.'[32] Similarly, prostitutes had little chance of successfully bringing prosecutions for rape, as
from the misogynistic perspective of the time they were 'asking for it'.

Glaring double standards can be found in society's attitudes towards
male and female sexual behaviour at this period, several of which made
it difficult for women to attain full legal redress for rape. One of the most
obvious concerned the social status of the victim. The middle-class
Victorian idealisation of female chastity and the horror at its violation did
not necessarily extend to working-class women and prostitutes in particular. The sexual assault of a middle-class woman in a railway carriage
was a brutal outrage but the rape of a female servant by her middle- or
upper-class master attracted far less opprobrium. For some the use of
female servants for sexual gratification, whether consenting or not, was
seen as being a master's right.[33] Furthermore, as work on sex and violence in mid-nineteenth-century Lancashire shows, certain sections of
working-class masculine society tolerated the sexual assault of single
women who socially interacted with men, whether it be during festivities,
merely accepting a lift or being alone in the same room with a man. If the
man was a significantly older male and a dominant figure in the community, like Harrison, then sexual assault was all the more acceptable,
and thus all the more difficult for the violated female to find redress.[34]

In this patriarchal and misogynistic social and legal climate it is no
wonder that women in general and those like Eliza in particular –
working-class, independent, working in the male environment of pubs
and inns – were reluctant to report cases of sexual assault. Considering
the usual defence tactic of questioning the moral probity of female com-
plainants, it could seem as if the victim was as much on trial as the

alleged rapist.[35] Why then did Eliza decide to go through the ordeal? She would have to endure the character assassination and mud of insinuation slung by the defence. Her friends, family and neighbours would be in the public gallery to hear it all. Her sexual history would be read by many thousands more in the newspapers. Furthermore, she must have also been fearful of Harrison's threat of bewitchment, and we have already seen what happened to Ritty Littlewood under similar circumstances. Eliza's overriding motive was probably not to see justice being done for a crime committed but rather the defence of her reputation within her own community. She only made a complaint, and that after much hesitation, after the gossip about her relations with Harrison had spread around the neighbourhood. Her experience is a vivid example of the huge import-ance placed on female sexual respectability. Eliza's social position and employability were at stake. In this respect her decision making was heavily influenced by the responses of the women rather than the men around her. Elizabeth Brown felt sexually threatened and clearly wanted Eliza out of sight. A female neighbour was instrumental in passing the gossip to the landlady of the New Cross Inn, who in turn showed little sympathy by immediately sacking Eliza. Only Hannah Wilson was sup-portive, but unfortunately we do not know what she said to convince Eliza to go to the police. It was certainly the case, though, that Eliza had to prove herself in the eyes of the female community in and around North Row and Meadow Lane and she could only do that by prosecuting Harrison and going public.

Eliza's position was boosted considerably by the fact that the magis-trates were unusually supportive and understanding of her precarious situation. She had, after all, been the means of trapping Harrison, a man who the local authorities considered a public enemy, a man who had embarrassed the reputation of the town. So they repaid her courage as best they could. They felt duty-bound to criticise what they considered Eliza's 'weakness, folly, and superstition', but were conscious of the public position she had put herself in: 'We can well comprehend that in the course of a long and severe examination, and the comments which have been made on her conduct, she may have exposed herself to some imputations.' Harrison had 'heaped upon this young woman charges and imputations of a most filthy and impure kind, which, if true, would stamp her with infamy for the rest of her life.' But the magistrates wanted to ensure that no one in the packed court, her neighbours, employers, family and friends, was in any doubt that Eliza was, 'in her station of life, a person of unblemished reputation, and that her general conduct and character have, from earliest life, been most exemplary and commendable.'[36]

Ferns began what was to be an impressive two-hour defence of his client, which focused almost entirely on the charge of assault. He expressed his satisfaction that what he described as the 'exceedingly incredible' accusation of rape was dropped, but thought that even the charge under the Aggravated Assaults Act was inappropriate. He pointed out that its provisions principally concerned domestic violence inflicted by husbands and fathers on wives and children and was not concerned with 'an assault upon a woman who submitted to his [Harrison's] amorous embraces.' In fact Ferns claimed the whole case had been trumped up to persecute Harrison, and suggested that 'but for the prejudice created against Harrison throughout the country, by the aid of the press, the prisoner would not then have been called upon to answer the charges preferred against him.' He politely queried Barret's motives for taking on the prosecution case, denounced Superintendent James's 'Jesuitical ingenuity' in procuring evidence, and offensively dismissed the evidence of constable Braithwaite, as 'they need only to look at his bloated face and lascivious mouth, to be satisfied as to his character.' Ferns's lashing tongue was rather less bold and rhetorical when it came to the charge of fortune-telling, primarily because there was no defence. He feebly suggested that 'some scraps of paper, old books and glasses' did not constitute evidence, and hoped the magistrates would not 'allow their minds to be warped by prejudice.'

Ferns finished speaking around a quarter past twelve and the magistrates retired to deliberate. Those in court waited expectantly. To while away the time one newspaper reporter thumbed through Harrison's manuscripts and books, which had been left on display in court as evidence of his occult trade. As he flicked through what turned out to be an account book the journalist came across an incriminating entry:

*Eliza Croft, 5s.*
*John Stephenson,*
*In love*
*—— at —— a fortnight.*

It proved that Harrison had lied about the sum given to him by Eliza. The book was immediately passed over to the magistrates who further asked for Superintendent James to bring them all the other books confiscated from Harrison's room.

The magistrates returned to give their judgment at one o'clock. Harrison was asked to stand up and then Lupton delivered his judgment. After going over the evidence, praising the work of the police and high-lighting the good character of Eliza Croft, he came to the verdict:

> We therefore, in respect of the offence of having imposed on Eliza Croft, by the arts and means to which we have referred (and of which you now stand convicted), adjudge you to be a rogue and vagabond, within the meaning of the Act of Parliament passed in the 5th year of the reign of George the Fourth, chapter 83, and for that offence we sentence you to be imprisoned, and kept to hard labour in the House of Correction for this borough, for the term of three calendar months. For the other offence of having assaulted and ill-treated Eliza Croft we adjudge that you be further imprisoned and kept to hard labour in the same House of Correction for the term of six calendar months, which term of imprisonment shall commence and take effect from and after the expiration of the first-mentioned period of three calendar months. And we further order that at the expiration of the said term of six calendar months, you do enter into recognizance in the sum of £100 for your good behaviour, for the six months then ensuing.

Both sentences were the maximum the magistrates could impose. There was a buzz of excitement as Lupton concluded but there was no further barracking of Harrison, who 'seemed to feel acutely his position.'[37] But just when the trial seemed to be at an end there was a sensational devel-opment. Before formally concluding the session Lupton asked the public gallery if anyone else wished to bring forward a complaint against Harrison. A careworn-looking woman stepped forward and announced, 'My name is Jane Harrison, and I am the wife of the prisoner. I am a mar-ried woman and have been married for twenty-three years. I live at Hunslet. The only complaint I have to make against the prisoner is for neglecting his wife and family. I was married to him on the 3rd of August 1833.' It was a set-up. The publicity of the Dove affair may indeed have boosted Harrison's fame but it also stirred the ghosts of his unsavoury past. Barret, like Ferns, had done his own muck-raking and found further means of punishing the man who had played such a profound part in the downfall of his former client. Barret now stood and addressed the court: 'This is his first wife. Mrs Brown we shall bring forward hereafter to show that she is his second wife.' Ferns loudly protested that 'they were hunting Harrison down'. The chase was relentless.

## 'This modern bluebeard'

The magistrates' bench reconvened at the courthouse on Saturday 8 November, where it became clear that Harrison was not charged with bigamously marrying Elizabeth Brown but rather her daughter. The story heard in court that day exposed the murky depths of Harrison's seedy life, rendering the claims of honour and probity expressed in his public letter to the press all the more worthless.

One day in late February 1846, not long after Harrison had begun lodging in the house of Elizabeth Brown in Moor End, he took advantage of his landlady being away to force her sixteen-year-old daughter Sarah Ann to have sex with him. It is worth pointing out that the legal age of consent at this period was only twelve years old. When Elizabeth returned, Sarah Ann told her what had happened. Instead of reporting Harrison to the police for rape, Elizabeth coerced him into marrying her daughter, and on 18 May they were wed at Rothwell Church. The only witnesses were Elizabeth, who being illiterate made a cross in the register, and the church sexton John Flockton, who signed his name in a shaky hand. Sarah Ann gave her age as eighteen. Although girls could marry at the age of only fourteen, to marry under the age of eighteen was uncommon and apparently not very socially acceptable. The marriage meant nothing to Harrison, of course, and when they arrived back home from the church Harrison asked for the wedding ring back.

Harrison only slept with his new wife for a few nights and then resumed sharing a bed with her mother in the same room (there were hisses and cries of 'shame' from the public gallery on hearing this revelation). Nine months later Sarah Ann gave birth. The confinement went badly and Sarah Ann fell seriously ill. Worse was to come as the baby was taken away by Harrison and given to a woman in Providence Street to nurse. The next time she saw her baby it was dead. When Sarah Ann gave this evidence in court it caused a sensation in the public gallery and her mother fainted and had to be taken out of court. Proceedings resumed with Sarah Ann telling how she continued to live under the peculiar domestic arrangements for a year or two after her shotgun wedding, and then went to live with her cousin Elizabeth Saxton. Sometime during this period she was told by a neighbour that Harrison was already married. Considering they were hardly living as a couple, this news may not have been too traumatising, and certainly did not stop her from bigamously marrying a man named John Sutcliffe at St Marks, Woodhouse, in 1851, albeit under her maiden name.

As if this was not sufficient evidence of Harrison's disgraceful behaviour, the court then heard from Maria Steel. Harrison had married her at St John's Church, Wakefield, in October 1850. They had met one night in a railway carriage as Harrison returned from a pleasure excursion to Liverpool. Like Harrison, Maria was already married, to a man named John Steel. She had lived with him for eleven months and then he left. When she met Harrison she had not heard from Steel for several years and so she considered the marriage void. Following the marriage ceremony Maria went to live with Harrison in his lodgings in the Dewsbury Road but their relationship lasted only another eight days. Her brother, John Wright, who worked on the power looms at Marshall's factory, got to hear that Harrison was already married and confronted him with this knowledge. Harrison denied it, but he was not a convincing liar. When Maria and her brother went to collect her things from Dove's room they found the door locked. Around five o'clock the next morning Maria got a ladder and climbed up to the bedroom window, where she saw Harrison in bed with Elizabeth Brown. She called upon her sister and told her what she saw and her sister then went to a policeman who demanded entry and returned Maria's clothes to her.

Ferns employed his usual tactic, staining Maria's character by suggesting she had been a prostitute, but Maria emphatically swore she 'never walked the streets'. After hearing all the witnesses the magistrates decided there was sufficient evidence for the case to be brought before a jury. Harrison was called upon to answer the charge of bigamy but declined to say anything, and so he was committed for trial at the next assizes in York.

The tangled web of bigamy laid bare in court was nothing particularly unusual. Bigamy was probably fairly widespread in working-class urban areas at the time, and certainly understandable considering the nature of the marriage laws. It was easy to get away with it in rapidly expanding towns like Leeds. Churches were dealing with so many marriages that clergymen and clerks had neither the time nor the resources to check the backgrounds of those requesting to be married. Furthermore, relatively few of those who were deserted by or who unwittingly married bigamists bothered to prosecute. Between 1853 and 1863, for example, only 884 cases were tried.[38] This is primarily because the offended parties preferred to avoid publicising their marital status. After all, from what we have seen already, some of those who married bigamists went on to commit bigamy. The alternatives were to cohabit openly with another man and incur social stigmatisation, pretend to be married or remain single. It was actually the Poor Law authorities who instigated many of the bigamy prosecutions. When deserted wives, like Jane Brayshay, requested poor relief the authorities would investigate why their husbands were not supporting them. Then the bigamy would be revealed and the police would be called in. A typical example was that of John Rouke of Leeds. He had first married Mary Ann Parker in Silkstone Church in 1844 when he was only sixteen, but abandoned her a few years later. In 1854 he married Jane Everett. He soon left her and she was reduced to poverty and had to enter the workhouse. After questioning her regarding her marital status the Leeds Poor Law tracked down Rouke and he was sentenced to a year in prison.[39]

Despite the preoccupation of the middle- and upper-class establishment with 'family values', little concern was expressed about the 'problem' of bigamy among the working classes. While uncommon middle- and upper-class prosecutions, such as that of the aristocrat William Yelverton in 1861,[40] attracted considerable attention, newspapers reported bigamy cases among the lower classes in a perfunctory and apathetic manner. *The Times*, in its brief record of Harrison's bigamy trial, remarked, 'The only feature of interest in the case was that the prisoner is the Leeds wizard who gave evidence on Dove's trial.'[41] Indeed, during the parliamentary debate over the Matrimonial Causes Act in 1856, the House of Commons was made aware that bigamy and cohabitation was widespread among the poor, and that the proposed Act would perpetuate this condition because the cost of divorce would be way beyond their means. The predominant feeling in the Lords and to a lesser extent in the

Commons, however, was that it was a far greater threat to the moral fabric of society to give the working classes access to divorce. With despicable hypocrisy Bishop Wilberforce warned that such a move 'would be purchased at the price of the introduction of unlimited pollution.'[42] Yet it was the lack of divorce that enabled pollutants like Harrison to sow discord and misery in the lives of women and trigger a chain reaction of bigamy and bastardy.

## Just deserts

So, Harrison found himself taking the same journey to York Castle that William had taken some eight months before. The circumstances were quite different of course. Harrison was not facing the death penalty and public interest in him outside Leeds had died down. There were an unusually large number of cases to be heard that winter assizes involving 116 prisoners. It was in fact one of the busiest York winter assizes on record, and among the indictments there were far more salacious and sensational cases to report on than that of Harrison's bigamy; besides, there were three other bigamists on trial including John Rouke.[43] Most public attention was focused on John Hannah, a Manchester tailor who murdered Jane Banham, the principal dancer of a troop of entertainers who toured around the towns of the West Riding. After Banham's husband had deserted her and emigrated to America, she lived with Hannah and had several children. When she decided to leave him he slit her throat. Naturally the court was packed to hear the judge sentence him to death.

Harrison was tried on Tuesday 9 December, before the judge William Erle. It was not a long affair, being just one of numerous cases dealt with by the judge that day. Nevertheless, Harrison's notoriety was enough to ensure that the public gallery was crowded. The prosecution presented the same incontrovertible evidence that had already been heard by the Leeds magistrates, and Harrison's defence lawyer, Mr Maule, faced an impossible task to elicit any sympathy from the jury. He pleaded with them to discard all prejudices they might have had, observing, probably correctly, that, had his client not given evidence at an important criminal trial, which he refrained from naming, the charge of bigamy would never have been raised. That trial, he said, had caused 'much talk and ill-feeling to be entertained' towards Harrison, and put in motion the project to 'unfairly crush' him. He asked them to consider the case as if it were 'against a man named John Smith, who belonged to some obscure village, and against whom they knew nothing.' The jury was not impressed and it took only a few minutes consultation to return a verdict of guilty, to the evident approval of the public gallery. Judge Erle turned to Harrison and told him he had been 'leading a life of unparalleled profligacy,' and sentenced him to four years' penal servitude.[44] So, as the wizard was led out of court, the curtain closed on an extraordinary public drama of poison, murder, rape and bigamy. Harrison no doubt cursed the day he first met William Dove but he had only himself to blame for his crimes. The 'great Yorkshire Astrologer' had been badly let down by his Book of Destiny. The stars had intimated nothing to him of his fate, of the consequences of reading aloud from *The Times* that fateful January day.

# Notes and references

**1** See Altick, *Evil Encounters*, ch. 4; Dallas Liddle, 'Anatomy of a "nine days' Wonder": Sensational Journalism in the Decade of the Sensation Novel', in Andrew Maunder and Grace Moore (eds), *Crime, Madness and Sensation* (Aldershot, 2004). My thanks to Andrew Maunder for a pre-publication draft of this book.

**2** *The Times*, 13 August 1856; *Western Flying Post*, 26 August 1856; *Leeds Times*, 16 August 1856.

**3** *Leeds Intelligencer*, 16 August 1856.

**4** *News of the World*, 21 September 1856.

**5** *The Times*, 13 August 1856.

**6** Cited in the *Leeds Mercury*, 19 August 1856.

**7** On provincial newspaper sensitivities in this respect see Owen Davies, 'Newspapers and the Popular Belief in Witchcraft and Magic', *Journal of British Studies*, 37 (1998), p. 151.

**8** *Western Flying Post*, 26 August 1856.

**9** *Leeds Times*, 1 November 1856.

**10** *Leeds Intelligencer*, 16 August 1856.

**11** Reprinted in the *Leeds Times*, 23 August 1856.

**12** *News of the World*, 17 August 1857; 'The Literature and Religion of Murder', *Saturday Review*, 16 August 1856.

13 *Leeds Times*, 15 November 1856.

14 *Leeds Intelligencer*, 16 August 1856. See also Davies, *Witchcraft, magic and culture*, pp. 51–4.

15 *News of the World*, 21 September 1856.

16 *Leeds Times*, 1 November 1856.

17 *Leeds Mercury*, 19 August 1856; *York Herald*, 23 August 1856; *Leeds Times*, 23 August 1856.

18 The following account of Harrison's trials is based on reports in the *Leeds Intelligencer*, 25 October 1856; 1 November 1856; 13 December 1856; *Leeds Mercury*, 11 December 1856; *News of the World*, 16 November 1856; PRO ASSI 41, 25.

19 *Leeds Intelligencer*, 16 August 1856. See also Davies, 'Newspapers and the Popular Belief in Witchcraft and Magic', p. 152; Davies, *Cunning-Folk*, p. 27.

20 *Punch*, 25 October 1856. On *Punch*'s satire of almanacs see Maureen Perkins, *Visions of the Future: Almanacs, Time, and Cultural Change* (Oxford, 1996), pp. 145–53; Perkins, *The Reform of Time: Magic and Modernity* (London, 2001), pp. 107–16.

21 *Punch*, 1 November 1856.

22 Shani D'Cruze, 'Sex, Violence and Local Courts: Working-Class Respectability in a Mid-Nineteenth-Century Lancashire Town', *British Journal of Criminology*, 39 (1999), p. 50.

23 John Webster, *Displaying of Supposed Witchcraft* (London, 1677), p. 311.

24 Davies, *Witchcraft, magic and culture*, pp. 216–7; Jason Semmens, *The Witch of the West: Or, The Strange and Wonderful History of Thomasine Blight* (Plymouth, 2004), pp. 36–7.

25 See John M. Riddle, *Eve's Herbs: A History of Contraception and Abortion in the West* (Cambridge, Mass., 1997).

26 See Angus Mclaren, *Reproductive Rituals* (London, 1984), pp. 102–6; David E. Allen and Gabrielle Hatfield, *Medicinal Plants in Folk Tradition* (Portland and Cambridge, 2004), pp. 65–6, 238–40; Roy Vickery, *A Dictionary of Plant-lore* (Oxford, 1995).

27 *Leeds Intelligencer*, 18 July 1857; *The Times*, 16 July 1857, 22 July 1857.

28 *Leeds Intelligencer*, 1 November 1856.

29 See Ann Clark, *Women's silence, men's violence: sexual assault in England, 1770–1845* (London, 1987); Gattrell, *Hanging Tree*, pp. 470–74.

30 McLaren, A *Prescription for Murder*, pp. 84–5.

31 Wiener, *Men of Blood*, pp. 255–70; Smith, *Trial by Medicine*, pp. 85–7.

32  *The Times*, 6 December 1856. See also Kim Stevenson, 'Observations on the Law Relating to Sexual Offences: The Historical Scandal of Women's Silence', *Web Journal of Current Legal Issues* (1999).

33  See Caroline Conley, *The Unwritten Law: Criminal Justice in Victorian Kent* (Oxford, 1991), pp. 81–95.

34  Shani D'Cruze, *Crimes of Outrage: Sex, Violence and Victorian Working Women* (London, 1998); D'Cruze, 'Sex, Violence and Local Courts', pp. 39–55; D'Cruze, 'Approaching the History of Rape and Sexual Violence: notes towards Research', *Women's History Review*, 1 (1993), pp. 377–97. See also Jill Barber, '"Stolen Goods": The sexual harassment of female servants in West Wales during the nineteenth century', *Rural History*, 4 (1993), pp. 123–36.

35  See Clive Emsley, *Crime and Society in England 1750–1900* (2nd edn, London, 1996), pp. 161–3.

36  *Leeds Intelligencer*, 1 November 1856.

37  *Leeds Intelligencer*, 1 November 1856.

38  Cited in Rebecca Gill, 'The Imperial Anxieties of a Nineteenth-Century Bigamy Case', *History Workshop Journal*, 57 (2004), p. 75.

39  *Leeds Mercury*, 11 December 1856.

40  See Gill, 'Imperial Anxieties', pp. 59–78; G. Frost, 'Bigamy and cohabitation in Victorian England', *Journal of Family History*, 22 (1997), pp. 286–306.

41  *The Times*, 11 December 1856.

42  Cited in Stone, *Road to Divorce*, p. 371.

43  *The Times*, 3 December 1856.

44  *Leeds Intelligencer*, 13 December 1856.

# Epilogue

'The closing scene of Dove's strange and eventful history forms one of those fearfully startling incidents which survive the record of the moment, and become as it were great landmarks in the annals of crime.' So stated the *Leeds Intelligencer* shortly after William's execution. What he did, the paper asserted, 'would remain for generations an object of fear and repugnance, there can be no doubt.'[1] Hindsight suggests otherwise. With Harrison finally behind bars and out of the public eye the name of William Dove became yesterday's news, no doubt much to the relief of his family. His trial certainly became a standard citation in textbooks on poisoning and medical jurisprudence.[2] Yet his crime did not resonate through history as the *Leeds Intelligencer* predicted. In contrast, the name of William Palmer had a lasting fascination for the media, later joined in the annals of 'true crime' by other sensational middle-class poisoners, such as Dr Harvey Crippen and Herbert Armstrong the 'Hay Poisoner'. In 1957 Palmer was even the subject of a sympathetic novel by Robert Graves, *They Hanged My Saintly Billy*. The same year he was mentioned in the popular comedy film *Doctor at Large* (1957) starring Dirk Bogarde. More recently, in 1998, he was the subject of a BBC drama, and in 2004 there was an exhibition dedicated to him at Stafford.

L. Perry Curtis, in his study on the press coverage of Jack the Ripper, pondered the question of why certain murders were given extensive press coverage in the Victorian period and others were treated as 'news in brief'.[3] As he suggests, all murders reflected the 'Victorian obsession with character and virtuous conduct', and those where women were the culprits or that involved multiple victims, appeared motiveless, or demonstrated excessive brutality were most likely to catch the newspaper editors' attention. Of equal cultural significance, though, is the question of why certain murderers endured in the public consciousness and others did not. I am not suggesting for one minute that William Dove *deserves* to be remembered nearly a century and a half later, but why is his name largely forgotten when Palmer's lives on? Both were middle class and committed the same type of murder. Both received blanket coverage in the press, though because Palmer was tried in the capital the column inches dedicated to the trial were greater in the London newspapers. Dove's notoriety may have been lessened by being seen as an imitator, but his case had the added spice of magic. The most significant difference between the two murderers was that Dove confessed and Palmer did not, and that is the key reason for the longevity of Palmer's name and the obscurity of Dove's. The act of confession largely killed off public interest. There were certainly doubts about his sanity and, therefore, his culpability, but such questions held little interest for those seeking entertainment from murder. What keeps notoriety alive is speculation. If the criminal did not confess, then there remained the tantalising possibility that he or she was innocent, that someone else was the culprit. Even when there was little public doubt about guilt, there was still the mystery, particularly in poisoning cases, of how and why the crime was committed. Had the prosecution been accurate in its reconstruction of events leading up to the murder? In Dove's case the speculation could have arisen later as to whether he had also poisoned his father in order to fulfil Harrison's prediction and so get his hands on his annuity; remember the unsubstantiated rumours that fed the sensational prospect of Palmer being a serial killer. Dove's confession of his guilt effectively rendered all further lurid conjecture pointless, and that was at least some comfort to his family.

While William Dove's impression on the public consciousness may have been fleeting, he and his crime obviously had a more lasting and profound influence on those individuals who knew him or were involved in his trial. We cannot fathom the depths of grief experienced by the Doves and the Jenkins, or how it resonated through the rest of their lives. The *Wesleyan Times* stated that several preachers' families related to the Doves had 'been thrown into deep affliction by this terrible catastrophe and deep humiliation.'[4] The *Watchman* talked of the 'fragrance' attached to the Dove name being tainted with murder and madness. 'An estimable family,' it wrote, 'is now plunged in humiliation and woe,' but the church, it promised, would 'not on that account disown their name, or withdraw its sympathy.'[5] After the trial, William's mother removed from her home of twenty-five years and went to stay with William Lord's family at Woodhouse Grove. According to one acquaintance, she 'bore with wonderful fortitude the terrible affliction of her son's crime, and its dreadful consequence; but she was heart-stricken by the woeful infliction, and welcome was the grave which opened up for her.'[6] She died in 1858 and, shortly after, Lord retired as governor of Woodhouse Grove School.[7]

In contrast with the concern and sympathy expressed towards the Doves and their reputation, the suffering of the Jenkins received hardly any compassionate acknowledgement by the Methodist press. One gets the impression that the murder of a daughter was worthy of less commiseration than the tarnishing of a respected name. The Jenkins remained in the media shadows because of their more humble social status. They no doubt, and quite understandably, considered this a blessing, but, as a consequence, there are few leads for the historian to discover how their lives were affected. We do know that John Sloggett Jenkins and his wife Sarah returned from Madras a few years after the trial. Jenkins evidently gave up his ministration and teaching and, by the mid-1870s, the couple had settled in Great Malvern, where Jenkins became the proprietor and editor of the *Malvern Advertiser*, a local mouthpiece of independent politics. He did not give up his faith, though, and continued to perform as a preacher.[8]

The trial and execution of William Dove certainly did no harm to Baron Bramwell's career. He went on to become a highly respected judge, harsh on criminals but also sometimes sensitive to miscarriages of justice.[9] He became a prominent exponent of *laissez-faire* liberalism, upholding in court the protection of employers against employees' claims for compensation due to injury. He was also ardently against Teetotalism and in 1885 wrote *Drink*, a best-selling pamphlet upholding the right to imbibe. As to Thomas Askren, who carried out the sentence imposed by Bramwell, he also went on to have a notable public career. For twenty years he was York's executioner and also carried out hangings in Leeds, Durham, Lincoln and Edinburgh. Over the years his skills with the rope showed no signs of improvement, indeed they seemed to get worse. In 1865 Askren presided over the hanging of the wife murderer Matthew Atkinson, at which the rope broke, letting Atkinson plunge fifteen feet to the ground. It was just as well for Askren that the next time such an incident happened, in 1877, it was not in public view, though several journalists were present to see the rope around John Henry Johnson's neck break, and subsequently witness his protracted death throes during Askren's bungled second attempt to hang him.[10] The hangman himself died the following year on 6 December 1878. Thomas Wright was so affected by his final hours with William that he stated shortly after his execution that he would not be visiting other condemned prisoners in the foreseeable future, and would concentrate on his other philanthropic ventures. Yet we find him ministering to William Jackson in Chester prison in December 1856, prior to his execution by Calcraft. A few days later, Wright was back at York consoling John Hannah, who was hung by Askren on 27 December before a crowd of some 5000 people.[11]

Not long after the trial of Harrison, Joseph Morton Barret became a Leeds town councillor, and it is likely that his role in the defence of Dove and the prosecution of the wizard was influential in his elevation in Leeds society. He died in 1870. Thomas Nunneley also joined the town council and was later appointed surgeon to the Leeds General Infirmary in 1864. Two years after the Dove affair he published a big book on *The Organs of Vision*. It attracted poor sales and some bad reviews evidently inspired by personal animosities – perhaps the consequence of the positions he had taken at the trials of Palmer and Dove.[12] Nunneley's colleague George Morley drifted back into relative obscurity, though he did give evidence at another poisoning trial in 1858. John Sagar, a one-time painter, druggist and innkeeper, but then master of the Keighley workhouse, stood accused of killing his wife using arsenic. Morley was the expert medical witness at the trial and testified that all his tests demonstrated a fatal amount of the poison was the cause of death. The workhouse doctor testified, however, that Sagar's wife had died of natural causes. The local surgeon who conducted the *post mortem* confirmed that Sagar's wife had died from inflammation of the bowels but declined to say whether he thought it was caused by the administration of arsenic.[13] As a consequence Sagar was found not guilty. Morley retired to Jersey a few years later and died in 1867.[14]

It is, perhaps, rather appropriate that the fate of Henry Harrison remains a mystery to me. I have been unable to trace his movements subsequent to entering prison. I could have engaged on a genealogical trail to trace his two children by Jane Brayshaw, but it would have served no academic purpose. For a few months Harrison was the most famous and reviled wizard in Britain, yet as with his former client, William Dove, his name faded into obscurity. The story of one of his professional predecessors, Mary Bateman, is still known in Leeds, and I guess this book might revive similar local interest in Harrison, though, if it does, I hope it provokes more than just titillation.

Most of the locations in this book have changed beyond all recognition. The villages of Burley and Normanton have been engulfed by the sprawling expansion of Leeds. While Park Square remains intact, and the Dove family home is now occupied by solicitors, much of the urban environment of mid-nineteenth-century Leeds has disappeared. The South Market, North Row, and the New Cross Inn were all torn down during the programmes of urban renewal of the twentieth century. Nevertheless, the childhood reminiscences of Richard Hoggart in *The Uses of Literacy*, his classic book on working-class urban culture, suggest that something of the flavour of life in Harrison's day survived into the early twentieth century. Hoggett grew up in the district of Hunslet, not far from where Harrison lived, and recalled some of the folk beliefs held by the locals and the continued presence of the herbalists' stalls at the local fair.[15]

Today there are still several locations where the curious can connect, however tenuously, with the events recounted in this book. You can visit Oxford Place Chapel, though due to later renovation and a fire in 1911 not much of the original building survives, and meditate on the influence of Methodism in William's life and how the Wesleyan community responded to his behaviour and death. Perhaps you might then move on to the Scarborough Hotel, where you can sup a pint of real ale and consider the influence of drink on William's actions in the same building where the first day of Harriet Dove's inquest was held. You could then move on to the Old Red Lion, one of Harrison's haunts in Meadow Lane, and cogitate on the central role of the pub in the wizard's life and business. I have an inkling the pub still accepts the magical fraternity. If you still have the afternoon to spare, and someone else is driving, then a drive up the A64, the old Turnpike Road to York, will take you past White Well Farm, though the stream of cars that bomb past on the way to join the A1 now gives little sense of the isolation that Harriet must have experienced at White Well. The Fox and Grapes pub, where Harrison and Dove went for a drink after sowing magical talismans around the farm, is still there serving thirsty travellers. This hypothetical journey ends at York, where one can experience a more sober reminder of William's fate by visiting the condemned cell in York Castle Museum.

If any reader does follow this itinerary, I hope they will reflect as much on the broad context of the story as on the lives of the people concerned. The crimes perpetrated by Dove and Harrison were not just the acts of individuals committed against individuals, they were also the product of the society in which were committed. Society creates and shapes criminal activity. Consider, for example, whether William would have murdered Harriet if they had been able to divorce rather than merely separate. Would the Matrimonial Causes Act, made law only a year later, have saved her life? As we have seen, for the urban working classes bigamy and cohabitation provided a way out of unhappy or abusive marriages, but for the Doves, bound by the restrictions of class and religion, such options were out of the question. In this sense Harrison was better off than his social superior, but then he was the sort of man to abuse that illicit freedom. But if society shapes crime, then crime, through its reporting, interpretation and punishment, also shapes society. Through the medium of the newspapers, the actions and ultimate fate of William Dove influenced society's understanding, or should that be misunderstanding, of poisoning. William's actions were also a significant influence upon the evolving role of psychiatry in English jurisprudence, and his death contributed to the national debate over execution, highlighting the issue of whether killing justified state-sanctioned murder. But while arguing that Dove's crime must be understood as a societal as well as an individual action, it is only fitting that this book ends by suggesting that one person above all deserves to be remembered. We will never know Harriet Dove's version of events: she was a victim in life and remains voiceless in history.

## Notes and references

1 *Leeds Intelligencer*, 16 August 1856.

2 See, for example, George Lathom Browne and Charles Stewart, *Reports of Trials for Murder by Poisoning* (London, 1883), pp. 233–68; James Fitzjames

Stephen, *A History of the Criminal Law of England* (London, 1883), vol. 3, pp. 426–37. Stephen's account was based on notes taken by Baron Bramwell.

3  Curtis, *Jack the Ripper*, p. 12.

4  *Wesleyan Times*, 4 August 1856.

5  *The Watchman*, 24 July 1856.

6  Spencer, *Men that are gone*, p. 151.

7  Lord died at Manningham in 1873 aged eighty-two; Slugg, *Woodhouse Grove School*, pp. 74 and 78.

8  See *The Post Office Directory of Worcestershire* (London, 1876), p. 1012; *Littlebury's Directory and Gazetteer of Worcestershire and District* (Edinburgh and London, 1879), p. 297; Slugg, *Woodhouse Grove School*, p. 142.

9  See Chadwick, *Bureaucratic Mercy*, pp. 151–6.

10  Bland, *Common Hangman*, p. 169.

11  *The Times*, 22 December 1856; McDermid, *Life of T. Wright*, p. 48.

12  *DNB*.

13  *The Times*, 19 March 1858.

14  Slugg, *Woodhouse Grove School*, p. 288.

15  Richard Hoggart, *The Uses of Literacy* (London, 1957), pp. 13, 17–19, 32.

# Bibliography

Abbott, Geoffrey, *William Calcraft: Executioner Extra-ordinaire!* (St Albans, 2004).

*A Historical Guide to Leeds and its Environs* (Leeds, 1858).

Allen, David E. and Gabrielle Hatfield, *Medicinal Plants in Folk Tradition* (Portland and Cambridge, 2004).

Alpert, Michael, *London 1849: A Victorian Murder Story* (London, 2004).

Altick, Richard D., *Evil Encounters: Two Victorian Sensations* (London, 1987).

Altick, Richard D., *Victorian Studies in Scarlet* (New York, 1970).

Andrews, Jonathan and Andrew Scull, *Undertaker of the Mind: John Monro and Mad-Doctoring in Eighteenth-Century England* (Berkeley, 2001).

Anning, S.T., 'Early Medical Education in Leeds', in Beresford and Jones (eds), *Leeds and its Region*.

Anning, S.T. and W.K.J. Walls, *A History of the Leeds School of Medicine* (Leeds, 1982).

Anning, S.T., *The History of Medicine in Leeds* (Leeds, 1980).

Augstein, H.F., *James Cowles Prichard's anthropology: remaking the science of man in early nineteenth-century Britain* (London, 1998).

Augstein, H.F., 'J.C. Prichard's Concept of Moral Insanity – A Medical Theory of the Corruption of Human Nature', *Medical History*, 40 (1996), pp. 311–43.

Baines, Edward, *The Life of Edward Baines* (London, 1851).

Baines, Edward, *History, Directory and Gazetteer of the County of York* (Leeds, 1822).

Barber, Jill, '"Stolen Goods": The sexual harassment of female servants in West Wales during the nineteenth century', *Rural History*, 4 (1993), pp. 123–36.

Barnard, Sylvia, *Viewing the Breathless Corpse: Coroners and Inquests in Victorian Leeds* (Leeds, 2001).

Barnard, Sylvia, *To Prove I'm not Forgot: Living and Dying in a Victorian City* (Manchester, 1990).

Barr, John, *A statement of facts, being a brief history of the measures adopted by the Leeds Wesleyan Methodist Society, in their opposition to the introduction of an organ into Brunswick Chapel* (Leeds, 1827).

Bartlett, Peter, 'Legal Madness in the Nineteenth Century', *Social History of Medicine*, 14, 1 (2001), pp. 107–31.

Bartrip, Peter, 'A "Pennurth of Arsenic for Rat Poison": The Arsenic Act, 1851 and the Prevention of Secret Poisoning', *Medical History*, 36 (1992), pp. 53–69.

Bartrip, Peter, 'Public opinion and law enforcement: The ticket-of-leave scares in mid-Victorian Britain', in V. Bailey (ed.), *Policing and Punishment in Nineteenth-Century Britain* (London, 1982).

Bate, Jonathan, *John Clare* (London, 2004).

Bateson, Charles, *The Convict Ships, 1787–1868* (Glasgow, 1959).

Bebbington, David, 'Gospel and culture in Victorian Nonconformity', in Jane Shaw and Alan Kreider (eds), *Culture and the Nonconformist Tradition* (Cardiff, 1999), pp. 43–62.

Beckworth, William, *A Book of Remembrance: Records of Leeds Primitive Methodism* (London, 1910).

Beier, Lucinda McCray, *Sufferers and Healers: The experience of illness in seventeenth-century England* (London and New York, 1987).

Beresford, M.W., *East End, West End: The Face of Leeds During Urbanisation 1684–1842* (Leeds, 1986).

Beresford, M.W. and G.R.J. Jones (eds), *Leeds and its Region* (Leeds, 1967).

Bland, James, *The Common Hangman* (Whitecroft, 2000).

Bleackley, Horace, *The Hangmen of England* (London, 1929).

Blécourt, Willem de and Owen Davies, *Witchcraft continued: Popular magic in modern Europe* (Manchester, 2004).

Bourke, Angela, *The Burning of Bridget Cleary: A True Story* (London, 1999).

Boyle, Thomas, *Black Swine in the Sewers of Hampstead: Beneath the Surface of Victorian Sensationalism* (London, 1990).

Bridges, Frederick, *Phreno-Physiometrical Characteristics of James Spollin, who was tried for the Murder of Mr. George S. Little* (London, 1858).

Bridges, Frederick, *Phrenology Made Practical and Popularly Explained* (4th edn, London, n.d.). First published 1857.

Briggs, Asa, 'Cholera and Society in the Nineteenth Century', *Past and Present*, 19 (1961), pp. 76–96.

Briggs, Katherine, A *Dictionary of Fairies* (London, 1976).

Browne, J. Crichton, 'Cranial Injuries and Mental Diseases', *West Riding Lunatic Asylum Medical Reports*, 2 (1872), pp. 97–136.

Brown, P.S., 'The vicissitudes of herbalism in late nineteenth- and early twentieth-century Britain', *Medical History*, 29 (1985), pp. 71–93.

Brown, P.S., 'Herbalists and medical botanists in mid-nineteenth-century Britain with   special reference to Bristol', *Medical History*, 26 (1982), pp. 405–21.

Bucknill, John Charles and Daniel H. Tuke, *A Manual of Psychological Medicine* (London, 1858).

Bucknill, John Charles, 'Plea of Insanity – The Trial of William Dove', *Journal of Mental Science*, 3 (1857), pp. 125–34.

Budd, K., 'Research into anaesthetic by a surgeon: Thomas Nunneley of Leeds', *Proceedings of the History of Anaesthesia Society*, 15 (1994), pp. 9–15.

Burney, Ian, *Bodies of Evidence: Medicine and the Politics of the English Inquest, 1830–1926* (Baltimore, 2000).

Burney, Ian, 'A Poisoning of No Substance: The Trials of Medico-Legal Proof in Mid-Victorian England', *Journal of British Studies*, 38 (1999), pp. 59–92.

Bynum, W.F. and Roy Porter (eds), *Medical Fringe and Medical Orthodoxy 1750–1850* (London, 1987).

Campbell, J. Menzies, *Dentistry Then and Now* (Glasgow, 1981).

Chadwick, Roger, *Bureaucratic Mercy: The Home Office and the Treatment of Capital Cases in Victorian England* (New York and London, 1992).

Clark, Ann, *Women's silence, men's violence: sexual assault in England, 1770–1845* (London, 1987).

Clough, W.C., 'Cases of paralysis cured by strychnine', *The Lancet*, 29, 757 (1838), pp. 805–6.

Cockburn, J.S., 'Patterns of violence in English society: homicide in Kent 1560–1985', *Past and Present*, 130 (1991), pp. 70–106.

Coley, Noel G., 'Alfred Swaine Taylor, MD, FRS (1806–1880): Forensic Toxicologist', *Medical History*, 35 (1991), pp. 409–27.

Conley, Carolyn A., *The Unwritten Law: Criminal Justice in Victorian Kent* (Oxford, 1991).

Cookson, Gillian, The *Townscape of Darlington* (Woodbridge, 2003).

Cooper, David D., 'Public Executions in Victorian England: A Reform Adrift', in Thesing (ed.), *Executions*, pp. 149–64.

Cooper, David D., *The Lesson of the Scaffold: The Public Execution Controversy in Victorian England* (London, 1974).

Cooter, Roger, *Phrenology in the British Isles: An Annotated, Historical Bibliography and Index* (Metuchen and London, 1989).

Cooter, Roger, *The cultural meaning of popular science: Phrenology and the organization of consent in nineteenth-century Britain* (Cambridge, 1984).

Currie, R., *Methodism Divided: A Study in the Sociology of Ecumenicalism* (London, 1968).

Curtis, L. Perry, *Jack the Ripper and the London Press* (New Haven and London, 2001).

Davies, Owen, *Cunning-Folk: Popular Magic in English History* (London, 2003).

Davies, Owen, *Witchcraft, magic and culture 1736–1951* (Manchester, 1999).

Davies, Owen, *A People Bewitched: Witchcraft and Magic in Nineteenth-Century Somerset* (Bruton, 1999).

Davies, Owen, 'Cunning-folk in the Medical Market-Place during the Nineteenth Century', *Medical History*, 43 (1999), pp. 55–73.

Davies, Owen, 'Newspapers and the Popular Belief in Witchcraft and Magic', *Journal of British Studies*, 37 (1998), pp. 139–66.

Davies, Owen, 'Cunning-folk in England and Wales during the Eighteenth and Nineteenth Centuries', *Rural History*, 8 (1997), pp. 93–109.

Davies, Owen, 'Urbanisation and the Decline of Witchcraft: An Examination of London', *Journal of Social History*, 30 (1997), pp. 597–617.

Davies, Owen, 'Methodism, the Clergy, and the Popular Belief in Witchcraft and Magic', *History*, 82 (1997), pp. 252–65.

Dawson, W. Harbutt, *History of Skipton* (London, 1882).

D'Cruze, Shani, 'Sex, Violence and Local Courts: Working-Class Respectability in a Mid-Nineteenth-Century Lancashire Town', *British Journal of Criminology*, 39 (1999), pp. 39–55.

D'Cruze, Shani, *Crimes of Outrage: Sex, Violence and Victorian Working Women* (London, 1998).

D'Cruze, Shani, 'Approaching the History of Rape and Sexual Violence: notes towards Research', *Women's History Review*, 1 (1993), pp. 377–97.

Dews, Colin D., *Oxford Place Methodist Centre, Leeds, 1835–1985: a history of one hundred and fifty years of worship and witness* (Leeds, n.d.).

Ditchfield, G.M., *The Evangelical Revival* (London, 1998).

Dungett, John (ed.), *Life and Correspondence of the late Mrs. Margaret Burton, of Darlington* (Darlington, 1832).

Eigen, Joel Peter, *Unconscious Crime: Mental Absence and Criminal Responsibility in Victorian London* (Baltimore, 2003).

Eigen, Joel Peter, *Witnessing Insanity: Madness and Mad-Doctors in the English Court* (New Haven and London, 1995).

Emmerichs, Mary Beth, ' "Getting away with Murder?" Homicide and the Coroners in Nineteenth-Century London', *Social Science History*, 25, 1 (2001), pp. 93–100.

Emsley, Clive, *Crime and Society in England 1750–1900* (2nd edn, London, 1996).

*Extraordinary Life and Character of Mary Bateman, the Yorkshire Witch* (Leeds, 1809).

Fairfield, Charles, *Some Account of George William Wilshere, Baron Bramwell of Hever* (London, 1898).

Falret, Jean-Pierre, *De l'hypochondrie et du suicide* (Paris, 1822).

Feldmann, Theodore, 'Bipolar Disorder and Violence', *Psychiatric Quarterly*, 72, 2 (2001), pp. 119–29.

Fields, C.D., 'The social structure of English Methodism: Eighteenth–twentieth centuries', *British Journal of Sociology*, 28 (1977), pp. 199–225.

Fissell, Mary, *Patients, Power, and the Poor in Eighteenth-Century Bristol* (Cambridge, 1991).

Forbes, Eric G., 'The Professionalisation of Dentistry in the United Kingdom', *Medical History*, 29 (1985), pp. 169–81.

Frost, G., 'Bigamy and cohabitation in Victorian England', *Journal of Family History*, 22 (1997), pp. 286–306.

Gattrell, V.A.C., The *Hanging Tree: Execution and the English People 1770–1868* (Oxford, 1994).

Gill, Rebecca, 'The Imperial Anxieties of a Nineteenth-Century Bigamy Case', *History Workshop Journal*, 57 (2004).

Goodman, David, *Foul Deeds and Suspicious Deaths in Leeds* (Barnsley, 2003).

Graham, Thomas and August Wilhelm Hofmann, *Report upon the alleged adulteration of Pale Ales by strychnine, etc.* (London, 1852).

Gream, G. T., 'On the use of Nux vomica as a remedy in hay-fever', *The Lancet*, 55, 1397 (1850), pp. 692–3.

Greenwald, Gary and Maria Greenwald, 'Medicolegal Progress in Inquests of Felonious Deaths: Westminster 1761–1866', *Journal of Legal Medicine*, 2 (1981), pp. 193–264.

Hammerton, A. James, *Cruelty and Companionship: Conflict in Nineteenth-Century Married Life* (London and New York, 1992).

Hargreaves, A., 'Dentistry in the British Isles', *Clio Medica*, 72, 1 (2003), pp. 171–330.

Harris, Michael, 'Social Diseases? Crime and Medicine in the Victorian Press', in W.F. Bynum, Stephen Lock and Roy Porter (eds), *Medical Journals and Medical Knowledge* (London and New York, 1992), pp. 108–25.

Hattersley, Alan Frederick, *The Convict Crisis and the Growth of Unity: Resistance to Transportation in South Africa and Australia, 1848–1853* (Pietermaritzburg, 1965).

Heaton, James, *Memoir of Mr. John Dungett, of Newcastle-upon-Tyne* (London, 1833).

Heaton, James, *Farther Observations on Demoniac Possession, and Animadversions on Some of the Curious Arts of Superstition* (Frome, 1822).

Helfand, William H., 'James Morison and his Pills', *Transactions of the British Society of the History of Pharmacy*, 1 (1974), pp. 101–35.

Hempton, David, *The Religion of the People: Methodism and Popular Religion c.1750–1900* (London, 1996).

Henderson, William, *Folk-Lore of the Northern Counties* (London, 1879).

Hillam, Christine, *Brass Plate and Brazen Impudence: Dental Practice in the Provinces, 1755–1855* (Liverpool, 1991).

Hodgkins, Sheilagh, 'The major mental disorders and crime: Stop debating and start treating and preventing', *International Journal of Law and Psychiatry*, 24 (2001), pp. 427–46.

Hoff, Joan and Marian Yeates, *The Cooper's Wife is Missing: The Trials of Bridget Cleary* (New York, 2000).

Houghton, J. Hyde, 'The use of Nux Vomica in cases of Constipation and Costiveness', *Association Medical Journal*, April 5 (1856), pp. 271–4.

Hoyle, Susan, 'The witch and the detective: mid-Victorian stories and beliefs', in de Blécourt and Davies (eds), *Witchcraft continued*, pp. 46–68.

Hughes, Robert, *The Fatal Shore: A History of the Transportation of Convicts to Australia* (London, 1987).

*Illustrated Life and Career of William Palmer of Rugeley* (London, 1856).

Ingram, Allan (ed.), *Patterns of Madness in the Eighteenth Century: A Reader* (Liverpool, 1998).

Jenkins, C.E., 'Treatment of the Malignant Cholera with Strychnine', *The Lancet*, 24, 625 (1835), pp. 657–8.

Jervis, Jervis, *A Practical Treatise on the Office and Duties of Coroners*, 2nd edn (London, 1854).

Kalikoff, Beth, 'The Execution of Tess d'Urberville at Wintonchester', in Thesing (ed.), *Execution*, pp. 111–121.

Kalikoff, Beth, *Murder and Moral Decay in Victorian Popular Literature* (Ann Arbor, 1986).

King, Francis X., *The Flying Sorcerer* (Oxford, 1992).

Knelman, Judith, *Twisting in the Wind: The Murderess and the English Press* (Toronto, 1997).

Knipe, William (ed.), *Criminal Chronology of York Castle* (York, 1867).

Lawson, Joseph, *Letters to the Young on Progress in Pudsey during the last Sixty Years* (Stanningley, 1887; reprint Firle, 1978).

Levine, Robert S., 'Uncle Tom's Cabin in Frederick Douglass' Paper: An Analysis of Reception', *American Literature* 64 (1992), pp. 71–93.

Liebig, Baron and Justus Liebig, 'Remarks upon the Alleged use of Strychnine in the Manufacture of Bitter Beer or Pale Ale', *The Lancet*, 59, 1501 (1852), pp. 551–2.

*Life and Recollections of Calcraft the Hangman* (London, *c.* 1880).

López-Ibor, Juan José, Hagop S. Akiskal and Mario Maj (eds), *Bipolar Disorder* (New York, 2002).

Loudon, Irvine, ' "The Vile Race of Quacks with which this Country is Infested" ', in Bynum and Porter (eds), *Medical Fringe & Medical Orthodoxy*, pp. 106–28.

Lyth, John, *Glimpses of Early Methodism in York* (York, 1885).

Macgowan, Douglas, *Murder in Victorian Scotland: The Trial of Madeleine Smith* (Westport, 1999).

Manson, Edward, *Bramwelliana: Or, Wit and Wisdom of Lord Bramwell* (London,1892).

Marland, Hilary, *Medicine and Society in Wakefield and Huddersfield 1780–1870* (Cambridge, 1987).

Marland, Hilary, 'The medical activities of mid-nineteenth-century chemists and druggists, with special reference to Wakefield and Huddersfield', *Medical History*, 31 (1987), pp. 415–39.

Marneros, Andreas and Jules Angst (eds), *Bipolar Disorders: 100 Years after Manic-Depressive Insanity* (Dordrecht, 2000).

Mathews, H.F., *Methodism and the Education of the People 1791–1851* (London, 1949).

Maunder, Andrew and Grace Moore (eds), *Crime, Madness and Sensation* (Aldershot, 2004).

Mayhew, Charles Henry, 'Acute Delirious Melancholia', *West Riding Lunatic Asylum Medical Reports*, 1 (1871), pp. 252–60.

Maziere, E., 'The Use of Opium in the Treatment of Melancholia', *West Riding Lunatic Asylum Medical Reports*, 2 (1872), pp. 254–77.

McDermid, Thomas Wright, *The Life of T. Wright, of Manchester, the prison philanthropist* (Manchester, 1876).

McLaren, Angus, *A Prescription for Murder: The Victorian Serial Killings of Dr Thomas Neill Cream* (Chicago, 1993).

Mclaren, Angus, *Reproductive Rituals* (London, 1984).

'Memoir of Mrs. Christopher Dove, Jun.', *Arminian Magazine*, 39 (1816).

Mitchell, Charles (ed.), *The Newspaper Press Directory* (London, 1856).

Moran, Richard, *Knowing Right from Wrong: The Insanity Defense of Daniel McNaughtan* (New York, 1981).

Morris, Beverley R., *A Theory as to the Proximate Causes of Insanity* (London, 1844).

Morris, R.J., *Class, sect and party: The making of the British middle class, Leeds 1820–50* (Manchester, 1990).

M'Owan, Peter, 'Memoir of Mr. Christopher Dove', *Wesleyan-Methodist Magazine*, 5th S., 11 (1856), pp. 966–77.

M'Owan, Peter, *The two Doves: or, Memoirs of Margaret and Anna Dove, late of Leeds* (London, 1839).

M'Owan, Peter, *Memoir of Christopher Dove* (London, 1837).

Obelkevitch, James, *Religion and Rural Society: South Lindsey, 1825–75* (Oxford, 1976).

*Olla podrida, from the Hull advertiser and exchange gazette* (Hull, 1800).

Olli, Soili-Maria, 'The Devil's pact: a male strategy', in Owen Davies and Willem de Blécourt (eds), *Beyond the witch trials: Witchcraft and magic in Enlightenment Europe* (Manchester, 2004), pp. 100–16.

Osborn, George, *A Man of God: or, Providence and Grace exemplified in a Memoir of the Rev. P. M'Owan, compiled chiefly from his letters and papers* (London, 1873).

*Partial Defences to Murder: Provisional Conclusions on Consultation Paper No. 173* (Law Commission, May 2004).

Pearson, Robin, 'Knowing one's place: Perceptions of community in the industrial suburbs of Leeds, 1790–1890', *Journal of Social History*, 26 (1993), pp. 221–44.

Perkins, Maureen, *The Reform of Time: Magic and Modernity* (London, 2001).

Perkins, Maureen, *Visions of the Future: Almanacs, Time, and Cultural Change* (Oxford, 1996).

*Pigot and Co.'s Royal National and Commercial Directory* (London and Manchester, 1841).

Poovey, Mary, *Uneven Developments: The Ideological Work of Gender in Mid-Victorian England* (Chicago, 1988).

Porter, Roy, 'Witchcraft and magic in Enlightenment, Romantic and Liberal Thought', in Marijke Gijswijt-Hofstra, Brian Levack and Roy Porter, *Witchcraft and Magic in Europe: The Eighteenth and Nineteenth Centuries* (London, 1999), pp. 191–283.

Porter, Roy, ' "I Think Ye Both Quacks": The Controversy between Dr Theodor Myersbach and Dr John Coakley Lettsom', in Bynum and Porter (eds), *Medical Fringe*, pp. 56–78.

Potter, Harry, *Hanging in Judgement: Religion and the Death Penalty in England* (London, 1993).

Prichard, James Cowles, *A Treatise on Insanity, and other disorders affecting the mind* (London, 1835).

Reid, T. Wemyss (ed.), *A Memoir of John Deakin Heaton, M.D. of Leeds* (London, 1883).

Riddle, John M., *Eve's Herbs: A History of Contraception and Abortion in the West* (Cambridge, Mass., 1997).

Rimmer, W.G., 'Leeds Leather Industry in the Nineteenth Century', *Thoresby Society* 46 (1960), pp. 119–64.

Robinson, George, *Observations on Some Recent Cases of Poisoning* (Gateshead, 1856).

Royle, E., 'The Church of England and Methodism in Yorkshire, *c.* 1750–1850: From Monopoly to Free Market', *Northern History*, 33 (1997), pp. 137–61.

Rule, John, 'Methodism, popular beliefs and village culture in Cornwall, 1800–1850', in R. Storch (ed.), *Popular culture and custom in nineteenth-century England* (London, 1982), pp. 48–70.

'Scientific Evidence: The Trials of Palmer, Dove, &c.', *The Rambler*, 18, Old Series (1856), pp. 226–31, 308–15.

Sellers, David, *Hidden Beneath our Feet: The Story of Sewerage in Leeds* (Leeds, 1997).

Semmens, Jason, *The Witch of the West: Or, The Strange and Wonderful History of Thomasine Blight* (Plymouth, 2004).

Semmens, Jason, ' "I will not go to the Devil for a Cure": Witchcraft, Demonic Possession, and Spiritual Healing in Nineteenth-Century Devon', *Journal for the Academic Study of Magic*, 2 (2004), pp. 132–55.

Semmens, Jason, 'The Dock Dæmoniac: Or, a Study of Possession, Dissent, and Healing in Early Nineteenth-Century Plymouth', MA Dissertation, Exeter University, 2001.

Shah, Nurun N., Patricia M. Averill and Andrew Shack, 'Mixed versus manic bipolar disorder: A comparison of demographic, symptomatic, and treatment differences', *Psychiatric Quarterly*, 75, 2 (2004), pp. 183–96.

Sharpe, J.A., *Crime in Early Modern England 1550–1750* (London and New York, 1999).

Sharpe, James, 'The history of violence in England: some observations', *Past and Present*, 108 (1985) pp. 206–15.

Shepherd, Michael, 'Psychiatric journals and the evolution of psychological medicine', in W.F. Bynum, Stephen Lock and Roy Porter (eds), *Medical Journals and Medical Knowledge* (London, 1992), pp. 188–206.

Sigsworth, Eric M. and Phillip Swan, 'Para-medical Provision in the West Riding', *Society for the Social History of Medicine Bulletin*, 29 (1981), pp. 37–9.

Sindall, Rob, *Street Violence in the Nineteenth Century: Media Panic or Real Danger?* (Leicester, 1990).

Sindall, Rob, 'The London Garrotting Panics of 1856 and 1862', *Social History*, 12, 3 (1987), pp. 351–9.

Slugg, J.T., *Woodhouse Grove School: Memorials and Reminiscences* (London, 1885).

Smith, F.B., *The People's Health 1830–1910* (London, [1979] 1990).

Smith, Kathryn C., 'The Wise Man and his Community', *Folk Life*, 15 (1977).

Smith, Roger, *Trial by Medicine: Insanity and Responsibility in Victorian Trials* (Edinburgh, 1981).

Snell, Keith and Paul S. Ell, *Rival Jerusalems: The Geography of Victorian Religion* (Cambridge, 2000).

Sonne, Susan C. and Kathleen T. Brady, 'Bipolar Disorder and alcoholism', *Alcohol Research and Health*, 26, 2 (2002), pp. 103–8.

Spencer, Henry, *Men that are gone from the households of Darlington* (Darlington and London, 1862).

Steele, Anthony, *History of Methodism in Barnard Castle* (London, 1857).

Steury, Ellen Hochstedler, and Michelle Choinski, ' "Normal" Crimes and Mental Disorder: A Two-Group Comparison of Deadly and Dangerous Felonies', *International Journal of Law and Psychiatry*, 18, 2 (1995), pp. 183–207.

Stevenson, Kim, 'Observations on the Law Relating to Sexual Offences: The Historical Scandal of Women's Silence', *Web Journal of Current Legal Issues* (1999).

Stone, Lawrence, *Road to Divorce: England 1530–1987* (Oxford, 1990).

Stone, Lawrence, 'The history of violence in England: a rejoinder', *Past and Present*, 108 (1985), pp. 216–24.

Stone, Lawrence, 'Interpersonal violence in English society, 1300–1980', *Past and Present*, 101 (1983), pp. 22–33.

Sullivan, Sheila, ' "What is the Matter with Mary Jane?" Madeleine Smith, Legal Ambiguity, and the Gendered Aesthetic of Victorian Criminality', *Genders*, 35 (2002).

Sutherland, Henry, 'The Change of Life, and Insanity', *West Riding Lunatic Asylum Medical Reports*, 3 (1873), pp. 299–314.

Sutherland, Henry, 'Menstrual Irregularities and Insanity', *West Riding Lunatic Asylum Medical Reports*, 2 (1872), pp. 53–72.

Sutherland, Henry, 'Arachnoid Cysts', *West Riding Lunatic Asylum Medical Reports*, 1 (1871), pp. 218–32.

Thackrah, C. Turner, *The effects of the principal arts, trades and professions and of civic states and habits of living, on health and longevity. With a particular reference to the trades and manufactures of Leeds* (London, 1831).

*The Heroes of the Guillotine* (London, *c.* 1868; reprinted 1975).

*The Last Moments and Execution of Wm. Dove!* (York, 1856).

Thesing, William B. (ed.), *Execution and the British Experience from the 17th to the 20th Century* (Jefferson and London, 1990).

*The Times edition of the last hours and execution of W. Palmer the poisoner* (London, 1856).

Thorne, Nicola, *My Name is Martha Brown* (London, 2000).

Torrey, E. Fuller, *Out of the Shadows: Confronting America's Mental Illness Crisis* (New York, 1996).

Tosh, John, *A Man's Place: Masculinity and the Middle-Class Home in Victorian England* (New Haven and London, 1999).

Turner, J.M., 'Methodist Religion 1791–1849', in Rupert Davies, A. Raymond George and Gordon Rupp (eds), *A History of the Methodist Church in Great Britain* (London, 1978), pp. 97–112.

Vandermeersch, P., 'The victory of psychiatry over demonology: The origin of the nineteenth-century myth', *History of Psychiatry*, 2 (1991), pp. 351–63.

Vickery, Roy, *A Dictionary of Plant-lore* (Oxford, 1995).

Vincent, David, *Bread, Knowledge and Freedom* (London, 1981).

Walkowitz, Judith, *City of Dreadful Delight: Narratives of Sexual Danger in Late-Victorian London* (London, 1992).

Walkowitz, Judith, 'Jack the Ripper and the myth of Male Violence', *Feminist Studies*, 8 (1982) pp. 543–75.

Ward, D., 'Environs and neighbours in the "Two Nations": residential differentiation in mid-nineteenth century Leeds', *Journal of Historical Geography*, 6 (1980), pp. 132–62.

Ward, James Lawrence, 'Mr Ward's Defence of Irregular Practitioners', *The Lancet*, 29, 754 (1838), pp. 699–701.

Watson, Katherine, *Poisoned Lives: English Poisoners and their Victims* (London, 2003).

Watts, Michael, *The Dissenters: The Expansion of Evangelical Nonconformity*, vol. 2 (London, 1995).

Webster, John, *Displaying of Supposed Witchcraft* (London, 1677).

West, Robert Athow, *Sermons by the Late Mr William Dawson, of Barnbow, near Leeds. With a sketch of the author* (London and Otley, 1860).

Wheater, William, 'Yorkshire Superstitions', *Old Yorkshire*, 4 (1883), pp. 265–71.

White, William, *Directory and Topography of the Borough of Leeds, Halifax* (Sheffield, 1858).

White, William, *General Directory of the Town, Borough, and Parish of Sheffield* (Sheffield, 1856).

White, William, *Directory of Leeds, Bradford* (Sheffield, 1854).

Wiener, Martin J., *Men of Blood: Violence, Manliness and Criminal Justice in Victorian England* (Cambridge, 2004).

Wiener, Martin J., 'Judges v. Jurors: Courtroom Tensions in Murder Trials and the Law of Criminal Responsibility in Nineteenth-Century England', in *Law and History Review*, 17, 3 (1999), pp. 467–506.

Weiner, Michael J., 'The Sad Story of George Hall: Adultery, Murder, and the Politics of Mercy in mid-Victorian England', *Social History*, 24, 2 (1999).

Williams, Caleb, *Observations on the Criminal Responsibility of the Insane; Founded on the Trials of James Hill and William Dove* (London and New York, 1856).

Wood, W. Charles, *Statistics of Insanity; Being a Decennial Report of Bethlehem Hospital from 1846 to 1855 Inclusive* (London, 1856).

Woods, Robert and John Woodward (eds), *Urban Disease and Morality in Nineteenth-Century England* (London, 1984).

Wyhe, John van, *Phrenology and the Origins of Victorian Scientific Naturalism* (Aldershot, 2004).

Younghusband, Pat, 'Joseph Lawson, Pudsey 1821–1890', *Lawson Times*, 5 (1998), pp. 8–10.

# Index